160619052

Alan R. Thomas, MA
Editor

Classification: Options and Opportunities

Pre-publication
REVIEWS,
COMMENTARIES,
EVALUATIONS . . .

"**M**ost American librarians, raised in a tradition of classification for "marking and parking" only, will be surprised at the variety represented in these papers editor Alan R. Thomas has assembled.

Reading part or all of this volume, or even browsing through its pages, quickly points to the inherent values and uses of classification for purposes other than just to "mark and park." The presence of "hidden" classification in thesauri, the purposes served by different classification schemes, and the possible new ways of accessing information through classification and technology are each reason to explore this interesting and useful book."

Lawrence W. S. Auld, PhD
Chair, Department of Library Studies and Educational Technology, School of Education, East Carolina University, Greenville, NC

The Haworth Press, Inc.

Classification:
Options and Opportunities

Classification: Options and Opportunities

Alan R. Thomas, MA
Editor

The Haworth Press, Inc.
New York • London

Classification: Options and Opportunities has also been published as *Cataloging & Classification Quarterly,* Volume 19, Numbers 3/4 1995.

The development, preparation, and publication of this work has been undertaken with great care. However, the publisher, employees, editors, and agents of The Haworth Press and all imprints of The Haworth Press, Inc., including The Haworth Medical Press and Pharmaceutical Products Press, are not responsible for any errors contained herein or for consequences that may ensue from use of materials or information contained in this work. Opinions expressed by the author(s) are not necessarily those of The Haworth Press, Inc.

The Haworth Press, Inc., 10 Alice Street, Binghamton, NY 13904-1580 USA

Library of Congress Cataloging-in-Publication Data

Classification: options and opportunities/Alan R. Thomas, editor.
     p. cm.
     "Has also been published as Cataloging & classification quarterly, volume 19, numbers 3/4, 1995"–T.p. verso.
     Includes bibliographical references and index.
     ISBN 1-56024-709-6 (alk. paper)
     1. Books–Classification. I.Thomas, Alan R.
Z696.A4C694 1995
025.4'3--dc20

                      95-14546
                      CIP

INDEXING & ABSTRACTING

Contributions to this publication are selectively indexed or abstracted in print, electronic, online, or CD-ROM version(s) of the reference tools and information services listed below. This list is current as of the copyright date of this publication. See the end of this section for additional notes.

- *Computing Reviews,* Association for Computing Machinery, 1515 Broadway, 17th Floor, New York, NY 10036

- *Current Awareness Bulletin*, Association for Information Management, Information House, 20-24 Old Street, London EC1V 9AP, England

- *Index to Periodical Articles Related to Law*, University of Texas, 727 East 26th Street, Austin, TX 78705

- *Information Science Abstracts*, Plenum Publishing Company, 233 Spring Street, New York, NY 10013-1578

- *Informed Librarian, The,* Infosources Publishing, 140 Norma Road, Teaneck, NJ 07666

- *INSPEC Information Services,* Institution of Electrical Engineers, Michael Faraday House, Six Hills Way, Stevenage, Herts SG1 2AY, England

- *INTERNET ACCESS (& additional networks) Bulletin Board for Libraries ("BUBL"), coverage of information resources on INTERNET, JANET, and other networks.*
  - JANET X.29:UK.AC.BATH.BUBL or 00006012101300
  - TELNET: BUBL.BATH.AC.UK or 138.32.32.45 Login 'bubl'
  - Gopher: BUBL.BATH.AC.UK (138.32.32.45). Port 7070
  - World Wide Web: http: //www. bubl.bath.ac.uk./BUBL/home.html
  - NISSWAIS: telnetniss.ac.uk (for the NISS gateway),
    The Andersonian Library, Curran Building, 101 Saint James Road, Glasgow G4 ONS, Scotland

- *Library & Information Science Abstracts (LISA),* Bowker-Saur Limited, Maypole House, Maypole Road, East Grinstead, West Sussex RH19 1HH, England

- *Library Hi Tech News*, Pierian Press, P. O. Box 1808, Ann Arbor, MI 48106

- *Library Literature,* The H.W. Wilson Company, 950 University Avenue, Bronx, NY 10452

(continued)

- *National Clearinghouse for Primary Care information (NCPCI)*, 8201 Greensboro Drive, Suite 600, McLean, VA 22102

- *Newsletter of Library and Information Services,* China Sci-Tech Book Review, Library of Academia Sinica, 8 Kexueyuan Nanlu, Zhongguancun, Beijing 100080, People's Republic of China

- *Periodica Islamica,* Berita Publishing, 22 Jalan Liku, 59100 Kuala Lumpur, Malaysia

- *Referativnyi Zhurnal (Abstracts Journal of the Institute of Scientific Information of the Republic of Russia),* The Institute of Scientific Information, Baltijskaja ul., 14, Moscow A-219, Republic of Russia

SPECIAL BIBLIOGRAPHIC NOTES

*related to special journal issues (separates)
and indexing/abstracting*

☐ indexing/abstracting services in this list will also cover material in any "separate" that is co-published simultaneously with Haworth's special thematic journal issue or DocuSerial. Indexing/abstracting usually covers material at the article/chapter level.

☐ monographic co-editions are intended for either non-subscribers or libraries which intend to purchase a second copy for their circulating collections.

☐ monographic co-editions are reported to all jobbers/wholesalers/approval plans. The source journal is listed as the "series" to assist the prevention of duplicate purchasing in the same manner utilized for books-in-series.

☐ to facilitate user/access services all indexing/abstracting services are encouraged to utilize the co-indexing entry note indicated at the bottom of the first page of each article/chapter/contribution.

☐ this is intended to assist a library user of any reference tool (whether print, electronic, online, or CD-ROM) to locate the monographic version if the library has purchased this version but not a subscription to the source journal.

☐ individual articles/chapters in any Haworth publication are also available through the Haworth Document Delivery Services (HDDS).

Classification:
Options and Opportunities

CONTENTS

ALTERNATIVE CLASSIFICATION SYSTEMS

COMBINATION PLATTERS AND RECLASSIFICATION

CLASSIFICATION AND THE NEW TECHNOLOGY

ABOUT THE EDITOR

Alan R. Thomas gained the professional qualifications of Associate and then Fellow of the Library Association. He received a research MA in Library and Information Studies from the Queens University of Belfast and an MA in Counselling and Guidance from the University of Reading. For many years he served as Head of the Division of Information Retrieval Studies at Ealing College (now Thames Valley University). He has taught at several American library schools, most recently as Associate Professor at St. John's University and currently as Visiting Associate Professor at Pratt Institute, New York. He has published many articles and book reviews and is a member of the editorial board of *Cataloging & Classification Quarterly.*

Introduction:
Exploring the Armamentarium

Alan R. Thomas

In the course of their professional education, training, reading, and practical experience, many librarians and information specialists may receive little exposure to the range and diversity of library and bibliographic classification. The richness that is available includes different ways of viewing and organizing knowledge, multiple functions of classification, a variety of systems, options within those systems, different procedures for constructing and applying schemes, new means of searching schedules and classified files. Because courses in cataloging and classification necessarily include descriptive cataloging, subject cataloging, and other concerns, their treatment of classification is consequently confined. Usually detailed theoretical and practical attention is given to just one or two classification schemes, with some other systems receiving shorter mention and without supporting practice work. The most-used textbooks tend to accord with the curricular emphases.

Many information professionals work exclusively in specialized areas such as technical services, reader services, or library management. Others may gain more variety according to some "dual-assignment" plan, thus becoming more aware of the difficulties of both the users and the catalogers/classifiers at first-hand. Not only catalogers/classifiers but all library staff members may be required or wish to contribute to decision-making on policies and practices concerning classification. If these professionals lack acquaintance with a span of solutions and are overly conditioned by those used on-site, they may be tempted to conclude too quickly that those adopted systems and procedures are inevitable and as good as can be had. They may not question enough that current local practice, use of established pseudo-standards, and so-called economized technical processing

[Haworth indexing entry note]: "Introduction: Exploring the Armamentarium." Thomas, Alan R. Published in *Classification: Options and Opportunities* (ed: Alan R. Thomas) The Haworth Press, Inc., 1995, pp. 1-5. Multiple copies of this article/chapter may be purchased from The Haworth Document Delivery Center [1-800-3-HAWORTH; 9:00 a.m. - 5:00 p.m. (EST)].

1

(the latter increasingly utilized partly due to competitive tendering) may repeatedly waste valuable time and energy of service staff and readers.

The intention in presenting this set of papers is to encourage fresh and wider interest in library and bibliographic classification decisions, the extent of choice, and the "best fit" of a system to local factors. It is perhaps timely to reaffirm that the arrangement and optimum navigation of the document collection and its records constitute key resources and responsibilities of the entire library staff. Their active and informed involvement in identifying user approaches, problems, and preferences is essential to any careful decision and implementation. Therefore it is hoped that the gathering of papers may help promote a more participatory propinquity or collocation of subjects, and that not only classifiers and catalogers as such but also reader and bibliographical services staff, library administrators, and others might take part. The "Great American Library Dream" has been described as "that dream of librarians which strives to reveal to readers the subject-contents in books."[1] But how to make that dream come true? Requirements include surveying readers' interests and behavior, considering how successful are the local policies and procedures in force, and then confirming, adapting, adopting or fashioning apt organizations of knowledge (explicit in the form of classifications, covert in the guise of syndetic references to and from related subject access points).

Information required for making choices in classification may be said to fall into two broad kinds: external information and internal information. External information includes appreciation of the available and the emerging technical repertory–that armamentarium used to withstand and more nearly accommodate turbulent changes in knowledge and user needs. Many theories and systems, whether old or new, have some relevance for today and therefore, first or closer acquaintance with them constitute useful "new" experiences. Internal environmental information relates to the current and future functions of the particular library or information center, characteristics of the collections, the performance and acceptability of the system in present use, and specific requirements or preferences of staff and users of various categories and levels. The individual reader must indeed "remain a 'gray' and 'ghostlike' individual until defined as to intelligence, interests, and motivation."[2] Comparative assessment of possible solutions, including those already employed, may be made and sample trials carried out on the most promising systems. Feedback on experience with Dewey Decimal Classification and Library of Congress Classification is widely available though there is need for more hard information as to why and how libraries use the internal options of those schemes. For lesser known classifications, some degree of reality-testing may be gleaned from visits, interviews, correspondence, and reading the reports of adoptions and modifications by other libraries and centers.

This collection of papers is necessarily limited and identifies, describes, and discusses only some of the variety of options and investigative approaches. Many more are being discovered, rediscovered, written about, devised, refined, researched, and evaluated. Some schemes are highly specialized and purposefully drawn up for individual collections yet embody partially transferable thought-provoking notions, structures, and devices. Advances in technology render further enhancements and innovations certain.

The enthusiasm and cooperation of the contributors in sharing their "gifts differing" is acknowledged with thanks, as is the sustained patience and guidance provided by Dr. Ruth C. Carter, editor of *Cataloging & Classification Quarterly*. Numerous arguments with former colleagues Pat Booth, James Shearer, Mary South, John Shinebourne, and Pnina Wentz always generated light rather than heat; the jury is still out on most of the issues.

Indexing of the text was undertaken by the LIS 634 Abstracting and Indexing class (Spring, 1995) of Pratt Institute School of Information and Library Science (Visiting Associate Professor Alan R. Thomas, project coordinator; Robert Armitage, Terrie L. Ashley, Frank Collerius, Derek A. Coursen, Rodger Friedman, Frank J. Girello, Delritta R. Hornbuckle, Steven W. Knittweis, Edward D. Meisner, Ricki L. Moskowitz, John J. Patrisco, and Rick L. Perdew).

The Contents List is just like any other classified arrangement in that certain contributions could have been placed equally well in other sections, clear cases for alternative location. The series or array of the sections themselves might have been ordered differently, while within each paper alternative sequencing of text would doubtless have suited certain readers better. The opening section, *BASIC DESIGN CONSIDERATIONS,* presents ideas and principles concerning the function, assessment, design, and construction of classifications. It is hoped that the papers therein may raise some of the initial questions for those with established library collections who are wondering whether to retain their present scheme or switch to a different system (in both cases with or without modifications). It is also hoped that those privileged and challenged to select or create a system for a quite new information center or library will find some clarification and benefit. Some relative weighing of particular schemes is included in the section *Combination Platters and Reclassification.*

The next section, *OPTIONS WITHIN STANDARD CLASSIFICATION SYS-TEMS,* covers the Library of Congress Classification and the Dewey Decimal Classifications. Because these two are used so much and emphasized in basic textbooks and consequently their general features well known, the focus of the contributed papers is on choices available in these systems. A paper considering the Library of Congress versus Dewey decision appears in the *Combination*

Platters and Reclassification section, while a description of electronic Dewey has been placed in the last section *Classification and the New Technology*.

ALTERNATIVE CLASSIFICATION SYSTEMS are generally less well known and therefore their chief contexts, characteristics, and developments are described. This section includes classifications intended for wide adoption as well as some prepared for particular local settings. The review of reader-interest classifications, which frequently co-exist with the Dewey Decimal Classification, is placed last so as to immediately precede the next section. That section *COMBINATION PLATTERS AND RECLASSIFICATION* covers use of multiple classifications within the same institution or even the same collection and includes also the related decision and planning of reclassification. The last section, *CLASSIFICATION AND THE NEW TECHNOLOGY*, features firstly a review which includes the present and potential support from our trusty "Three Musketeers"–the computer, telecommunications, and information storage technologies. A second paper provides a guide to features of electronic Dewey.

Kelley, well experienced in both classifying and readers' advisory work, investigated the contribution of classification in her day. Her holistic approach and creative scepticism may perhaps find some echo and extension in recent books by librarian Thomas Mann.[3,4] Though Kelley identified many limitations she later concluded: "As I pondered thus upon the unified nature of library service, I discovered that classification could be thought of only in relation to the part it contributed to a final goal. Again it resumed a kind of central position; but this time, instead of resuming also its separate entity, it seemed to radiate throughout the structure shafts of illumination, lighting up and strengthening all library service. It seemed to me that classification could be made to reinforce the framework of our service and prevent the whole from collapsing into a formless and undirected tangle."[5]

Today there beckons a replete repertoire available of principles, perspectives, models, applications, practices, feedback, and research results. Searchable specifications from several schemes and thesauri may be added to a record, diverse strategic paths for a literature search devised, displayed and recorded to suit group and individual preferences. The contribution of classification now and increasingly offers added value, variety, and versatility.

NOTES

1. Grace O. Kelley, *The Classification of Books: An Inquiry into its Usefulness to the Reader.* (New York:Wilson, 1937), 5.

2. Grace O. Kelley, "The Classification of Books in Retrospect and in Prospect: A Tool and a Discipline". In, William M. Randall, ed. *The Acquisition and Cataloging of Books.* (Chicago: University of Chicago Press, 1940), 163-186, p. 169.

3. Thomas Mann, *A Guide to Library Research Methods.* (New York: Oxford University Press, 1987).

4. Thomas Mann, *Library Research Models: A Guide to Classification, Cataloging, and Computers.* (New York: Oxford University Press, 1993).

5. Grace O. Kelley, "The Classification of Books in Retrospect and in Prospect: A Tool and a Discipline," p. 164.

BASIC DESIGN CONSIDERATIONS

Alternative Starting Points
in Classification

Derek W. Langridge

SUMMARY. The necessity of knowledge of structure of a classification not only to compilers of systems but also to those who classify documents or search is emphasized. American and European assumptions are contrasted. The relationship of a special classification to a general classification is considered. Some differences in the construction of three general schemes are noted. The concept of a "main class" is elucidated. Alternative starting points for dividing knowledge by its forms or by phenomena are exemplified. The idea that the treatment of main classes reflects a world view is offered and supported by illustrations. Principles for determining degree of detail are presented. The case for specificity is argued. Procedures for making a science class are contrasted with those for making a humanities class.

Derek W. Langridge taught for many years at the Polytechnic of North London and served also as a visiting faculty member in the United States. He is Classification Consultant and an active member of the Classification Research Group. He has authored several books and papers on classification and indexing.

Address correspondence to: 37 Brick Lane, Cerne Abbas, Dorset DT2 7JW, United Kingdom.

[Haworth co-indexing entry note]: "Alternative Starting Points in Classification." Langridge, Derek W. Co-published simultaneously in *Cataloging & Classification Quarterly* (The Haworth Press, Inc.) Vol. 19, No. 3/4, 1995, pp. 7-15; and: *Classification: Options and Opportunities* (ed: Alan R. Thomas) The Haworth Press, Inc., 1995, pp. 7-15. Multiple copies of this article/chapter may be purchased from The Haworth Document Delivery Center [1-800-3-HAWORTH; 9:00 a.m. - 5:00 p.m. (EST)].

7

ALTERNATIVE STARTING POINTS IN CLASSIFICATION

The starting point in classification is not a simple concept, but considerations must include purpose, the relevance of theory, the relation of technique and substance, general and special approaches, methods of dividing knowledge, principles for defining classes, and degree of detail required.

Misconceptions and Basic Assumptions

There are probably many people who believe that the structure of classification schemes is a theoretical subject, a matter of interest only to those concerned with their making and nothing to do with the "practical" librarian. This "practical" begs the question, of course. What is practical? In a matter as complex as the classification of knowledge the practical course is the one based on sound theory. Understanding how schemes are made is of equal importance to those who operate them, whether in classifying and indexing or in searching. Above all it is necessary to be aware of the most fundamental decisions made in establishing the main characteristics of a scheme. To take a very obvious example: it is essential for anyone using the *Dewey Decimal Classification* (DDC) or the *Library of Congress Classification* (LCC) to know that in a library arranged by either of these schemes probably no more than half of the history books will be in the class named History, that major branches of history such as religious and economic will be found elsewhere, and that every main class will contain some history books. The most important implication of this fact is that the library's index should contain many entries under history, showing where the various aspects may be found. In this era of computers such elementary, essential matters are often ignored. I have been in libraries using DDC where the only index entry reads "History–900." This distribution of history results from a quite legitimate decision concerning one of the major alternatives in a scheme's construction. Knowledge of such normal structural details is essential to the practitioner of any scheme. In respect of the older schemes, there must also be an awareness of their structural defects.

Before we look at the major alternatives in scheme construction we should remind ourselves that there are some big differences in basic assumptions. One set of these assumptions is prevalent in the USA, the other widespread in Great Britain. The typical American view sees classification and cataloguing as separate functions, the first concerned with arrangement of books, the second with the construction of catalogues. This American point of view is epitomised in the separate LCC and the

Library of Congress Subject Headings (LCSH). The opposite view sees classification as applying equally to books and to catalogues, making a significant difference to what one expects of a scheme. In particular, it expects a high degree of specificity so that the catalogue can spell out not only the precise subjects of books but also of analytical entries for parts of books and periodical articles. The American method is satisfied with much broader classes, for shelf arrangement only, and it leaves precise specification of subjects to alphabetical headings in the catalogue. Even here, the LCSH procedure is a hit-and-miss affair, falling far short of any theoretical ideal.

American pragmatism contrasts with a more rigorously systematic approach common in the European countries. Europe looks to a philosophic foundation for classification schemes. Such basis is not considered important in America though study of American classification in the eighteenth and nineteenth centuries will show that this was not always the case. True, there was Henry Evelyn Bliss in more recent times, but he was a prophet without honour in his own land.

General and Special

Most people being asked about differences between classification schemes are likely to think first of the general and the special. Superficially it appears that university, public, and national libraries need a scheme for the whole of knowledge while special libraries need one only for their subject. In fact, there is no such thing as a special library in this sense: all special libraries contain a range of subjects in addition to their central interest. Thus the *London Classification of Business Studies* is not confined to the narrow subject of business management but contains a wide range of subjects for those people with an interest in management. A special scheme, therefore, is not one limited to a single class of knowledge but one in which that class is given more prominence than the rest. This means that even if a special scheme is made for this core subject it must be extended well beyond the centre; alternatively, a general scheme must be drawn on to supply the whole range of subjects required.

In making a special scheme one should always start from the general, from knowledge as a whole. Every subject takes its place in a context and has ramifications throughout the tree of knowledge. It is impossible to define the limits and enumerate the parts of a subject without first considering its relationship to the whole of knowledge. One should not attempt a classification for the arts without considering their connections with other major subdivisions of knowledge such as philosophy, history, and science; a classification for music without considering its place among other arts; a classification for jazz without considering its relationship with other forms of music.

Although the amount of work involved is vastly different, the starting point for a general or a special scheme should therefore always be the same. There are obvious implications here for anyone faced with choosing how to classify a special library. There are always practical limitations, of course, determined by what is available and whether the making of a new scheme is feasible. In principle, however, everything appears to favour the use of a general scheme. In the past this alternative has frequently been rejected owing to the inadequacy of existing general schemes. This objection no longer applies since the new edition of the *Bliss Bibliographic Classification* (BC2) is in such detail that it serves both general and special needs. For example, the medicine class is more detailed than any special classification for medicine yet published. The scheme has the further advantage of providing many alternatives for the treatment of particular subjects.

Some Differences in General Schemes

DDC, LCC, and BC2 represent very different approaches to the task of classification making. Dewey has told us himself that he was obsessed with the idea of decimal numbers and their usefulness. As the name of his scheme implies, it attempted to fit knowledge into a regular pattern of successive tenfold divisions. The form of his scheme was paramount, the contents took second place. There is clearly no such uniformity in knowledge, and even the genus-species relationship implied is only one of a number. It should be no surprise that the result was a scheme inappropriate in structure and incompetent in its method of levelling specific subjects.

Although it was developed in a particular library, the intention behind DDC was to provide a scheme for general use. As everyone knows, LCC on the other hand, was devised for use within the Library of Congress, and only afterwards was deemed suitable for other libraries. Despite the general scope of the Library of Congress itself, the LCC scheme reveals the special approach. In making the scheme, the contents of the Library of Congress were divided first into main classes based upon an earlier classification. Teams allocated to the various subjects then developed their classes independently. The scheme was not conceived as a whole but as an aggregate of special schemes. The classes do look similar because of the notation and layout but these are superficial matters of presentation. The scheme is lacking in a more fundamental common pattern of organisation. One might call it a minimalist classification in that it frequently uses alphabetical order within broad classes rather than pursuing systematic order throughout. Another significant feature is the defining of classes by reference to the total contents of books, rather than basing them on the analysis of knowledge incorporated in books. The classes were, in fact, developed by moving books on the shelves until a suitable arrangement was found and used to make the schedule. This is a very useful way of checking the suitability of an arrangement but not the best way of devising one.

DDC and LCC both demonstrate unsatisfactory approaches to classification. Subject specialists, believing that these two schemes are representative of classification, become disenchanted when they find so little correspondence in the systems to their own mode of thinking. However, classification does not need to have such faults. The alternative is a completely systematic approach subordinating all technical considerations to those of content and purpose. The model for this was the *Colon Classification* of S.R.Ranganathan, the fully developed representative of which is BC2. This latter scheme shows rigorous analysis of subjects by categories, making possible all necessary combinations of ideas in the many complex subjects that exist. It provides exhaustive enumeration of concepts for complete specificity, and the subordination of notation to content.

Main Classes

If the general schemes show significant differences there is one major respect in which they are alike. They all use the same principle for arriving at the first division of knowledge. The term "main class" is used for the result of this division. Main classes are a practical device, the final presentation of knowledge in a way considered most helpful to users. They represent a second stage following an examination of the nature of knowledge. What are its main divisions? One can think of knowledge in two ways: what form it takes or what topic is discussed. On the one hand there are kinds of knowledge such as science, philosophy, history, and art; on the other hand there are the phenomena studied by these fundamental forms. The phenomena of nature, animals, plants, and rocks are dealt with in art as well as in science, but the kind of knowledge we gain from art is quite different from that produced by science.

The distinction between forms and phenomena gives us two possible starting points for a general classification scheme. We could begin with the forms of knowledge. All works of science, for example, would constitute one major division, and within that very broad class the various scientific disciplines such as physics, chemistry, and zoology would be distinguished. Alternatively, we could begin with phenomena. In this approach a typical class would be rabbits, bringing together all works on that topic whether of zoology, animal husbandry, cookery, or any other way of dealing with rabbits. This second method has only once been attempted by a general scheme designer, namely James Duff Brown. He demonstrated the result in his now defunct *Subject Classification*. Contrary to general belief and despite the term "discipline scheme" applied commonly to all other general classifications, the former method of beginning with forms of knowledge has never been used. The test is whether each main class consists of all and nothing but what its name implies, for example that the Philosophy class is all philosophy and nothing but philosophy, that the History class is all history and nothing but history, and so forth. It is easy to confirm that this is far from being the case in all existing general schemes. In these systems, all major forms of knowledge–even science– are distributed to some degree. The physics of music, for example, is a scientific subject that would be located in music and not in physics. All main classes include material from other forms of knowledge, and especially include history and philosophy of a subject.

The method actually used in the general schemes is probably best described as "field of interest." The aim is to bring together those documents regarded as most useful to persons interested in a particular sphere of thought or action. Thus the Religion class contains works that may belong to the form of theology, history, philosophy, sociology, or psychology; all such writings are considered of interest to anyone whose central concern is religious activity.

The use of phenomena as the first principle of division has been advocated as a way of overcoming the supposed problem of disappearing disciplinary boundaries. In fact, it is only *within* fundamental forms of knowledge that this problem arises, not between them. It may well be that literature of the natural sciences would now be best organised by starting with the phenomena rather than with the individual scientific disciplines. It is doubtful whether beginning with phenomena is applicable to the social sciences as a whole. It is certain that the method has no relevance to the wide-ranging humanities including philosophy, religion, history, literature, and the study of the arts. Primary division by phenomena is not possible throughout a general scheme. A pure discipline scheme is possible although nobody has yet thought it desirable.

The number, scope, and order of main classes represents a conscious or unconsciously held view of the world. DDC, LCC, and BC2 differ little in the number and definition of main classes. BC2 considers the order of classes much more carefully. Yet all three systems, samples of a liberal

humanist attitude, look alike when compared with Marxist schemes
devised for use in Russia and China or with mediaeval schemes. The latter
systems are themselves all very similar in their fusion of Aristotelian and
Christian thought. We can also see that changes over long periods of time
make different classifications appropriate to different epochs. The knowledge of the ancient world, the middle ages, and modern times are best
accommodated by different schemes. An interesting question for today is
whether we are at the beginning of a new era as some people claim. There
is considerable literature of the New Age relating to scientific, religious,
and social matters which may be pointing to a new configuration of
knowledge.[1]

Treatment of Detail

The principle for deciding the kind and degree of detail in classification
is known as literary warrant. Since there are many possibilities, choice
must be based on what has actually been written.

There are two ways of proceeding. In the first method, the subjects of
whole books can be used to define classes in a scheme. This approach was
advocated in the early 20th century by the English librarian Wyndham
Hulme and was practised by the Library of Congress. In the second
method, the knowledge in books is analyzed and the resulting elements
used to define the classes. This second method is much more versatile,
providing infinitely more subjects of books and not limited in its usefulness to shelf arrangement. When Hulme wrote about literary warrant, he
saw a clear distinction between the broad subjects of whole books and the
very precise subjects of periodical articles. If this distinction was ever
valid it is no longer so. The Hulme definition is useful only as an addition
to deal with a purely bibliographic aggregation of materials that does not
correspond to any normal division of knowledge, that is to say with the
small proportion of books whose scope cannot be defined by the analytical
method.

Hulme argues that even if there were only one book corresponding to a
given subject description it should be provided for in a scheme. This is
virtually impossible to achieve using his method, as the lack of specificity
in LCC amply demonstrates. By using the analytical method, however, it
is possible to anticipate a very large number of subjects that may occur.

A very large number of books now published cannot be specified by the
LCC schedules. The LCSH also fails to express the exact scope of a book
in one specific heading, and employ a loose procedure in which a detailed
subject is represented by several overlapping, non-specific headings.
Complete specificity of any subject, however complicated that subject

may be, is the aim of BC2. Specificity demands both analysis into categories and the exhaustive enumeration of concepts within each category. Specificity is not only essential to efficient information retrieval but also for accurate classifying. Unless the precise subject of a document is listed in the schedules of a scheme it may prove difficult to discern that broader class to which it belongs.

The deficiencies of LCC may be attributed to lack of awareness rather than any deliberate pursuit of a non-specific policy. A broad approach was explicitly utilised in the *BSO Broad System of Ordering,* designed for classifying information centres rather than documents. The BSO formed part of a European communications project.

Sciences and Humanities

Among main classes of a general scheme the scientific are purest in content, the humanities being more heterogeneous. The procedure for making a science class is to start by analysing the categories of phenomena belonging to the subject. Such matters as history and philosophy of science are treated as mere adjuncts and are provided by common subdivisions at the beginning of a class.

In the humanities one must start with the forms of knowledge contributing to the study of a subject. For example, in any particular one there are three distinct major areas. The area of social aspects includes social history, sociological, economic, political and other aspects. The area of theory and practice contains prescriptive technical writings concerned with the creation of the art concerned. The last area consists of descriptive writings that discuss the achievement within the art–writings in the form of history, biography, and criticism. A class designed from this starting-point will be noticeably different from one beginning with categories of phenomena. The latter method would produce a class for each musical instrument and that class would bring together books on the manufacture, maintenance, technique of playing, role in ensembles, biography and criticism of performers, etc., for the particular instrument. Such an arrangement may suit players of the instrument concerned. However, that arrangement is unlikely to be the one preferred by other users. The latter would surely be served better by that method that begins with the forms of knowledge. This would collocate different kinds of writing about an instrument with similar kinds of writing on other instruments. Thus one class would include how to play the violin, viola, cello, etc., while another class would include biographies of violinists, violists, cellists, etc.

Certain fundamental issues raised in this paper have received expanded treatment in other publications.[2,3,4]

REFERENCES

1. D.W. Langridge, "Bliss, the disciplines and the New Age," *Bliss Classification Bulletin* no.34 (1992): 8-13.

2. D.W. Langridge. *Subject analysis: principles and procedures.* London: Bowker-Saur, 1987.

3. D.W. Langridge, "Classifying knowledge." In, A.J. Meadows, ed. *Knowledge and communication.* London: Library Association, 1991.

4. D.W. Langridge. *Classification: Its kinds, elements, systems and applications.* London: Bowker-Saur, 1992.

Blissful Beliefs:
Henry Evelyn Bliss Counsels
on Classification

Alan R. Thomas

SUMMARY. Study of the organization of knowledge and of theories, systems, and practices of library classification provides a foundation for considering the design of an effective scheme. Use of existing standard systems has disadvantages and requires a library to either adapt itself to a standard or adapt that standard to the library. Prompt reclassification to an effective system will produce ultimate economy in service. Helpful order within a system is secured by application of certain principles. The scheme should be plastic to accommodate differing requirements and include alternative locations and citation orders of components. Construction and application of a relative classification present persistent problems.

INTRODUCTION

Many ideas of Henry Evelyn Bliss (1870-1955) on choices in design and application of library and bibliographic classification appear relevant for today and they may well stimulate discussion. Moreover, new technology enables many of the notions to be implemented or extended–thus an OPAC allows both classified and alphabetical subject approaches; reclassification of the catalog records can be more readily effected and the ability to reclassify "virtual" documents is at hand; while automatic construction and display of classmarks for both regular and alternative combinations could be accomplished.

Bliss himself declared that his main interest lay in the organization of

[Haworth co-indexing entry note]: "Blissful Beliefs: Henry Evelyn Bliss Counsels on Classification." Thomas, Alan R. Co-published simultaneously in *Cataloging & Classification Quarterly* (The Haworth Press, Inc.) Vol. 19, No. 3/4, 1995, pp. 17-22; and: *Classification: Options and Opportunities* (ed: Alan R. Thomas) The Haworth Press, Inc., 1995, pp. 17-22. Multiple copies of this article/chapter may be purchased from The Haworth Document Delivery Center [1-800-3-HAWORTH; 9:00 a.m. - 5:00 p.m. (EST)].

knowledge in relation to social organization and "*not* my proposed system of classification."[1] This paper does not deal with his Bibliographic Classification as such, though a need for light-heartedness in the sober subject of classification grants but one indulgence. In wartime Britain, the then secretary of the (British) Library Association assured the government censor that the schedules were "purely bibliographical and without any military significance whatever."[2]

The main source of information for the material that now follows was the Henry E. Bliss Papers[3] in the Rare Book and Manuscript Library of Columbia University. The original material has been selected, rearranged, synthesized, and paraphrased in the interests of continuity and brevity.

FOUNDATION STUDIES
FOR LIBRARY CLASSIFICATION DECISIONS

The system of knowledge was considered from several viewpoints: historical, scientific, philosophical, and educational.[4] The organization of knowledge was examined in relation to social organization, the organization of science (Wilhem Ostwald was among the thinkers studied), and the organization of research.

The practical task was to facilitate helpful arrangements of documents and their catalog records. To this end, library collections, their classification practices, library classification theories and schedules (including the pioneer work of Cutter and Dewey) were investigated. Ideas were applied and refined through technical experience and consultation with readers in the library of City College. Many letters have been exchanged with professional librarians. An annual pilgrimage was made to the Pratt library school for discussion with Josephine A. Rathbone,[5] regarded as an "aunt"[6] of the Bibliographical Classification scheme.

PURPOSE OF LIBRARY CLASSIFICATION

Library classification should be educative, not simply utilitarian.[7] Its educational value "dignifies the library as an embodiment of knowledge."[8]

It follows that a complete library service for library staff, readers, and students requires the application of the classification system not only to documents on shelves but also to their bibliographic records in the form of a systematic subject catalog.[9,10]

SOME PROBLEMS OF USING STANDARD SYSTEMS

Librarians and bibliographers considering the issue of standardization are cautioned to "watch your step in boarding this platform."[11] It should be remembered that "more time is spent in using classifications than in compiling them."[12]

It is "more effectual to have your classification fit your collection than have it conform to some standard . . ."[11] It may appear advantageous to use a detailed, ready-made system, especially a so-called standard. Yet a widely-used system is not necessarily research-based, well-designed, or efficient. The question arises "are the makeshifts in vogue really standards?"[13] An individual reader has his/her own private organization of subject-matter that can never be fully reflected. However, should this reader then encounter another idiosyncratic organization of knowledge within the library then the prospects for good subject searching and extension are diminished further.[14] Of the well-known systems, the Library of Congress Classification is not a valid choice for standardization because it is not typical (i.e., not designed and verified for a type or class of library) and neither is the arbitrary Universal Decimal Classification.[15] The Dewey Decimal Classification "is not grate, tho it has don grate things. It groo like the oak, becaus no other tree wus thair."[16]

One choice is to adapt the library to the straightjacket of the standard. Another option is to change the restrictive standard on-site to fit the particular library but this course of action carries the danger of confused tinkering. Standard systems without adequate options result in "irksome confinement and a profitless burden."[12] To be helpful in a given situation the standard may require alterations to serve national, language, special purposes, the needs of users (staff and readers), the particular document collection, nature of the subject or domain, and various local conditions, requirements, and resources. The work of adapting the inflexible standard may prove equal to or even greater than that of creating a better, more efficient scheme.

Standards of different purposes and levels should be relatively compatible. Consistency does not demand "complete conformity in view, outline, structure or detail."[17]

Many problems relating to using standards apply also to the home-made schemes of other libraries.

RECLASSIFICATION

Antiquated, restrictive library buildings are constantly being replaced. Because a good classification scheme secures economy in service, there is an equal need for the interior reconstruction of "our true temple of knowledge."[8] New, better constructed systems should be applied to libraries "even if only to the more recent books."[18] The reclassification decision involves "weighing an initial expense against an ultimate economy."[19] The longer "the change is postponed, the more it will cost."[8]

PRINCIPLES FOR CONSTRUCTING A CLASSIFICATION

The efficiency of a system turns mainly on ensuring adequate specificity, logical subordination, and a helpful collocation of subdivisions. The degree of detail provided should match that of ever-developing human interests. Inclusion of any subject is warranted when it is well defined and if several books have been published about it.[20] Each specific subject is logically subordinated to its relevant generic subject. Fundamental sciences, derivative studies, and applied sciences are graded by their relative speciality and successively subordinated.

The main consideration is the ordering of closely related classes and details to secure the greatest convenience for users. Communally accepted patterns of subject order and relationships, such as those reflecting the organization of knowledge maintained in scientific and pedagogical systems and conventions produce the most useful and lasting results. The resultant order is then modified to serve bibliographical and practical requirements.[21]

ADAPTIVENESS OF A CLASSIFICATION

There should be plasticity within a system to suit divergent needs of libraries: the different constituencies, purposes, services, interests, or the courses of professors and teachers. A general scheme cannot host all requisite viewpoints and relations but to be efficient it should provide for the general and the most common ones.[22] Alternatives sought but not included in a published classification scheme may be devised and implemented by the library concerned.

ALTERNATIVE LOCATION

Alternative locations should be provided in subject schedules for major and minor subjects and in tables of common subdivisions. Alternative locations are justified when a given subject or form is related closely to two or more others. For example, photography has candidacy for inclusion in technology or within the arts; economic history in general history or with economics; constitutional law within law or in political science; paleontology could be subordinated to either biology or geology. The preferred collocation of the scheme should be based on that relationship most important to current dominant interests. Any other important interests should be served by listing alternative placings.[23]

Where a library does not require some members of a series of logically equal, coordinate classes, the unwanted ones may be excised to juxtapose the wanted subjects.[23,24]

With the device of adaptation to nationality, a favored nation or language may be brought to the front of a series, overriding its normal position in the series.

ALTERNATIVE METHODS OF CLASSIFYING SUBJECTS

Within a subject or form the order of application of successive characteristics of division may be varied, that is there are different sequences in which the various components of a composite class may be combined. For instance, several modes for classifying a literature and its history, biography, and criticism might be offered. The literature in a given language could be divided first by period and then by form, or vice versa; literary texts could be separated from works about the literature and each major group then divided in various ways, or the division into texts and literary history made after prior division by period and/or form. As with alternative locations, alternative methods may be justified in both regular subject schedules as well as in lists of recurring subdivisions. That sequence most suitable for a given collection and readership is selected.

Where appropriate to attach two or more common subdivisions in a table to a regular subject classmark, any of these auxiliary specifications can be combined in duplex or complex classification, "any of them may precede, others being secondary, and tertiary" as required.[25] In a given library choice would be decided there of, say, one of the following patterns:

Shipbuilding–History–New Hampshire–18th century
Shipbuilding–History–18th century–New Hampshire
Shipbuilding–New Hampshire–History–18th century.

PERSISTENT PROBLEMS IN CLASSIFICATION

The tasks of making and applying a relative subject classification and resolving the claims of specialist interests remain "very complicated and difficult."[26] Furthermore, there are problems caused by incomplete knowledge of subject-matters and uncertain comprehension of scientific and educational systems by the cataloger/classer of books within a library.[27]

NOTES

1. Letter from Bliss to George B. Utley, June 11, 1925.
2. Letter from P.S.J. Welsford to the Censor, January 29, 1940.
3. Henry E. Bliss Papers, Rare Book and Manuscript Library, Columbia University in the City of New York. The Bliss archive was transferred from the School of Library Service in 1974. It consists of approximately 1,300 items dating from 1904 to 1951 and is contained and organized in four boxes and three scrapbooks. The material includes correspondence with many librarians and editors, journal articles, pamphlets, etc.
4. Application by Bliss to the John Simon Guggenheim Memorial Foundation, October 7, 1938.
5. Letter from Bliss to Josephine A. Rathbone, March 29, 1912.
6. Letter from Bliss to Dorkas Fellows, September 8, 1993.
7. Letter from Bliss to Grace Osgood Kelley, March 6, 1933.
8. Henry E. Bliss, "Conservatism in library classification," *Library Journal* 37(12), (December 1912):659-668, p. 667.
9. Letter from Bliss to Grace Osgood Kelley, May 23, 1927.
10. Letter from Bliss to J.C.M. Hanson, May 5, 1933.
11. Henry Evelyn Bliss, "Billionaire bibliography," *Library Journal 56* (May 15, 1931): 435-439, p. 438.
12. Letter from Bliss to Eric and Georgette de Grolier, February 26, 1932.
13. Henry E. Bliss, "What do you mean by practical classification?" *Special Libraries* 24(2), (March 1933): 35-37, p. 35.
14. Letter from Bliss to Grace Osgood Kelley, April 21, 1933.
15. Letter from Bliss entitled "Classification for bibliography of science–a problem." Published in Letters to the Editor, *Nature* 127(3215), (June 13, 1931): 889-890, p. 890.
16. Letter from Bliss to Dorkas Fellows, October 11, 1933.
17. Letter from Bliss to Cyril C. Barnard, September 29, 1936.
18. Letter from Bliss to Grace Osgood Kelley, December 10, 1926.
19. Letter from Bliss to Ernest D. Burton, June 23, 1910.
20. Letter from Bliss to Grace Osgood Kelley, December 21, 1926.
21. Letter from Bliss to Eric and Georgette de Grolier, August 11, 1932.
22. Letter from Bliss to Eric and Georgette de Grolier, June 9, 1937.
23. Henry E. Bliss. Bliss Classification [letter], *Library Association Record* 41 (4th series,volume 6) (June 1939): 281-282, p. 281.
24. Letter from Bliss to Muriel Almon, February 7, 1930.
25. Henry Evelyn Bliss, *The organization of knowledge and the subject-approach to books*, 2nd edition (New York: Wilson, 1939), p. 45.
26. Henry Evelyn Bliss, Foreword, *Bliss Classification Bulletin* I(2), (March 1955): 1-2.
27. Henry E. Bliss, "Why the library's classification differs from that published." [Typescript dated February 24, 1936. Probably a report to a superior at City College].

Library Classification
and Information Retrieval Thesauri:
Comparison and Contrast

Bella Hass Weinberg

SUMMARY. Thesauri–structured controlled vocabularies, designed for information retrieval–are compared with classification schemes developed for the arrangement of library materials and/or bibliographic records. The syndetic structure (BTs and NTs) within the alphabetic sequence of thesauri constitutes a hidden classification, but many thesauri include an explicit hierarchical display; some feature notation. The various structures and applications of thesauri are surveyed, with an emphasis on their increasing role in electronic information retrieval. The skills required for thesaurus construction are similar to those for the development of classification schemes. The distinction between these activities is expected to blur in the future.

INTRODUCTION AND TERMINOLOGY

American librarians have generally considered classification and subject cataloging two distinct activities: the former designed for the arrange-

---

Bella Hass Weinberg, DLS, is Professor in the Division of Library and Information Science, St. John's University, Jamaica, NY. She chaired the committee of the National Information Standards Organization which developed the revised American national standard for thesaurus construction.

The author gratefully acknowledges research support from St. John's University, as well as assistance in the production of the paper from her former graduate assistant, Toni Marie Burke, and Patricia-Ann Tansky, formerly a secretary in the Division of Library and Information Science. Thanks are also due to the thesaurus managers who gave permission to include illustrations from their thesauri in this paper. © 1995 by Bella Hass Weinberg

[Haworth co-indexing entry note]: "Library Classification and Information Retrieval Thesauri: Comparison and Contrast." Weinberg, Bella Hass. Co-published simultaneously in *Cataloging & Classification Quarterly* (The Haworth Press, Inc.) Vol. 19, No. 3/4, 1995, pp. 23-44; and: *Classification: Options and Opportunities* (ed: Alan R. Thomas) The Haworth Press, Inc., 1995, pp. 23-44.

ment of physical documents in a logical sequence on shelves, and the latter for retrieval of bibliographic records representing documents on specific topics via alphabetically arranged subject headings. European and Third World librarians have more experience with bibliographic classification schemes, designed for the arrangement of document surrogates–records representing the information contained in books–in a classified catalog. The most widely used bibliographic classification scheme, though little known in the United States, is the Universal Decimal Classification (UDC), an expansion of the Dewey Decimal Classification (DDC) employing special symbols to indicate relationships between subjects.

Classified catalogs are complemented by an alphabetic index–in one or more languages–and usually the index entries serve instead of subject headings. Indexes to classified catalogs and alphabetical subject catalogs have different structures and functions; librarians who construct the former generally do not also maintain the latter.

Interest in the classified catalog has increased in the U.S. in the past few years as a result of Karen Markey's work with the online display of DDC.[1] Liu and Svenonius have experimented with the use of chain indexing in the electronic version of DDC.[2] Chain indexing is an economical indexing technique that complements the hierarchy of a classification scheme.[3] It is applied primarily to the indexing of classified catalogs, but Liu and Svenonius used this technique for indexing the DDC schedules, with an eye toward its eventual application to online bibliographic databases.

These developments indicate an end to the "marking and parking" approach to classification and an interest in using classification, in conjunction with alphabetic indexes, for subject retrieval as well as for the physical arrangement of materials. The Dewey experiments are notable in that they represent a return to this classification's original dual purpose: shelf classification and use in a classified catalog. The closest thing to a classified catalog in American experience is the *shelflist*. The difference between the two is that in a classified catalog, there are often multiple access points for a single document–just as a book may be assigned more than one subject heading–while a shelflist contains only one record per title. Electronic shelflists are familiar to American librarians, while online classified catalogs are on the horizon.

The purpose of this paper is to compare information retrieval thesauri with library classification–both shelf and bibliographic classification schemes. The phrase *information retrieval thesaurus* is used here in contrast to the widely used reference work, *Roget's Thesaurus*. Hans Wellisch, a member of the committee which developed the revised American National Standard for thesaurus construction,[4] provided an interesting note in the glossary to distinguish the two types of thesauri: *Roget's Thesaurus* suggests synonyms to those who want stylistic variation in their writing, while information retrieval thesauri indicate which of two synonyms is preferred. In the balance of this paper, the term *thesaurus* represents *information retrieval thesaurus*.

The full form of the term serves to point out a primary difference between shelf classification schemes and thesauri–their field of application. The most frequent application of thesauri is in the indexing or content analysis of *parts* of documents, e.g., articles in periodicals, while shelf classification schemes are intended for the physical arrangement of books, complete runs of journals, and other media.

The phrase *information retrieval thesaurus* also serves to point out the origin of the concept–outside the library world. Those who began using computers for information retrieval seemed to consciously avoid library science terminology. One of the pioneers of information science, Mortimer Taube, reportedly said, "Advanced cataloging sounds so dull–call it documentation!" (*Documentation* was the former name for the discipline of *information science*.)

Information scientists coined the term *descriptors* for *subject headings* and *thesauri* for *subject heading lists*. It is interesting to note that *thesauri* are now often being renamed *knowledge bases*, as vogue words from the domain of artificial intelligence enter the information science literature.[5]

A major difference in the application of subject heading lists and thesauri, which perhaps warranted the change in terminology, is that the former were designed for *precoordination* and the latter for use in *postcoordinate* information systems.

Subject headings originated in the environment of card and book catalogs. Relationships between two concepts, such as "Religion and Science," had to be indicated in a single heading, as the print medium was inflexible: one could not efficiently scan all the entries under *Religion* to find those with the additional subject heading *Science*. With postcoordinate information systems (which, incidentally, preceded computers) the two concepts could be represented by separate descriptors and combined at the point of search.

The Library of Congress adopted thesaurus notation for its subject heading list in December 1986. (Thesaurus notation appeared first in the microfiche edition with that date. The first "red books" with thesaurus notation were dated 1988, the 11th edition of *Library of Congress Subject Headings* [LCSH].) Dykstra considered the change in notation inappropriate because LC subject headings are precoordinate, and hence LCSH does not constitute a true thesaurus.[6]

Librarians who work with online catalogs are now cognizant of the power of postcoordination and realize that their former deliberations over the order of elements in subject heading lists are often irrelevant in the online environment. To take an example from the classic *topic–place* vs. *place–topic* debate, it matters little in the online mode whether a subject heading is structured as "Boston–Museums" or "Museums–Boston," since the Boolean combination "Museums AND Boston" will retrieve either string.

Svenonius has pointed out that precoordination is useful even in the online environment because it avoids *false drops*–the retrieval of unwanted combinations of terms. For example, a search on "Philosophy AND History" will retrieve documents on both the "philosophy of history" and the "history of philosophy"–two very different topics.[7] (A false drop could also occur in the case of a postcoordinate search on "Boston AND Museums," not because the order of the words is significant, but owing to the possibility of false coordination, as in the case of a document on "Museums in London and Art Galleries in Boston.")

The first thesauri consisted of *uniterms*–single words–but the false drop problem quickly became apparent, and the idea of *bound terms* was developed: allowing multiple words representing a single concept to be established as descriptors. *Concept* is a very difficult term to define, however, and most thesauri include precoordinate terms, mainly because the indexes based on them are published in both print and electronic versions. Rogers has pointed out that *Medical Subject Headings* (MeSH) has to serve both the precoordinate environment of printed *Index Medicus* and the National Library of Medicine *Current Catalog* as well as the postcoordinate MEDLINE database.[8]

Frequency of a concept in a domain often leads to precoordination in a thesaurus. For example, MeSH includes many terms on the model of "Kidney Neoplasms." Such terms could be split without introducing the problem of false drops due to word order. One can, however, imagine the number of entries that would be found in *Index Medicus* under each of the separate terms.

Like LCSH, MeSH includes a list of standardized subheadings that are linked with headings in accordance with detailed rules. Although some would say that this precoordinate feature disqualifies MeSH from consideration as a thesaurus, the linked headings and subheadings are very useful in online searches as they convey aspects of topics, such as "adverse effects," which cannot efficiently be formulated through Boolean combinations of concrete terms. The powerful classified array of MeSH is discussed in a subsequent section of this paper.

Subject headings and thesauri are both types of controlled vocabulary. In the literature one often encounters definitions of *controlled vocabulary* that include classification schemes. The revised American thesaurus standard categorizes classification schemes as a type of *indexing language*, but not as controlled vocabulary, since the terminology (i.e., the words in the feature headings) of a classification scheme is not really *controlled*: the notation may be viewed as an artificial language representing terms in any natural language. Synonyms in the index to a classification scheme can (or should) both point to a class number; a preferred term is generally not indicated, as it would be in a controlled vocabulary. An exception occurs where there are many subheadings for an index term and it is not economical to display them in a printed index under two synonyms. A cross reference is provided in such cases by the indexer, but the vocabulary is not controlled from the outset.

Having defined the primary terms relating to classification and thesauri, we now proceed to a comparison of their major features.

NOTATION

Although a maxim taught in library school is "a classification is not its notation," American librarians often associate classification with the use of a specific notation–decimal numbers in the case of DDC, and alphanumeric characters in the case of Library of Congress Classification (LCC). Subject heading lists, in contrast, are thought of as alphabetic arrays of terms.

Standard thesaurus notation, in the form of BT/NT (broader term-narrower term) references, makes the hierarchical relationships between terms more explicit than the *see also* references used in subject heading lists, which represent two kinds of relationship: hierarchical and associative. Yet it was recognized even in the days of *see also* references that the syndetic structure of a subject heading list creates a hidden classification, which can be made explicit. Richmond studied the hierarchy of *cats* in LCSH and compared it with the corresponding zoological classification.[9]

Sinkankas attempted to build a hierarchy from LCSH, but found that its rule of providing only downward *see also* references–from broad to narrower terms–was often violated.[10] Thus it was difficult for a librarian or user to distinguish hierarchical *see also* references from associative ones, which were provided in both directions.

Weinberg created hierarchical displays from an edition of LCSH featuring thesaurus notation and contrasted these with the corresponding sections of LCC. The LCSH hierarchies were often deeper and more detailed than those in LCC.[11]

Some thesauri contain an explicit hierarchical display, without notation, generated from the BT/NT references in the alphabetic sequence of descriptors. An example of this is found in the *Thesaurus of ERIC Descriptors* (Figure 1). A slight variation on this structure is found in the *INSPEC Thesaurus* (Figure 2), which, in addition to the codes BT and NT, introduces the abbreviation TT for *top term*, i.e., the broadest term in the hierarchy. In a separate sequence, the top terms are arranged alphabetically, and all of their narrower terms, on all levels, are featured. Whereas

---

FIGURE 1. Broader term (BT) and narrower term (NT) references in the alphabetic display of the *Thesaurus of ERIC Descriptors,* 12th ed. (Phoenix, AZ: Oryx Press, 1990) compared with full hierarchical display.

Library Systems
USE   LIBRARY NETWORKS

Library Technical Assistants
USE   LIBRARY TECHNICIANS

LIBRARY TECHNICAL PROCESSES
                                              Jul. 1966
              CIJE: 803   RIE: 813   GC: 710
SN   Acquisition, preparation,
         and organization
         of library materials for use
UF   Technical Processes (Libraries)
         Technical Services (Libraries)
NT   Library Acquisition
BT   Library Services
RT   Abstracting
         Bibliographic Utilities
         Cataloging
         Classification
         Indexing
         Information Processing
         Information Technology
         Integrated Library Systems
         Libraries
         Library Administration
         Library Automation
         Library Expenditures
         Library Materials

: : :METHODS
: :EVALUATION METHODS
:SURVEYS
LIBRARY SURVEYS

: : :SERVICES
: : INFORMATION SERVICES
:LIBRARY SERVICES
LIBRARY TECHNICAL PROCESSES
.LIBRARY ACQUISITION
..LIBRARY MATERIAL
    SELECTION

: : :GROUPS
: : PERSONNEL
:LIBRARY PERSONNEL
LIBRARY TECHNICIANS
.MEDICAL RECORD
    TECHNICIANS

in the ERIC thesaurus' hierarchical display, every descriptor is an access point, in the top-term structure only the broadest descriptors are.

Another type of thesaurus display gives the full hierarchy within the primary alphabetic sequence of descriptors. In contrast to the "flat format" BT/NT notation, which provides only one level of hierarchy at a time, the variant structure shows all the levels. The *International Energy Subject Thesaurus* (Figure 3), for example, employs the notation BT1, BT2, etc., and NT1, NT2, etc. to indicate one level broader, two levels broader; one level narrower, two levels narrower, etc. The *NASA Thesaurus* (Figure 4) has an equivalent structure with different coding. It contains

---

FIGURE 2. Broader term (BT), narrower term (NT), and top term (TT) references in the *INSPEC Thesaurus* (Stevenage, Herts: Institution of Electrical Engineers, 1993). The TT references lead to the alphabetical array of top terms, which displays the full hierarchy.

interference (signal)
NT	crosstalk
	electromagnetic interference
	intersymbol interference
BT	interference
TT	interference
RT	interference suppression
	noise
	noise measurement
	reception
CC	B5230: B6200
DI	January 1977
PT	interference
	noise

interference (wave)
NT	acoustic wave interference
	electromagnetic wave interference
BT	interference
TT	interference
RT	interference spectrometers
	interferometers
	interferometry
DI	January 1977
PT	interference

interference
. interference (signal)
.. crosstalk
.. electromagnetic interference
... radiofrequency interference
.... atmospherics
.... jamming
.... radar interference
..... radar clutter
.... whistlers
.... white noise
... telephone interference
... television interference
.. intersymbol interference
. interference (wave)
.. acoustic wave interference
.. electromagnetic wave interference
... light interference
... moire fringes

FIGURE 3. Multi-level broader (BT1, BT2) and narrower (NT1, NT2) terms in the *International Energy Subject Thesaurus* (Paris: International Energy Agency, 1990). There is no auxiliary hierarchical display.

Semiconductor Counters
DA	December 1, 1974
USE	Semiconductor Detectors

SEMICONDUCTOR DETECTORS [01]
DA	December 1, 1974
UF	*Semiconductor Counters*
BT1	Radiation Detectors
BT2	Measuring Instruments
NT1	Bulk Semiconductor Detectors
NT1	CDTE Semiconductor Detectors
NT1	Ge Semiconductor Detectors
NT2	High-Purity GE Detectors
NT2	Li-Drifted Ge Detectors
NT1	Hgl2 Semiconductor Detectors
NT1	InSb Semiconductor Detectors
NT1	Junction Detectors
NT2	Li-Drifted Junction Detectors
NT1	Li-Drifted Detectors
NT2	Li-Drifted Ge Detectors
NT2	Li-Drifted Junction Detectors
NT2	Li-Drifted Si Detectors
NT1	Si Semiconductor Detectors
NT2	Li-Drifted Si Dectors
NT1	Surface Barrier Detectors
RT	Dosemeters
RT	Radiator Counters
RT	Semiconductor Devices

Reprinted with permission.

---

no BT/NT references–only the code GS (generic structure), with dots and indention indicating levels of hierarchy.

The tree structures of *Medical Subject Headings* (Figure 5) illustrate best the close relationship between thesauri and classification. The descriptors are not linked hierarchically through BT and NT references. Instead, each is assigned one or more classification notations, called *tree numbers*. The notation is alphanumeric and expressive, i.e., the longer the tree number, the more specific the term.

The tree-structure display provides a complete hierarchy–containing all

FIGURE 4. Generic Structure (GS) in the *NASA Thesaurus* (Springfield, VA: National Technical Information Service, 1988). There is no auxiliary classified display.

IONIZATION COUNTERS
 USE   IONIZATION CHAMBERS
        RADIATION COUNTERS

IONIZATION CROSS SECTIONS
 RT   ABSORPTI0N CROSS SECTIONS
        ∞CROSS SECTIONS
        NONADIABATIC THEORY
        SCATTERING CROSS SECTIONS

IONIZATION FREQUENCIES
 GS   FREQUENCIES
        . IONIZATION FREQUENCIES

IONIZATION GAGES
 UF   ION GAGES
 GS   MEASURING INSTRUMENTS
        . PRESSURE GAGES
        . . VACUUM GAGES
        . . . IONIZATION GAGES
        . . . . ALPHATRONS
        . . . . BAYARD-ALPERT-IONIZATION
                GAGES
        . . . . PENNING GAGES
        . . . . PHILIPS IONIZATION GAGES
        VACUUM APPARATUS
        . VACUUM GAGES
        . . IONIZATI0N GAGES
        . . . ALPHATRONS
        . . . BAYARD-ALPERT IONIZATION
                GAGES
        . . . PENNING GAGES
        . . . PHILIPS IONIZATION GAGES
 RT   HOT CATHODES
        KNUDSEN GAGES
        MCLEOD GAGES
        ORBITRONS
        PIRANI GAGES
        PRESSURE MEASUREMENT

FIGURE 5. Tree structure from *Medical Subject Headings*, 1994 (Bethesda, MD: National Library of Medicine, 1993). There is no hierarchical information in the alphabetic display of the thesaurus, except for the tree number(s) of the descriptor.

•**Psychologic Processes and Principles (Non MeSH)**	**F2**
Mental Competency	**F2.410**
Mental Health	**F2.418**
Mental Processes	**F2.463**
Cognition	**F2.463.188**
Awareness	**F2.463.188.150**
Cognitive Dissonance	**F2.463.188.305**
Consciousness	**F2.463.188.409**
Imagination	**F2.463.188.634**
Dreams	**F2.463.188.634.309**
Fantasy	**F2.463.188.634.507**
Learning	**F2.463.425**
Association	**F2.463.425.69**
Association Learning	**F2.463.425.69.296**

Reprinted with permission.

narrower, broader, and *sibling* terms. The last-mentioned are terms on the same level that share a "parent" or broader term. Siblings of the accessed descriptor are absent from the flat format (BT/NT), the multilevel format (BT1, NT1), and the generic structure (GS). They can be found in the auxiliary hierarchical displays of the ERIC and INSPEC thesauri, but there is much redundancy in these structures while there is none in MeSH: hierarchical information is given only in the tree structures.

An even greater advantage of the tree structure than economy of space is its power in searching. In the electronic versions of MeSH it is possible to "explode" a descriptor through its tree number, with the result that all the narrower terms under it are automatically searched. With other thesauri, it is necessary to use Boolean OR to connect a broad descriptor and its narrower terms on more than one level–a rather time-consuming procedure. In the typical DIALOG thesaurus display, line numbers can be cited in a search statement to link a descriptor and its first-level narrower terms. To examine the second level of narrower terms requires another command.

The allocation of notation to the tree structures of MeSH was done very carefully, and the system continues to serve indexers and searchers well some three decades after implementation. The tree structures have been emulated recently by MEDLINE's commercial rival, Excerpta Medica.[12]

It is, however, also possible to assign non-expressive notation to thesaurus descriptors, the simplest form being computer-generated line numbers. These are found in the *Art & Architecture Thesaurus* (AAT), which also has lengthy alphabetic expressive notation designed for computer manipulation (see Figure 6). The advantage of the line numbers is that they can be revised automatically when new descriptors are added.

There is thus a continuum of thesaurus structures from alphabetical arrangement of descriptors with a single level of hierarchy indicated for each, to full hierarchical displays with expressive notation. Liu and Svenonius, in contrasting thesauri and classification, suggested that in the former, hierarchies are generally flatter. Responding to their paper, Weinberg noted that this may be true in thesauri that limit the indication of hierarchy to single-level broader and narrower terms, but in their depth of hierarchy, thesauri such as MeSH and the AAT rival library classification schemes.[13] In thesauri with systematic (classified) displays, the alphabetic array of descriptors is often secondary–functioning as an index to the hierarchical display.

Liu and Svenonius also implied that thesauri lack another feature found in classification–hierarchical levels denoting concepts that cannot be expressed by a single term; but MeSH features "non-MeSH" terms to express these general concepts (see Figure 5), while the AAT has node labels to indicate the characteristics of division, e.g., <houses: by shape> (see Figure 6). The *thesaurofacet* concept, developed in England,[14] represents a complete synthesis of thesaurus and classification structures.

PRINCIPLES AND METHODS OF COMPILATION

Library classification schemes may be divided into those that are based on a philosophical division of knowledge and those based on literary warrant. LCC is the best example for the latter category, while DDC is often considered to be in the former (although in the author's recent experience serving on a committee monitoring the revision of the DDC religion schedule, literary warrant is now a primary consideration in the expansion of the classification).

Thesauri may be categorized in the same way: many are developed empirically, with descriptors added as the documents being indexed warrant. Others–especially those with expressive notation and those which are based on the concept of facets–reflect the structure and categories of a domain (field). The AAT is explicitly based on the concept of facets, and this concept is implicit in MeSH. For example, one of the MeSH trees is devoted to "Diseases," a primary facet of medicine.

FIGURE 6. Top: Computer-generated line numbers in the hierarchical display of the *Art & Architecture Thesaurus,* 2nd ed. (New York: Oxford University Press, 1994). Bottom: The alphabetic display in the 1990 edition gives the expressive notation for each descriptor, following the code CN. This was omitted from the 1994 edition, but is included in the MARC record for each AAT term.

<visual works>
<visual works by medium or technique>

VC.246	**mail art**
VC.247	**montages**
VC.248	**photomontages**
VC.249	**mosaics**
VC.250	**multimedia works**
VC.251	**niellos**
VC.252	**paintings**
VC.253	*<paintings by form>*
VC.254	**cabinet pictures**
VC.255	**dummy board figures**
VC.256	**easel paintings**
VC.257	**miniatures (paintings)**
VC.258	**panel paintings**
VC.259	**scroll paintings**
VC.260	**handscrolls**
VC.261	**emakimono**
VC.262	**shaped canvases**
VC.263	**tondi**

chests of drawers
	TG.475	(L,N)
ALT	chest of drawers	
SN	Type of case furniture usually having four drawers but sometimes made with three, five or more; generally supported on feet and sometimes resting directly on the floor.	

Use **commodes** for similar case pieces generally supported on short legs. Use **chests with drawers** for chests with one or more tiers of drawers below a deep storage space.

UF	bureaus (chests of drawers)
	chests, dressing (chests of drawers)
	drawers, chests of
	dressers (chests of drawers)
	dressing chests (chests of drawers)
CN	V.TG.AFU.AFU.AXC.ALO.BCW

Reprinted with permission.

MeSH is not a true faceted scheme because it features a great deal of *polyhierarchy*, i.e., many of its descriptors occur in multiple trees. *The Tree Trimmer* is a recent publication designed to let the searcher know whether the narrower terms of a given MeSH descriptor are identical in all hierarchies.[15] The AAT, in contrast, does not admit of polyhierarchy; each descriptor is assigned to only one facet.[16]

Classifiers and library science students are familiar with the relative index of DDC and may think that the "distributed relatives"–the multiple contexts of a topic–constitute a case of polyhierarchy. This is not true, however; DDC, like LCC, has discipline as the primary facet and disperses concrete topics, such as *women*, among the various disciplines, depending on the *aspect* from which the topic is treated, e.g., psychology or sociology. Thesauri may contain hierarchies of disciplines, but concrete topics would not be enumerated in such hierarchies; the concrete topics would be descriptors in separate hierarchies. A discipline descriptor and a concrete term can be postcoordinated in search statements such as "women AND psychology" or synthesized in index strings such as "women–psychology."

Many thesauri are linked to a bibliographic database, and the addition of descriptors is dependent to a large extent on literary warrant, i.e., the number of documents on a topic. This is a factor in the expansion of LCSH as well. Another factor that is considered in the expansion of MeSH is the retrievability of a topic through free-text searching in the MEDLINE database; if the term is unambiguously retrievable by limiting a search to the title field, a descriptor may *not* be added to the thesaurus.[17] The AAT is not linked to a single database, but indexers and searchers from any of the institutions that employ the thesaurus may propose new descriptors (candidate terms); thus literary warrant is a factor in this thesaurus as well, along with user warrant.

Subject experts play a greater role in the design of systematic thesauri than they do in the development of alphabetic thesauri. Classified thesauri are often developed in a top-down approach, while alphabetic thesauri are expanded in a bottom-up approach. In other words, if the designers of a thesaurus plan to assign expressive notation to descriptors, they must carefully circumscribe the domain, identify the primary facets (top terms), and then proceed to enumerate the narrower terms. Thesaurus development in such situations is generally done by committee: information specialists collaborating with subject experts.

Alphabetic thesauri may, in contrast, be developed empirically in a bottom-up approach, with descriptors and hierarchical relationships added as the literature requires. Subject experts may be consulted regarding the preferred form of a descriptor or the correctness of a given BT/NT link, but no general outline of the structure of a domain is necessary a priori. This approach is probably the best one for mission-oriented indexing services, which draw on the literature of multiple disciplines. (An example of a mission-oriented secondary service is *Pollution Abstracts*.) In contrast, the structure of a discipline such as zoology is quite stable and lends itself to classification.

Whether a top-down or bottom-up approach is used for thesaurus construction, "[a] formal classification . . . can assist in the formation of references by displaying the hierarchical structure of the subject."[18]

MAINTENANCE AND UPDATING

Thesauri, like classification schemes, are growing organisms and need to be monitored and maintained. Thesauri that do not reflect the latest developments and terminology in a field give an impression of out-of-dateness and hence are underutilized.

Thesauri usually have a narrower scope than library classification schemes, and perhaps this is one of the reasons why thesauri tend to be updated more quickly than classification systems. Whereas DDC is issued in a revised edition approximately once in seven years, a new print edition of the MeSH thesaurus is published annually. If one considers LCSH a thesaurus, we may note that a new edition in hard copy is issued annually, and that addenda and revisions are published weekly. All of these tools are now available in electronic versions as well, and the latter are generally more up-to-date than their print counterparts.

Thesauri are generally maintained with the assistance of software.[19] In fully automated environments, proposals of new descriptors can be made on an on-screen form and approved quickly by a thesaurus editor for application in indexing. (The approval of new subject heading proposals at LC takes somewhat longer.)

There is perhaps less resistance to the revision and expansion of thesauri than there is to the restructuring of classification schemes because of the implications of the latter for the "integrity of notation," i.e., the consistent meaning of a class number over time. The revision of descriptors does, however, have serious implications for searching, as few indexing operations can afford to reindex older documents when descriptors are modified. A thesaurus should therefore contain a record of the term history of each descriptor. Minimally, this should include the date the term was added to the thesaurus. For descriptors that are changed to entry terms (USE references), thesauri often indicate the years during which the term was a valid descriptor. *Annotated MeSH*, the version designed for indexers and searchers, provides a detailed history of changes in cross references in addition to the status of descriptors.

While it is relatively easy to implement one-for-one replacements of descriptors in databases, it is more difficult to deal with the addition of specific descriptors when older documents were indexed by broader ones. Reindexing in such cases cannot be done automatically, as some older documents are appropriately described by the broader term, while others have narrower scope and should be reindexed by a more specific descriptor.

In theory, thesauri have a policy of ultimate specificity, but in practice there are attempts to control their size. The earliest lists of *descriptors*–a term coined by Calvin Mooers–were designed to be very small.[20] The power of postcoordination was expected to obviate the need for the enumeration of many descriptors. Weinberg and Cunningham have posited that thesauri feature very detailed vocabulary for the core concepts of a domain, but include less specific terms for the peripheral concepts.[21] (This is analogous to special library classification schemes, which are very detailed for the primary subject, and less so for peripheral subjects.) Thus, for example, MeSH features very detailed vocabulary for parts of the body, but only a few general terms for environmental concepts. MeSH currently contains more than 17,000 descriptors,[22] which seems like a lot, but a 1983 paper noted that Excerpta Medica's vocabulary consisted of an order of magnitude more: 220,000 preferred terms and 250,000 synonyms.[23]

Bates has made a case that thesauri designed for end-users require a much larger entry vocabulary (i.e., more cross references) than thesauri designed for intermediaries because end-users are unaware of the basic grammar of descriptor formulation, e.g., the preference for nouns. She thus suggests that a *"Superthesaurus"* include references from other parts of speech, such as verbs and adjectives–forms often input by end-users in free-text searches.[24]

The greater the number of terms in a thesaurus, the more expensive it is to maintain, the harder it is to generate all the appropriate relationships, and the less the likelihood of consistent assignment of descriptors by indexers. In the literature of classification, one also finds the observation that the only scheme for which consistent application is assured is one that consists of a single number. The earliest library classification scheme reportedly contained two classes: sacred works and secular works. Immediately, borderline cases arose! In both classification and thesaurus management, there is thus a conflict between the needs for specificity and economy.

INNOVATIVE AND FUTURE APPLICATIONS

Innovative applications of thesauri include their use at the searching stage rather than the indexing stage. With a searching thesaurus, no descriptors are assigned to documents; the thesaurus is used instead to link synonyms and related terms at the point of searching. One problem that cannot be handled reliably in this way is the disambiguation of homographs, e.g., *cranes* (birds) and *cranes* (equipment). To some extent, co-occurrence data can be used for automatic selection of the correct descriptor-parenthetical qualifier combination. For example, the word *cranes* in the sense of birds is likely to co-occur with zoological and botanical terms, while *cranes* in the sense of equipment will generally co-occur with engineering terms.

More serious than the homograph problem is that of implicit concepts. Until we have natural language understanding by computers, only a human being can recognize unstated concepts in reading a text. Brenner, in reporting on computer-assisted indexing based on the matching of thesaurus terms to the natural language of abstracts, noted that 70% of descriptors could be assigned by computer. He thus concluded that only 30% of what human indexers do is intelligent.[25]

This leads to the application of thesauri in artificial intelligence (AI). Thesaurus concepts underlie most *knowledge bases*, structured representations of knowledge in a domain. Many AI researchers do not have a library-information science background, however; thus they have invented new terms for semantic relationships and have either neglected or reinvented the concept of the *reciprocal* of the cross reference, a powerful control device.

As noted above, since AI has become a hot field, many information scientists have adopted AI terminology, referring to thesauri as *knowledge bases*. The latter are far more complex structures than thesauri, with much more refined coding of hierarchical relationships than *broader term* and *narrower term*. Some thesauri refine the traditional BT/NT coding by distinguishing the "is-a" (class membership) relationship from the *part-whole* relationship, employing the codes BTP (broader term partitive) and NTP (narrower term partitive) for the latter. The cognitive science literature, however, indicates that there are six types of part-whole relationship.[26] While it may be necessary to distinguish these in a knowledge base to allow for correct inferences, the history of information science has shown that complicated coding systems are difficult to apply consistently in both indexing and retrieval.

Thesauri also underlie good hypertext systems: the links between parts (nodes) of a machine-readable text should be based on semantic relationships between descriptors–both hierarchical and associative. The latter type of relationship is generally coded RT (related term) in thesauri.

Given the focus of this paper on hierarchy, little attention has been paid to associative relationships, but it should be noted that the rules for establishing related-term references in certain thesauri are dependent on their hierarchies; for example, descriptors in the same hierarchy may not be linked by RT references. There is currently interest in coding a variety of types of related-term references, for example, in the AAT.

The latest interfaces to online catalogs designed for direct use by children feature a menu of categories, i.e., a classification, complemented by an alphabetic index.[27] We do not yet have research results that allow us to state whether the classified or alphabetic approach is preferred, but it is clear that they are complementary. A user beginning with a specific term should be able to see its position in a hierarchical display, while a user beginning with a broad category should be led to the narrower terms.

Little has been done with hierarchical display in thesauri mounted on the major online vendor systems.[28] For example, on DIALOG, as noted above, one can view the first-level broader and narrower terms of a given descriptor in the relatively small number of databases that have mounted thesauri. A full classified display is available only for thesauri that have such explicit structures, for example, MeSH. The display format of MeSH on DIALOG is, however, not as good as it is in the printed tree structures, in which one can view all of the broader terms of a selected descriptor, as well as the narrower terms. BRS, which until a few years ago had no online thesauri, mounted MeSH in 1991; according to a description by Van Camp,[29] only one level above and one level below the requested term are displayed–not the full hierarchy.

The systematic display of the AAT has been mounted on the Research Libraries Information Network (RLIN). Given the limitations of video-display terminals with respect to the number of lines that can be displayed on a screen, the panorama of the printed page is still preferable for viewing the complete hierarchy of a thesaurus. The electronic version, however, offers such possibilities as displaying the hierarchy to any desired level. A description of the newly mounted second edition of the AAT shows the *node labels* (facet indicators) of the hierarchy of visual works, e.g., <visual works by form>.[30] This is analogous to the summary outlines of classification schemes.

CONCLUSIONS

James D. Anderson has posited that indexing and classification are the same thing; the only difference is display.[31] Alphabetic thesauri possess hidden classifications which may be converted to explicit ones. Thesauri developed recently on the principle of faceting resemble synthetic classification schemes to a remarkable extent.

The Special Interest Group (SIG) of the American Society for Information Science (ASIS) that is most concerned with indexing is SIG/CR–Classification Research. Since 1990, SIG/CR has held an annual Classification Research Workshop in conjunction with the ASIS Annual Meeting; thesauri are the subject of many of the papers. The proceedings of the first three workshops have been published;[32] papers from the 1993 and 1994 workshops have been summarized[33] and are also scheduled to be published.

One of the most interesting papers presented at the 1993 workshop focused on the Music Thesaurus, a project of the Music Library Association. Hemmasi described how music subject headings from LCSH were decoordinated and structured hierarchically. A similar process took place in the development stage of the AAT.[34] Hemmasi made the intriguing proposal that experts in various domains extract the terms in their field from LCSH, restructure them, and return them to LCSH. Adoption of Hemmasi's idea would turn LCSH into a *macrothesaurus*–more general than, but compatible with, the microthesauri developed for specific fields.

Most extant thesauri have been developed for narrow domains, often because LCSH did not provide the requisite specificity for exhaustive analysis of documents. There has been little success in the automatic mapping of terms from disparate thesauri.[35]

Credit is due to Pauline Atherton Cochrane for pointing out the need for enhanced subject access to books.[36] This is being provided at present–to some extent–through keyword searching of machine-readable tables of contents. Analytical subject cataloging using descriptors derived from a microthesaurus compatible with LCSH would be far superior to keyword searching in terms of recall and precision. Furthermore, this would permit the integration of subject indexes to the serial literature with subject catalogs. As machine-readable indexes to periodicals are mounted alongside catalogs of monographs, the differences between cataloging and indexing methods have become apparent. The compatibility of the descriptive cataloging practices of databases and catalogs has been studied by Giral and Taylor;[37] subject access requires more attention.

The merger of monographic catalogs with analytical indexes, and the use of compatible thesauri for these two types of bibliographic databases, will blur the distinctions between library science and information science, and perhaps lead to a restructuring of the journals in the field. The majority of publications on thesauri currently appear outside the traditional cataloging periodicals; this should change as catalogers become increasingly concerned with thesaurus development.

This author does not expect paper-based documents to disappear in the foreseeable future. There will thus still be a need for the maintenance of physical libraries, as opposed to virtual libraries. A lot of research is currently focused on browsing, and the findings should be relevant both to those who develop shelf classification schemes and to those who design electronic information access systems.

Perhaps librarians who apply shelf classification schemes can truncate the notation of systematic thesauri to provide logical groupings without unnecessary specificity. We do not know what level of specificity is desirable in the physical arrangement of documents. Ranganathan argued for ultimate specificity–"co-extensiveness"[38]–but the notation he developed to accommodate this was impractical, and his Colon Classification was rarely implemented in the West.

On the basis of transaction log analysis, however, we do know that users of machine-readable files need and want specificity. End-users sometimes enter more general search terms than they really require, but a machine-readable thesaurus should display the narrower terms to them–without being asked. Computers are ideal for handling lengthy, complex notation that is unsuitable for humans to process; the user need not see the complexity of the underlying structure.

This article has demonstrated the complementarity of alphabetic thesauri and classification. We do not yet know enough about search habits–nor do we have enough online classified displays–to state whether the alphabetic or hierarchical approach is primary, but the computer will allow us to move from one to the other with ease. The fact that classification theorists and thesaurus designers are now part of the same professional societies and exchange ideas at conferences[39] suggests that principles and practices from each of the fields will inform the other.

The adoption of thesauri with complementary hierarchical displays may lead to the elimination of redundant practice in content analysis in the library community–the assignment of subject headings as well as shelf classification numbers representing identical topics.

NOTES

1. Karen Markey, "Searching and Browsing the Dewey Decimal Classification in an Online Catalog," *Cataloging & Classification Quarterly* 7:3 (Spring 1987): 37-68.

2. Songqiao Liu and Elaine Svenonius, "DORS: *DDC* Online Retrieval System," *Library Resources & Technical Services* 35:4 (Oct. 1991): 359-375.

3. T. D. Wilson, *An Introduction to Chain Indexing* (Hamden, CT: Linnett Books, 1971).

4. National Information Standards Organization. *Guidelines for the Construction, Format, and Management of Monolingual Thesauri.* Bethesda, MD: NISO, 1994. (ANSI/NISO Z39.19-1993). Many of the points made in this paper are developed and illustrated further in the standard.

5. Bella Hass Weinberg, "Vogue Words in Information Science," *Bulletin of the American Society for Information Science* 16:4 (April/May 1990): 15.

6. Mary Dykstra, "LC Subject Headings Disguised as a Thesaurus," *Library Journal* 113: 4 (March 1, 1988): 42-46.

7. Elaine Svenonius, "Proposal #2: Arguments in Favor," in *The Future of Subdivisions in the Library of Congress Subject Headings System:* Report from the Subject Subdivisions Conference, 1991, Martha O'Hara Conway, ed. (Washington, DC: Library of Congress, Cataloging Distribution Service, 1992), 36-38.

8. Frank B. Rogers, "Problems of Medical Subject Cataloging," *Bulletin of the Medical Library Association* 56 (Oct. 1968): 355-364.

9. Phyllis Allen Richmond, "Cats: An Example of Concealed Classification in Subject Headings," *Library Resources & Technical Services* 3 (Spring 1959): 102-112.

10. George M. Sinkankas, *A Study in the Syndetic Structure of the Library of Congress List of Subject Headings* (Pittsburgh: University of Pittsburgh, Graduate School of Library and Information Sciences, 1972). (The Pittsburgh Studies in Library and Information Sciences, 2), 53-58.

11. Bella Hass Weinberg, "The Hidden Classification in Library of Congress Subject Headings for Judaica," *Library Resources & Technical Services* 37:4 (Oct. 1993): 369-379.

12. *EMTREE Thesaurus 1992.* Volume 1: Tree Structure (Amsterdam: Excerpta Medica, 1992). The Introduction notes that "EMTREE was introduced in 1988 to integrate . . . various indexing systems" (p. I-1). These include several special classification schemes.

13. Bella Hass Weinberg, "Letter," *Library Resources & Technical Services* 36:1 (Jan. 1992): 123-124.

14. Aitchison, J. et al., comps., *Thesaurofacet: A Thesaurus and Faceted Classification for Engineering and Related Subjects* (Whetstone, Eng.: English Electric Co., 1969). Described in: F. W. Lancaster, *Vocabulary Control for Information Retrieval* (Washington, DC: Information Resources Press, 1972), 66-69.

15. William A. Clintworth, *The Tree Trimmer: A Search Tool for Multiple 'Tree Explosions' in Medical Subject Headings–1992* (Los Angeles: Clintworth Publications, 1991).

16. The distinction was clarified by David Batty at an "Open Forum on the NISO Thesaurus Standard" held at the ASIS Annual Meeting, Oct. 29, 1991. A report on the session is in: Steve Hardin, " '91 ASIS Conference Highlights Standards," *Information Standards Quarterly* 4:1 (Jan. 1992): 13-16. A correction notice is in: Bella Hass Weinberg, "Thesaurus Construction Update," *Information Standards Quarterly* 4:2 (April 1992): 22.

17. Policies of the National Library of Medicine regarding expansion of MeSH are reported in: Bella Hass Weinberg and Julie A. Cunningham, "The Relationship Between Term Specificity in MeSH and Online Postings in MEDLINE," *Bulletin of the Medical Library Association* 73:4 (Oct. 1985): 371.

18. Rita Marcella and Robert Newton, "Indexes, Thesauri and Classification," Chapter 5 of their: *A New Manual of Classification*. Aldershot: Gower, 1994: 154.

19. A directory is found in: Jessica L. Milstead, "Thesaurus Software Packages," American Society for Information Science, *Proceedings of the ASIS Annual Meeting* 27 (1990): 3-13. An outline of features is in: Jessica L. Milstead, "Specifications for Thesaurus Software," *Information Processing & Management* 27:2/3 (1991): 165-175.

20. F.W. Lancaster, "Vocabulary Control in Information Retrieval Systems," *Advances in Librarianship* 7 (1977): 4.

21. Bella Hass Weinberg and Julie A. Cunningham, "Term Specificity and Online Postings: Inverse Relationship?" American Society for Information Science, *Proceedings of the ASIS Annual Meeting* 21 (1984): 144-147.

22. Peri Schuyler, Head, MeSH, National Library of Medicine, reports that the 1994 edition contains 17,678 descriptors and approximately 15,000 cross references; the online version of the thesaurus contains 100,000 cross references (telephone conversation, March 17, 1994). At a meeting held at NASA in April 1993, Schuyler reported that MeSH had added 750 terms in the preceding year, and she expressed concern about the impact of this on indexing consistency in MEDLINE.

23. David F. Mayhew, "Indexing the Biomedical Literature," in *Indexing Specialized Formats and Subjects*, Hilda Feinberg, ed. (Metuchen, NJ: Scarecrow Press, 1983), 99. The introduction to the EMTREE Thesaurus (see note 12) reports that the controlled vocabulary contains 35,000 terms and 7,000 synonyms.

24. Marcia J. Bates, "Rethinking Subject Cataloging in the Online Environment," *Library Resources & Technical Services* 33:4 (Oct. 1989): 400-412.

25. The project was described in: E. H. Brenner et al., "American Petroleum Institute's Machine-Aided Indexing and Searching Project," *Science & Technology Libraries* 5:1 (Fall 1984): 49-62. The conclusion was drawn in: Everett H. Brenner, "Vocabulary Control," in: *Indexing: The State of Our Knowledge and the State of Our Ignorance: Proceedings of the 20th Annual Meeting of the American Society of Indexers, New York, 1988*, Bella Hass Weinberg, ed. (Medford, NJ: Learned Information, 1989): 66.

26. Morton E. Winston, Roger Chaffin, and Douglas Herrmann, "A Taxonomy of Part-Whole Relations," *Cognitive Science* 11 (1987): 417-444.

27. "Catalogs for Kids: Organization, Access, and Interfaces," Congress for Librarians, St. John's University, Feb. 21, 1994. Sherry Vellucci, Chair. Proceedings to be published by Learned Information, Medford, NJ. In response to my query at the conference, Virginia Walter reported that a doctoral study focusing on the primacy of the alphabetic or classified approach is in progress at UCLA.

28. Bella Hass Weinberg and Julie A. Cunningham, "The Design of Online Thesauri," National Online Meeting *Proceedings*, 9th, 1988 (Medford, NJ: Learned Information, 1988), 411-419.

29. Ann J. Van Camp, "The MEDLINE Integrated Thesaurus on BRS," *Online* 16:6 (Nov. 1992): 99-102. (Subsequent to the submission of this paper, BRS was acquired by CDPlus, and the interfaces were reported to have changed.)

30. "Art and Architecture Thesaurus (AAT) Second Edition Now in RLIN," *RLIN Focus* 6 (Feb. 1994): 8-9.

31. James D. Anderson, "Indexing and Classification: File Organization and Display for Information Retrieval," in: *Indexing: The State of Our Knowledge and the State of Our Ignorance* (1989), 69-83. (See note 25 for full bibliographic data.)

32. *Advances in Classification Research: Proceedings of the 1st ASIS SIG/ CR Classification Research Workshop*, Toronto, 1990. Susanne M. Humphrey and Barbara H. Kwasnik, Editors (Medford, NJ: Learned Information, 1991). Vol. 2 . . . 2nd, Washington, DC, 1991. Barbara H. Kwasnik and Raya Fidel, Editors (1992). Vol. 3 . . . 3rd, Pittsburgh, PA, 1992. Raya Fidel et al., Editors (1993).

33. Bella Hass Weinberg, "ASIS '93: An Indexer's Perspective," *Key Words: The Newsletter of the American Society of Indexers* 1:9 (Nov./Dec. 1993): 12-15, 22; "ASIS '94: An Indexer's Commentary," *Key Words* 2:6 (Nov./Dec. 1994): 1, 11-19.

34. Cathleen K. Whitehead, "The Art and Architecture Thesaurus as an Alternative to Library of Congress Subject Headings," in: *Cataloging Heresy: Challenging the Standard Bibliographic Product*: Proceedings of the Congress for Librarians, 1991, St. John's University, New York. Bella Hass Weinberg, ed. (Medford, NJ: Learned Information, 1992), 59-74.

35. For reviews of the compatibility of indexing languages, see: Linda C. Smith, "UNISIST Revisited: Compatibility in the Context of Collaboratories," in: *Classification Research for Knowledge Representation and Organization* (1992), 337-346 (see note 39 for full reference); Lei Zeng, "Compatibility of Indexing Languages in an Online Access Environment: A Review of the Approaches," in: *Advances in Classification Research* vol. 3 (Medford, NJ: Learned Information, 1993), 161-181.

36. Pauline Atherton, Director, *Books are for Use: Final Report of the Subject Access Project to the Council on Library Resources* (Syracuse, New York: Syracuse University, School of Information Studies, Feb. 1978).

37. Angela Giral and Arlene G. Taylor, "Indexing Overlap and Consistency Between the *Avery Index to Architectural Periodicals* and the *Architectural Periodicals Index*," *Library Resources & Technical Services* 37:1 (Jan. 1993): 19-43.

38. S.R. Ranganathan, *Prolegomena to Library Classification*. 3rd ed. (London: Asia Publishing House, 1967), 287-290.

39. Many papers on thesauri are found in: *Classification Research for Knowledge Representation and Organization: Proceedings of the 5th International Study Conference on Classification Research*, Toronto, Canada, June 24-28, 1991, Nancy J. Williamson and Michele Hudon, eds. (Amsterdam: Elsevier, 1992).

How to Study Classification Systems and Their Appropriateness for Individual Institutions

Robert M. Losee

SUMMARY. Answers to questions concerning individual library decisions to adopt classification systems are important in understanding the effectiveness of libraries but are difficult to provide. Measures of classification system performance are discussed, as are different methodologies that may be used to seek answers, ranging from formal or philosophical models to quantitative experimental techniques and qualitative methods.

INTRODUCTION

Classification systems provide an ordering for documents, taken here as books or any recording of knowledge using any medium. The ordering is based upon a classification number assigned to the book, representing the main focus of the work and acting as a subject surrogate. The classification system essentially supplies a browsing path from one document to another such that those patrons who browse follow the path, where the path may be through library stacks, a bibliography, classified files, etc. Patrons may search for materials located on the path in a systematic manner or in a more haphazard fashion. The path is designed so that

Robert M. Losee, PhD, is Associate Professor, School of Information and Library Science, University of North Carolina, Chapel Hill, NC 27599-3360.

[Haworth co-indexing entry note]: "How to Study Classification Systems and Their Appropriateness for Individual Institutions." Losee, Robert M. Co-published simultaneously in *Cataloging & Classification Quarterly* (The Haworth Press, Inc.) Vol. 19, No. 3/4, 1995, pp. 45-58; and: *Classification: Options and Opportunities* (ed: Alan R. Thomas) The Haworth Press, Inc., 1995, pp. 45-58. Multiple copies of this article/chapter may be purchased from The Haworth Document Delivery Center [1-800-3-HAWORTH; 9:00 a.m. - 5:00 p.m. (EST)].

neighboring books on the path are in most cases about similar topics. An exception to this would be at transition points, such as between the end of the 400s and the beginning of the 500s in a collection classed by the Dewey Decimal Classification (DDC). Additionally, it may be desirable in some libraries to have the starting point on the path be made easy for a human to determine, without using a sophisticated locating system such as would be provided by an online catalog. It is necessary for information professionals considering the use of a particular classification system to have evidence about (1) the administrative efficiency of different paths, (2) the ease of use and relevance of materials found for the patron, and to understand (3) the formal characteristics of a path.

Most library and information center classification systems are designed for one dimensional applications, with multiple entry points to the classification system being provided by a catalog which acts as a front end for the applied classification system. The library is conceptually one long shelf, with the subjects of documents changing slowly as one moves from one document to another. DDC and Library of Congress Classification (LCC) systems are one dimensional systems. Two and n-dimensional classification systems add power as well as a great deal of complexity to the organization of a document collection. The reader might wish to consider the problems that would arise if a library decided to develop and implement a classification system that worked in two dimensions. In traditional library shelving, the books above and below a particular volume would be similar to it, as well as those books to the left and right of the volume. How would this work and, more importantly for our purposes, how should we study the impact of such a system on a library? The ability to answer questions such as these is becoming more important as the introduction of computerized systems of various sorts appear capable of greatly improving the classification of documents. Important choices will need to be made.

Classification systems are facing increasing challenges due to the ability of computer systems to perform massive searches of electronic full-text databases in an effort to find related material and present it in an organized fashion to the searcher. Hypertext systems may contain different types of links (e.g., "about," "is-a," "refers to," etc.) allowing the user to move along a path of subject relationships. As hypertext on the Internet appears to be moving towards a standard based on the Mosaic protocol, which will probably be the initial standard for the United States government's "Information Infrastructure," computer programs are being produced and updated which can automatically produce links, producing statements in the hypertext markup language HTML. These statements and links represent a form of classification. Computerized document access systems such as these are relatively easily studied; traditional library classification systems are much harder to study, for a variety of reasons discussed below.

MEASURES OF CLASSIFICATION PERFORMANCE

Research on the applicability of specific classification systems to specific institutions may examine several aspects of the relationship existing between an individual or community of users and a classified collection. At the lowest level, one can count events that occur in the information environments, e.g., the number of books circulated. A better measure of quality is provided by indicators of satisfaction. If a user indicates that he/she is satisfied, this can be understood as correcting for count errors, e.g., circulated works the user reportedly found to have been worthless or a satisfying work that was not circulated. Best is a measure of effectiveness that determines the actual usefulness. For example, if a problem is solved based on a book, the book can be said to be effective in terms of the information need that prompted its circulation. We refer to this use/satisfaction/effectiveness hierarchy of potential measures as the "USE" hierarchy.

Research studies of classifier performance often present results graphically, with precision graphed on the y axis and with recall, the proportion of relevant documents that have been located so far, graphed on the x axis.[1] If all the documents that are "relevant" to an information need are to be retrieved, then variations in recall are not of concern. In this case, the number of documents that are expected to be retrieved to obtain all relevant documents is measured as the average search length (ASL), the average number of documents that will likely need to be examined to arrive at a randomly selected member of the set of relevant documents.[2] The ASL is easily understood by patrons because knowing that they will have to look at an average of 5 documents to get to a randomly selected relevant document is relatively simple when compared with understanding the more common recall/precision graph. Using this form of measure and economic cost data about each book or an "average" book, the expected cost of retrieving the relevant documents can be obtained and understood.

Measures may take a global view of the set of classified documents and attempt to minimize or maximize some relationship between all neighboring documents. For example, if the degree of subject similarity can be measured between neighboring documents and this is understood to be the primary goal, then the classification system which maximizes the similarity of all neighboring pairs may be the "best" classification system. A simplistic way of doing this is to count the number of matching subject headings in neighboring pairs of documents.[3] Similarly, the amount of information that one document provides about a neighboring document can be measured based on almost all available features using information theoretic techniques.

METHODS FOR STUDYING A CLASSIFICATION SYSTEM

Several methods have been profitably used in examining the idiosyncratic relationships between classification systems and users.[4] A preliminary factor that must be considered before using any of these methods is the defining characteristics of the user population. For example, libraries often survey their users and then declare that the community is pleased with the services provided. Those answering such a survey are not representative of the population of potential users; instead, they represent primarily those who found the library's services of greater benefit than the cost associated with getting to the library. Mail or telephone surveys of randomly sampled members of the community are far more likely to give a balanced picture of both those who find the library and its classification system useful and those who find it less than satisfactory. Regular users, for example, are far more likely to be comfortable with an existing classification system than the library avoider.

Libraries have recently begun to express more concern about equality of service to all members of the community. Researchers must make difficult decisions in this regard, such as to what extent should those considered unlikely to use the library be considered in the choice of a classification system. Librarians wishing to consider all alternatives might want to study classification systems considering several different populations; many aspects of classification system performance may be the same or similar across populations, while other population and subject specific aspects will vary considerably. Based on this knowledge, librarians can attempt to make a reasoned decision that will be relatively fair to all probable users.

Surveys and interviews are effective means for determining patrons' attitudes about classification systems. Questions may be open ended or closed. The former allows the user to respond as they wish, while closed ended questions ("I was satisfied with the finding tools in the library: Yes or No") force the user to select one or more of several possible responses. Closed ended questions are easier to analyze, while open ended questions can often provide information new to the researcher. Consider a situation where an inexperienced librarian makes up a question for a survey asking what categories of materials the user intends to circulate if they are found.

A closed end question that leaves out categories such as Gothic novels or war stories might force lovers of these genres to select other related genres on the survey; an open ended question would allow fans of these categories to be heard. This is particularly important where one is not certain what categories of materials or mental models the users find most beneficial when searching. Open ended responses can often be tabulated by looking at the solicited responses and categories developed *post facto* for data tabulation.

Research projects are often experimental in nature. Contrived situations that simplify processes and the use of random sampling allow for the control of extraneous variables in experimental settings, increasing the generalizability of results beyond the institution in which the research was performed. Experimental methods usually involve several different groups of subjects that are randomly assigned to groups, resulting in large sized groups being nearly equal when it comes to factors relating to the variables to be studied. Existing libraries usually fail to provide such an experimental setting. One is often tempted to use a different classification system in one or more libraries and then claim that noted differences are due primarily or solely to the classification system. However, many other factors could be responsible for the results, such as the interest or devotion that originally motivated the change also influencing other aspects of library services. A librarian motivated enough to change the classification system is unlikely to stop at this point; instead, numerous other improvements would probably be made and these may be responsible wholly or in part for the observed changes.

Quasi-experimental methods using existing systems attempt, through processes such as the random assignment of experimental subjects to treatment or control groups, to evaluate existing systems. For example, one might take two nearly identical libraries with "similar" populations (such as might be found with two branches of the same library system) and use two different classification systems on the two collections. Libraries could alternate days on which they were open. Studying the circulation figures for each library would indicate which system provided more circulating material and, by implication, which library had the superior classification. A detailed analysis of the different categories of materials can provide a window into the strengths and weaknesses of each system. Studying the transaction logs from online catalogs can provide a similar look at what the patrons found useful and where search and retrieval problems occurred.[5] These logs are one of the best non-reactive and unbiased records of patron search habits and provide one of the best data sets on which to base quantitative measures.

Qualitative methods often take one of two emphases. They may emphasize methods that are inherently non-quantitative. For example, a study of sexual bias in subject headings might use qualitative methods to determine whether an individual subject heading was biased. Given these qualitative judgements, statistical tests may then be used to determine whether the results are "significant." The term "qualitative" is also used to represent a particular philosophical view, often advocated by deconstructionists. They suggest that no theories should be imposed upon a particular situation and that the collected data should be used to suggest a theory.

Philosophical argumentation has been prominently used in the analysis of classification systems. Ranganathan, for example, developed his Colon Classification system using what can be termed philosophical arguments. These philosophically based systems still may be studied empirically in many cases. For example, Ranganathan's system attempts to provide independent facets. The independence of these facets may be easily tested statistically. Similar systems may be developed using principle components analysis[6] and then compared to philosophically developed faceted systems. The choice of the number of facets may be studied empirically by letting statistical methods "choose" the best factors or facets.

Investigations of classification systems may use more formal methods. Although these are seldom used in the library and information sciences, they are common in the "hard" sciences. A formal proof attempts to show, based upon a set of explicit assumptions and a set of reasoning principles, that a certain conclusion is justified. To a formalist, these conclusions are in fact *stronger* than the inferential results obtained from social scientific data analysis. A variety of classification techniques have been developed based on formal reasoning, primarily for classification by computers.[7] Formal work on library classification systems have included such formally based work as Larson's attempts to automatically classify books using Bayesian methods[8] and Losee's classification system which formally minimizes the subject-distance or maximizes the information between neighboring books.[9]

Where should research on classification systems take place? Studying a system already adopted by one's own library is far easier than studying a system in someone else's institution. When a system is in-house it may be manipulated to see the effects of variation. For example, a subset of a classified collection might be reclassified into a different system. After the initial outrage by the patrons, the reactions can be studied over time.

The encoding of one system into a second system can be beneficial for such work. A numeric system can always be encoded using letters and vice versa. Such substitutions allow for subcollections to be converted to other systems producing visually different classification numbers which are modified to "fit in" with the existing classification system, reducing the reactivity of patrons and some staff and making the results of a study less tainted.

STAFF NEEDS

A major determining factor in deciding how to study a classification system is who the users of the system are to be. Two categories of classification system users exist in a library: staff doing work and patrons using materials for their own purposes. Staff needs, in some senses, are far less important than the needs of patrons. As professionals, we should be willing to accept a system that is somewhat inefficient at directly addressing our needs. Patrons supply the vast majority of material uses and it may be argued that the library is there to serve them. In addition, the majority of staff searches are known item searches: a patron wants a specific book, a book is needed for recataloging, the shelves are being checked for a book the patron claims to have returned, etc.

A number of factors affect the decision by library directors on which classification system to use or adopt. If the proposed system differs from the current system, a major factor will be the cost of conversion, with the cost measured in expenses to convert the collection, lost opportunities for the staff who could be doing something else, and the cost to patrons who must learn a new system. After a new system is adopted, there are day to day expenses associated with classifying each document. This may depend on the complexity or "naturalness" of the classification system, as well as the ability to obtain classification numbers from other sources than the library (e.g., national bibliographic centers or OCLC). The ease of use of the system is important. Consider how often readers of essays such as this proceed into a small to medium sized DDC collection without stopping at the catalog; despite all the drawbacks of the DDC approach, it certainly passes the usability test!

Another factor that has received little attention is the extent to which a particular classification system results in errors being made by the staff when classifying books. These may be due to the intrinsic difficulty of using the system or ambiguities within the system, or mundane matters such as small typefonts used for computer displays or in printing books that contribute to misreadings on the part of the classifying librarian.

PATRONS' NEEDS

What do readers need from a classification system? Surprisingly, there is relatively little information about the browsing habits of different categories of patrons in different types of libraries. Some preliminary studies have been made in specific types of libraries and for specific types of patrons, but little progress has been made toward a general science of library or information system classification.[10]

One excellent study that focused on a special category of classifying habits is methodologically typical of the qualitative genre.[11] Following earlier works in anthropological studies of workers in "typical" office settings, Kwasnik studied how faculty members classified incoming mail, that is, what they did with the mail once it was received. A parallel set of studies of the use of existing classification systems by different categories of patrons might lead to valuable insights about the mental rules or procedures used by patrons in locating works through browsing.

A valuable study of OPACs by Solomon suggests another approach that might be useful in determining the subject searching behavior of users.[12] Solomon, as a part of his study, noted that for one group of children, the 7 most popular search terms were, in order of frequency of use, (1) cats, (2) dogs, (3) mystery, (4) animals, (5) magic, (6) poetry, and (7) dinosaur. This suggests that for groups serving similar types of patrons, particular care must be taken in making these most popular topics *easily* accessible through the classification system. If these topics cannot be placed together, they at least need to be cross referenced in the catalog and shelf dummies in the stacks, showing browsing patrons what other classification numbers would be worth examining.

What do users really need? This question will likely remain unanswered because humans can use virtually anything and could find some benefit in almost any piece of information. As long as users typically view the library and the information that they might find there in preconceived ways, it will be effectively impossible to learn the "information needs" of patrons in such a way that the library will be able to develop classification systems that can be shown empirically to be optimal.

NON-FICTION

Readers use two broad categories of materials: fiction and non-fiction. The use of classification systems is often understood to serve primarily the browser of non-fiction collections, with fiction being alphabetized by author within one, or at most, a few categories. Classification systems for non-fiction should collocate works on similar topics and separate dissimilar works. Determining the extent to which a classification system meets the needs of a population is thus simply the degree to which documents found helpful to patrons in the past are placed together by a system and the extent to which the documents used by different individuals have been separated. Data for a given library and each of a number of existing classification systems would be meaningful for the decisions made by that library, given an assumption of the stability of the qualities of information needs and requests of the user population. The experiences of other libraries may not be generalizable to your own. However, if most libraries of a particular type (e.g., public, school, etc.) find one classification system to be superior to another for their needs, it is safe to assume that it might be beneficial for all similar libraries to use that system viewed as superior by most.

Sawbridge and Favret report that for two libraries in the UK, non-fiction circulation increased 30% compared to the same period in a previous year after a more reader oriented classification system was introduced.[13] Note that because an experimental methodology was not used, it is difficult to say that the increase in circulation was due to the modified classification system. Librarians may have become more concerned with the patrons than they were in previous years; this attitude may have resulted in the change in classification policy. There may have been a general increase in library circulation due to any of a number of other reasons.

Classification systems also provide for "creative mental exploration"[14] of the collection, pointing out related topics to the user that might not have been considered when the collection was initially approached. Users often do not realize that certain categories of materials may exist in the library, or that a certain aspect of a subject has been written on. Studying the value of creative mental exploration is exceedingly difficult. One of the few tools available to study the value of this experience is economic in nature. Patrons who found material somewhat outside the original domain of their searches may be asked to rate the value of the discovered works in comparison to the value of another book or tangible objects or service. This comparison between a tangible entity and the less tangible entities provided by library service can provide an economic foundation for the study of library effectiveness.

As information systems move toward greater automation, dynamic classification systems can present documents classified with the particular user in mind. Thus, one user might find certain documents clustered one way, while a different user would find a different arrangement, each arrangement being optimized for the individual. This may be found in multiple entry catalogs or OPACs which can incorporate relevance feedback provided by the searcher. Optimization will be based upon criteria determined by the system designers and the end-users; the measurement of classification performance (vis-à-vis certain desirable classification characteristics) in these cases will be, in some senses, unnecessary as the system will be performing at the optimal level.

FICTION

Fiction is most commonly used in libraries for recreational purposes. Patrons often try to find enjoyable fiction that is similar in some way to other material they have been exposed to. Similarity may be based upon authorship, genre, reading level, historical period, or other attributes.

Shay Baker and Gay Shepherd suggest three useful principles for classifying fiction.[15] First, patrons should be able to "find the types of fictional work they want." This can be easily studied if, following the USE model, we measure patron use by studying circulation records or a similar form of information use. A superior approach would be to show patrons a randomly selected set of materials and see whether these individual volumes are inferior or superior to the volumes found using the classification system. The percent of materials outside the area in which they looked that patrons found helpful can help determine the degree to which relevant materials were clustered together.

Secondly, fiction classification systems should provide subdivisions by broad subject, genre, format of work, and other literary qualities that can help patrons. Questions about this principle can be most easily studied in experimental ways by placing some randomly selected works into a classified collection and placing other works into a more conventional, single alphabetized-by-author's-last-name collection.

Finally, patrons should be exposed to authors they might otherwise overlook. This may be tested in a manner similar to the first principle. Patrons may be asked to answer questions about what they intend to look for before approaching either of two forms of a collection. After potentially useful materials have been removed from the shelf, the works the patrons found interesting may be studied or circulation records may be examined. The differences between what the user intended to use and what they actually found in the differently classified collections can be studied qualitatively and quantitatively.

BROWSING AT THE SHELF OR IN THE CATALOG?

In countries such as the U.S. where open stacks are the norm, a fundamental question that is rising in importance in classification research is whether browsing can best be done at the catalog through the use of browsing through subject headings or through the use of ordering collections by classification numbers at the shelf. Historically, library classification systems have been relatively successful at placing similar materials in an arrangement that users found helpful in locating material based on subject. Classification numbers and subject headings placed in the card and more recently in online catalogs have provided other useful tools for subject access including a virtual classification bibliography. As computerized catalogs incorporate more expert knowledge about the relationships among the subject headings, organizing displays of bibliographic records based on material other than traditional classification numbers can be expected to improve.

Weinberg has noted that subject headings contain "hidden classification" information that can be used to automate, enhance, or simplify the classification process.[16] Other studies have shown that users remember things about books that are not commonly provided as access points in OPACS or by classification schemes, such as height, cover illustrations, condition of binding, etc. While the development of an OPAC that can organize material for an individual user may be based on book attributes other than or in addition to classification numbers, the relative performance of such an OPAC as compared to an OPAC supporting browsing by classification number or browsing at the shelf must be determined empirically.

Browsing paths may be stationary for a given population; this is a static classification system. Library classification systems, such as DDC, the Bliss Bibliographic Classification, second edition, and LCC, are essentially static. Dynamic classification information obtained from a computerized system that remembers what the searcher has found useful in the past may be based on circulation records. For example, a user who continually looks up "information" in an OPAC might find it helpful to have those books on information in the B, Q, T, and Z sections of a collection classified by LCC brought together by a classification system more responsive to that patron's needs. Such an approach has obvious applications in a system where the documents do not have permanently affixed classification numbers or are not directly accessed by patrons, such as an electronic document system like a large word processor or a closed stack library in which browsing must be done through the catalog.

Dynamic systems have the capability to "learn" the characteristics of either individuals or groups. They can therefore adapt to local needs. Research on dynamic systems is far more difficult than studying static systems. While these systems are optimized for one or more variables, other characteristics of the systems may be rather easily measured. If these variables are relatively important, they should be included in the system design for future systems.

CONCLUSION

Evaluating a classification system, either by itself or with a particular library collection as the object to be classified, is difficult. However, such studies are essential if we are to provide for effective browsing by patrons. We have relatively little empirical evidence about the intersection of classification systems and patron browsing behavior.

Part of this is due to the relative lack of interest in effectiveness measures by librarians and information scientists. In addition, classification systems are probably more difficult to study than many other functional aspects of librarianship. Because a classified collection is so expensive to produce, it cannot be simply studied using experimental methods allowing results to be generalized to other environments. Qualitative methods provide tools for studying individual or small numbers of cases. The inability to generalize from these studies makes them less valuable to the library community at large.

A proper study of classification systems will involve both quantitative methods and detailed qualitative studies of specific cases. This combination will likely lead to an understanding of the nature of classification systems, an insight that is asserted by different classification specialists but for which there is little empirical evidence. Improved research will undoubtedly result in both improved classification systems and in better choices being made by librarians who need to choose classification systems for their collections.

NOTES

1. Robert M. Losee, *The Science of Information* (New York: Academic Press, 1990), Gerard Salton and Michael McGill, *An Introduction to Modern Information Retrieval* (New York: McGraw-Hill, 1983), and Jerry D. Saye, ' "The Library of Congress Classification System in an Online Environment: A Reaction," *Cataloging & Classification Quarterly* 11, no. 1 (1990): 27-35.

2. William Cooper, "Expected Search Length: A Single Measure of Retrieval Effectiveness Based on Weak Ordering Action of Retrieval Systems," *Journal of the American Society for Information Science* 19, no. 1 (1973): 30-41.

3. Robert M. Losee, "A Gray Code Based Ordering for Documents on Shelves: Classification for Browsing and Retrieval" *Journal of the American Society for Information Science* 43, no. 4 (1992): 312-322.

4. Numerous books address research methodologies. The two most popular social scientific books are Earl Babbie, *The Practice of Social Research* (Belmont, CA: Wadsworth, 1992) and Fred N. Kerlinger, *Behavioral Research* (New York: HRW, 1986). In the library and information science area, readers might want to examine a general textbook such as Stephen P. Harter, *Research Methods in Librarianship: Techniques and Interpretation* (NY: Academic Press, 1980) or Robert M. Losee and Karen A Worley, *Research and Evaluation for Information Professionals* (San Diego: Academic Press, 1993). Those interested in primarily qualitative methodologies might best be served by Jack D. Glazer and Ronald R. Powell, *Qualitative Research in Information Management* (Englewood, Colo: Libraries Unlimited, 1992) or the *Library Quarterly* 63, no. 4 (October 1993), issue devoted to the topic. Some of the fundamental research questions for classification systems are outlined in Robert M. Losee, "Seven Fundamental Questions for the Science of Library Classification," *Knowledge Organization* 20, no. 2 (1993): 65-70.

5. Micheline Hancock-Beaulieu, "A Comparative Transaction Log Analysis of Browsing and Search Formulation in Online Catalogs," *Program* 27, no. 3 (July 1993): 269-280. Jerry Saye at the SILS, UNC-Chapel Hill has extensively studied transactions logs from the UNC OPAC system; the author has found Dr. Saye's discussions of this work over the years enlightening.

6. H. Borko, "Research in Computer Based Classification Systems," in *Theory of Subject Analysis: A Sourcebook*. (Littleton, CO: Libraries Unlimited, 1985): 287-305.

7. The bible in this area is the aging but still widely respected Richard O. Duda and Peter E. Hart, *Pattern Classification and Scene Analysis* (New York: Wiley, 1973). As an example of helpful literature outside LIS, the reader might wish to examine C. S. Wallace and D. M. Boulton, "An Information Measure for Classification," *The Computer Journal* 11 (1968): 185-194.

8. Ray R. Larson, "Experiments in Automatic Library of Congress Classification," *Journal of the American Society for Information Science* 43, no. 2 (March 1992): 130-148.

9. Robert M. Losee, "A Gray Code Based Ordering for Documents on Shelves."

10. Robert M. Losee, "The Relative Shelf Location of Circulated Books: A Study of Classification, Users, and Browsing " *LRTS* 37, no. 2 (1993): 197-209.

11. Barbara H. Kwasnik, "The Importance of Factors that are not Document Attributes in the Organization of Personal Documents," *Journal of Documentation* 47, no. 4 (December 1991): 389-398.

12. Paul Solomon, "Children's Information Retrieval Behavior," *Journal of the American Society for Information Science* 44, no. 5 (1993): 245-264.

13. Lynn Sawbridge and Leo Favret, "The Mechanics and the Magic of Declassification," *Library Association Record* 84, no. 11 (November 1982): 385-386.

14. Francis L. Miksa, "The Concept of the Universe of Knowledge and the Purpose of LIS *Classification,"* in N. J. Williamson and M. Hudon, editors, *Clas-*

sification Research for Knowledge Representation and Organization (Amsterdam: Elsevier, 1992).

15. Sharon L. Baker and Gay W. Shepherd, "Fiction Classification Schemes: The Principles Behind Them and Their Success," *RQ* 27, no. 2 (Winter 1987): 245-251.

16. Bella Hass Weinberg, "The Hidden Classification in Library of Congress Subject Headings for Judaica," *LRTS* 37, no. 4 (1993): 369-379.

Knowledge and the Educational Purposes of Higher Education: Implications for the Design of a Classification Scheme

Edmund C. Short

SUMMARY. The author proposes that a knowledge classification scheme be organized around four educational purposes of higher education. These purposes correspond to four curricula that are taught in institutions of higher education–the general education curriculum, the specialist education curriculum, the curriculum for the education of researchers, and the curriculum for the education of educators. Implications for the design of such a classification scheme are also suggested.

Classification of knowledge for the purpose of serving the college or university's teaching function is the focus of this article. Higher education uses knowledge for several purposes including research, service, and teaching, and thus requires diverse forms of knowledge classification. It will be the task here to suggest a framework for a classification scheme appropriate to higher education's teaching function and to do so with a theoretical, not merely a pragmatic, grounding.

If it were clear that the teaching function of higher education required access to knowledge in some standard or universally accepted form, it

Edmund C. Short, BS, MEd, EdD, is Professor of Education, College of Education, The Pennsylvania State University, University Park, PA.

[Haworth co-indexing entry note]: "Knowledge and the Educational Purposes of Higher Education: Implications for the Design of a Classification Scheme." Short, Edmund C. Co-published simultaneously in *Cataloging & Classification Quarterly* (The Haworth Press, Inc.) Vol. 19, No. 3/4, 1995, pp. 59-66; and: *Classification: Options and Opportunities* (ed: Alan R. Thomas) The Haworth Press, Inc., 1995, pp. 59-66. Multiple copies of this article/chapter may be purchased from The Haworth Document Delivery Center [1-800-3-HAWORTH; 9:00 a.m. - 5:00 p.m. (EST)].

59

would not be too difficult to prescribe a common scheme by which to classify knowledge for teaching or educational purposes in higher education and consequently a standard pattern by which to arrange various sources and documents. The problem, of course, is that the curriculum in higher education is not a standard or universal curriculum across all institutions of higher education. The diversity of curricula that presently exists is enormous, and the variety of curricula within a given institution may not resemble that of other institutions as much as one might think. Add to this circumstance the constant effort to change and update curricula.[1]

Is there any way that knowledge might be organized for educational purposes that would facilitate the teaching function in higher education given this diversity within and across curricula and institutions? Some analysis of the educational uses of knowledge in higher education would be helpful as a basis for thinking about optional ways of organizing knowledge for curricular and instructional purposes.[2] Such an analysis follows.

FOUR EDUCATIONAL PURPOSES OF HIGHER EDUCATION

There are, in my judgment, four distinct purposes for education at the level of colleges and universities. Confusion and conflation among these purposes have been at the heart of the difficulties faced in developing coherent curricula in higher education to say nothing of identifying and using the knowledge appropriate for such curricula. It can be argued, however, that distinctly different purposes are involved in curricula designed for the general education of students, for specialist education in various arts and professions, for the education of researchers, and for the education of teachers and/or professors who will teach curricula of the other three types. It can be argued that different classifications and organizations of knowledge are necessary for use in curricula designed to fulfill each of these four educational purposes.

Let me characterize each of these briefly and indicate how the knowledge required for each is of a different order and must be generated and organized differently. *General education* recognizes the need for all students to acquire the skills and knowledges that are required for citizenship and their activities as human persons. General education is designed to help people interpret their world and use knowledge wisely in a variety of personal and civic activities. Knowledge required for general education is knowledge of how to conduct one's activities as a citizen and as a person. In *specialist education* the student learns to function in a specialized field of practice as a professional or in some other technical specialty. Knowledge for specialist education is knowledge of how to carry out a particular human activity or profession. For example, knowledge of how to do accounting, how to teach, how to do electrical engineering, how to govern, how to do commercial art, how to perform music or drama, and so forth. In the *education of researchers,* the university must prepare competent researchers in all specialties, academic disciplines, and fields of study. Knowledge for research education is knowledge of how to conduct inquiry and research by any of the several varieties of research approaches that are possible within particular research disciplines or fields of study. The *education of educators* prepares those teachers and professors who work with students in their general education, their specialist education, or in their education as researchers to know how to assist students to learn the knowledge and skills associated with each of these matters. Knowledge for educator education is knowledge of how to teach and to facilitate student learning so that they can achieve educational purposes associated with either general education, specialist education, researcher education, or educator education.

Regardless of how research and the results of knowledge creation are structured within the university, it is inappropriate for research scholars to generate knowledge and for faculty to teach it and have students learn it in the natural units used to organize the research enterprise (except in the case of researcher education). Knowledge must be reorganized in such a way as to match each of the four educative purposes identified above. The educational purposes of students will naturally fall in line with one or more of these four educative functions of the university. Coherent curricular programs can be conceived and designed in relation to each of these functions. Students can be expected to understand and readily pursue such programs because they can see the obvious connections between what they are studying or learning and some human activity in which they may wish to engage. Whether students should pursue all four types of programs simultaneously or have them spread out over both undergraduate and graduate years is an issue which university faculties must decide, although it can be argued that no student's education is complete unless he/she has matriculated through programs of all four types.

Whichever program of studies students may be pursuing at a given time (general education, specialist education, researcher education, or educator education), they must be able to make the knowledge they encounter their own. They must have the opportunity to validate that knowledge by checking and understanding how that knowledge was generated. They must in some way test its validity in practice in their own actions and reflections. And they must not be burdened with the task of confronting and testing knowledge that has not been selected to serve the purposes of the pertinent curricular program, as is often the case in the current configuration of the curriculum. It is inappropriate, for instance, for a prospective elementary teacher to have to take the first few courses in a sequence of mathematical knowledge designed for math majors when what is needed is a broad grasp of many different areas of mathematics. A well-designed college or university curriculum should be organized so that the different types of knowledge find their proper place in relation to one of the four educational programs with distinct purposes.

SELECTING KNOWLEDGE FOR EACH TYPE OF PROGRAM

The form of curriculum organization proposed here calls for knowledge to be selected from appropriate bodies of knowledge and to be reorganized to serve the purposes of each practical mission-oriented program of study.

General education. In a program of general education, knowledge would be sought from any discipline or field of study which is considered relevant to the task of learning to act as a citizen and human person. Research on this particular dimension of human activity (one of the mission-oriented fields of inquiry) would shed light on just what specific practical and theoretical or disciplinary knowledge might best serve the purposes of general education and how it might efficaciously be organized. Unfortunately, in the past there has been very little systematic study of general education and, consequently, little understanding of what knowledge may be required to achieve the goals of general education.[1] In this proposed pattern of relating research and the curriculum, there is some hope of obtaining helpful answers to questions about the what and the how of general education. Research in other fields of practical education suggests that no form of organizing the content of general education would become the standard pattern but that any pattern would be structured around the various facets of the actual tasks of a citizen and a human person. Each faculty would have to make choices and defend them as persuasively as possible, arranging courses specifically designed to achieve the purposes of general education. No longer could the simple device of establishing distribution requirements among chunks of available research knowledge be considered adequate for the purposes of general education. Decisions about what constitutes an educated person and citizen, choices about what knowledge and activities might substantively contribute to that goal, and planning on how to design courses and sequences of courses to facilitate the necessary learning would have to be made. With clear goals and a sense of the different kinds of knowledge that may be relevant to the task, curricular programs for general education should not be as difficult to establish as has been the case in the past.

Specialist education. It is necessary in learning to do any particular kind of practical or theoretical work to draw upon knowledge of many kinds related to the specific practice to be mastered. This may include knowledge of the tasks, parameters, purposes, and competence standards associated with doing the practice itself. It will also include knowledge of pertinent disciplines or fields of knowledge that a practitioner would draw upon in determining plans and actions to be taken. It will involve knowledge of philosophical and cultural values that impinge upon the practice. And, perhaps most importantly, it will require practical knowledge acquired from research and reflection on the ongoing experience of the particular practitioner involved as he or she moves from novice to expert in the particular specialized practice. Whether we are concerned with educating criminal justice professionals, architectural designers, teachers, or musicians, all of these types of knowledge will need to be generated and made available for the instructional purposes of educating people into these specialized practices. The array of knowledge appropriate for each specialization is often quite extensive and must be selected and organized to match the educational demands of students in each of the particular specialist curricula. As a matter of convention, these programs, regardless of specialty, are often divided into professional studies, related theoretical or disciplinary studies, supervised and reflective practice, and finally self-initiated and self-assessed practice, and the knowledge to be learned is consequently organized to match each of these phases of the program.

Researcher education. The education of researchers is a matter about which many university faculty members have considerable expertise. The design of explicit programs to accomplish this task is, however, not as frequently undertaken as one might suppose, given the high level of faculty expertise in research. The primary vehicle in this domain has been the research apprenticeship. More often than not, however, even this approach has been utilized less frequently than that of assuming that students can grasp the fundamentals of the research process by reading research reports in their specialty or by reading books on research methods. If we recognize that doing research is a practical activity (whether it addresses disciplinary research questions or mission-oriented questions), we will be compelled to design educational programs for researchers in each type of research that are practice-oriented and knowledge-based, just as has been suggested for general education, specialist education, and will also be suggested for educator education. Knowledge should be drawn into these research internships that is derived explicitly from studies of research practices. In addition, knowledge of many kinds may be gleaned from related disciplines or fields of inquiry that may inform the decisions of practice, including knowledge pertaining to ethical questions in research, technical knowledge related to research tools and techniques, philosophical knowledge related to making and justifying knowledge claims of pertinent types, etc. All too many researchers are equipped with a modicum of understanding about how to do their particular kind of research and are left to stumble and recover on their own from their lack of thorough preparation. Systematic programs for educating researchers are necessary if the quality of research and knowledge generation is to be improved. As with the other educative functions of the university, the education of researchers should not be left to chance.

Educator education. The education of educators is a domain of the curriculum of higher education that is most often ignored. This domain pertains to the education of those who will prepare general education faculty members, specialized education faculty members, research education faculty members, and educator education faculty members. Ordinarily this task is placed with the graduate faculty, but their expertise is largely in research methods or in a special field of knowledge and not in the knowledge and skills of how to teach people to act as faculty members or educators in any of the four kinds of curricular programs. The few exceptions to this dearth of experience and expertise may be in certain graduate faculty members in teacher education or in higher education departments who have specifically acquired expertise in preparing people for these roles. The point of highlighting this as a valuable educative function for which curricula should be available is based once again on the fact that knowledge is being generated about this process which could and should be utilized systematically in preparing such educators of faculty for higher education. Such persons should be the most knowledgeable and skilled in the arts of fulfilling one or more of the four educative functions of higher education. The absence of the appropriate research knowledge related to this task, curricula to prepare people to carry out these functions as high quality professionals, or curricula within which their students may acquire their own university education is bound to leave negative effects throughout the entire higher education system.

IMPLICATIONS OF THE FOUR EDUCATIONAL PURPOSES OF HIGHER EDUCATION FOR THE ORGANIZATION OF KNOWLEDGE

Perhaps the most obvious implication of thinking about how educational purposes might affect the way knowledge resources and documents are organized and classified would be to recognize that the same system will not work for all four educational purposes outlined above. Each one of these four purposes and the kind of higher education curricula developed to accomplish each of them requires a different system of organizing the relevant knowledge. This means that the same chunk of knowledge quite possibly could appear in different configurations in different programs depending upon whether the guiding purpose is general education, specialist education, researcher education, or educator education. Historical knowledge on how the U. S. institutionalizes freedom of expression, for example, would be placed in a skills-of-the-citizen context in a college general education program, in a legal context for the prospective attorney specializing in first amendment law, in the context of historical verification for a scholar learning to conduct historical inquiry, and for a teacher of high school history in the context of how to help adolescents grasp the concept of freedom and its implications. On the other hand, certain knowledge may be appropriate only in one of these programs. Techniques of motivating students to learn, for instance, would probably be appropriate for the education of educators.

What usually happens under current practice is that every professor or instructor who is responsible for teaching a specific portion of a curriculum is left the difficult task of personally searching through knowledge recorded and organized for the convenience of researchers for those pieces that seem to be relevant to the educational goals at hand. If classification and cataloging schemes could be devised that would order available knowledge around educational purposes such as the ones stipulated here, it would no doubt be much easier for professors to locate and utilize the knowledge that is relevant to their instructional purposes and to avoid overlooking relevant knowledge that is actually available.

To bring this about, professors and teachers in each of the four curriculum programs and their natural curricular subdivisions should be called upon to lend their expertise to classifiers and catalogers to help determine a workable and usable scheme for organizing knowledge in each of the curriculum areas. It is quite possible that such schemes, when devised, would need to be modified from time to time, but that has been necessary under previous systems of classification as well. It is also quite possible that such an undertaking as this would require a sizable increase in the force of classifiers and cataloguers over what has been devoted to this work in the past. And there would need to be differentiation in new ways among such workers (and different training) to accommodate this new way of organizing knowledge by educational purposes. Luckily, those who now have expertise that pertains to classifying and cataloging research knowledge should be able rather easily to adjust to the demands of educational purpose number three–that of educating researchers–although even here some new dimensions might need to be introduced.

RECAP

My intent in this article has been to suggest a basis for deriving a classification system compatible with the uses of knowledge in four curricular program areas in higher education. I urge that work toward such a system be initiated. It may be quite difficult to devise a system of classification that well serves the complex and diverse needs of faculty as they focus on educational purposes such as general education, specialist education, researcher education, and educator education. An optimal system of knowledge classification would be based on scholarly work that identifies and organizes knowledge in relation to its various uses in teaching in higher education corresponding to each of the four curriculum program areas and their distinct purposes.

NOTES

1. William Toombs and William Tierney, *Meeting the Mandate: Renewing the College and Department Curriculum.* Washington, D.C.: The George Washington University, School of Education and Human Development, 1991. (ASHE-ERIC Higher Education Report No. 6).

2. Edmund C. Short, "Knowledge and the Educative Functions of a University: Designing the Curriculum of Higher Education," *East China Normal University Journal (Educational Sciences).* In Chinese. In press. [English Version, December, 1992. ERIC Document Reproduction Service No. ED 359 870].

OPTIONS WITHIN STANDARD CLASSIFICATION SYSTEMS

Library of Congress Classification: Alternative Provisions

Lois Mai Chan

SUMMARY. The Library of Congress Classification (LCC), being a system originally and specifically designed for the Library's own collection, generally eschews alternatives. Within the LCC schedules, alternatives are found occasionally in earlier editions; there are no alternative numbers in recently developed or revised schedules. On the other hand, many alternative numbers representing different treatment of specific types of materials such as bibliographies and monographic series are provided in LC MARC records. Such numbers may be used by other libraries that prefer the alternative treatment. In addition, many LC MARC records also include class or call numbers based on other classification schemes, including the Dewey Decimal Classification (DDC), the National Library of Medicine Classification (NLM), and the Superintendent of Documents Classification. The alternative class numbers assigned from other classifi-

Lois Mai Chan is Professor, School of Library and Information Science, University of Kentucky, Lexington, KY 40502.

[Haworth co-indexing entry note]: "Library of Congress Classification: Alternative Provisions." Chan, Lois Mai. Co-published simultaneously in *Cataloging & Classification Quarterly* (The Haworth Press, Inc.) Vol. 19, No. 3/4, 1995, pp. 67-87; and: *Classification: Options and Opportunities* (ed: Alan R. Thomas) The Haworth Press, Inc., 1995, pp. 67-87. Multiple copies of this article/chapter may be purchased from The Haworth Document Delivery Center [1-800-3-HAWORTH; 9:00 a.m. - 5:00 p.m. (EST)].

cation systems are provided as services to libraries not using the Library of Congress Classification.

INTRODUCTION

In traditional classification schemes in which the hierarchical structure is laid out in linear fashion, cross classification, i.e., the placement of subjects belonging to more than one hierarchy, is often resolved by providing alternatives. The alternatives may be different locations for the same subject or alternative citation orders for a class of subjects. Yet a third alternative is arranging some or all material in the collection according to a different classification scheme.

Discussing classification in general in 1933, Henry Evelyn Bliss advocated the provision of alternatives in classification systems:

> Classifications are relative and should be adaptive, and systems should, so far as is feasible, serve various tho not incompatible interests. Alternative locations should therefore be provided in the schedules for certain studies or sciences regarded from different points of view or preferred in other allocations.[1]
>
> A system that does not provide for alternatives may be the less efficient as a generally adaptable system.[2]

J. Mills explains the need and types of alternatives:

> *Alternatives.* No general classification is likely to be acceptable in its order and collocation to all Librarians. The 'consensus' as to the relations adhering between subjects, which Bliss claims exists, is not an absolute one but is both relative and temporary. Therefore, a general classification should be as far as possible adjustable to differing views and needs. There are two main problems involved:
> (a) *Alternative locations*: this refers simply to the moving of any given class to another position–e.g., in the BC [Bibliographic Classification] moving Theology from Class P to AJ so as to collocate it with Philosophy, the internal division of the class is not affected–only its neighbours are changed.
> (b) *Alternative treatments*: this refers to the provision for varying the facet formula in a subject. For examples, allowing Literature to be divided according to the formula Literature–Language–Form–Period–Author, *or* Literature–Language–Period–Author.[3]

Arthur Maltby defines *alternative locations* as "provision of two or more locations for a topic, from which a single one must be chosen and the other left blank . . . "[4] He recognizes the importance of providing alternatives in a classification:

> Many libraries will insist on a certain number of alternative arrangements in any classification, or else will make their own. Biography . . . and geography are two subject areas which come to mind as being especially vulnerable to the improvisations of individual libraries.[5]

Bliss discusses and provides two types of alternatives: (1) Indicated alternatives, including alternative locations and alternative methods; and (2) Systematic alternatives. Alternative locations, such as placing biochemistry under biology or chemistry or placing social psychology under sociology or psychology, allow collocations by different points of view. Alternative methods provide different citation formulae for arranging a particular body of literature, such as literature. Systematic alternatives, on the other hand, refer to the classification of certain types of material, such as subject bibliography, biography, and periodicals by subject or by type of material regardless of subject.[6]

According to Leo E. LaMontagne, the Library of Congress Classification (LCC), being a system originally and specifically designed for the Library's own collection, generally eschewed alternatives. As more and more libraries adopted the scheme, "some consideration was given to the problem, chiefly in correspondence, unfortunately not in published statements."[7]

Nonetheless, LaMontagne recognizes the need for alternative provisions:

> It is true that a unanimity of opinion concerning the divisions and their order does not always exist, especially in the newer branches of learning. It is also true that the objects of knowledge and the specialties which deal with them frequently do not coincide. There are overlapping and twilight zones, and fission and fusion of subjects. . . . All these the classifier must solve on the basis of theory or the practical needs of a library or libraries. He may select one place and refer from alternate places; he may also make alternative provisions so that each library may select the classes which best suit its needs. . . . In actual classing, the library's interests, even if of secondary importance, determine the class.[8]

With regard to alternative classes in LCC specifically, LaMontagne states two purposes:

> (1) develop the classification to meet the needs of libraries in fields where the emphasis on subject collocation differs from Library of Congress practice, and (2) develop a classed catalog representing the various relationships of a subject with other fields.[9]

Currently, there are very few "indicated alternatives" in the LCC schedules; those that exist appear mostly in earlier schedules. On the other hand, many "systematic alternatives" are provided in LC MARC records. In addition, many LC MARC records also include class or call numbers based on other classification schemes.

ALTERNATIVES IN LCC SCHEDULES

Within the LCC schedules, alternatives are found occasionally in earlier schedules; there are no alternative numbers in recently developed or revised schedules. Alternatives are often not indicated as such, but given in the form of parenthesized numbers with "Cf." notes, "Prefer" notes, or *see* references, so that other libraries using LCC may consider using these numbers as alternatives that are better suited to their needs.[10] In more recently developed or revised schedules, numbers enclosed in parentheses are "abandoned numbers," indicating relocations, and are not considered true "alternatives."

Because the classification of Biography, Language and Literature, and Philosophy "differs markedly from the canons of classification which prevailed when the schedules were developed,"[11] many alternative provisions are found in these classes.

Biography

LaMontagne discusses the different citation orders that may be applied to classifying biography: "by form in a biography class, regardless of subject; by form subarranged by subject; and by subject."[12] He provides the following illustration:

1.	Form class:	Biography
	Biographees:	Bach, Johann S.
		Bache, Franklin
		Bacon, Francis

2. Form class: Biography
   Subject: Philosophy
   Biographee: Bacon
   Subject: Music
   Biographee: Bach
   Subject: Science
   Chemistry
   Biographee: Bache
3. Subject: Philosophy
   Biographee: Bacon
   Subject: Music
   Biographee: Bach
   Subject: Science
   Chemistry
   Biographee: Bache

A note found at the beginning of Subclass CT states Library of Congress policy with regard to the classification of biography:

> Class here general collective or individual biography only. For collective or individual biography representative of special classes or subjects of the classification system, *see* the class or subject, e.g., H57+, Social scientists; TA139+, Engineers

Class CT contains biography restricted to the following divisions taken from the third edition of the schedule:[13]

BIOGRAPHY

CT	
21-22	Biography as an art or literary form
93-206	General collective biography
206	Portraits
210-3150	National biography
3200-9999	Biography by subject
3200-3910	Women
(4150-9950)	Special subjects

The second edition of Class C provided here, by means of parenthesized numbers, an alternative treatment of subject biography, namely, an arrangement by subject in one location. Because these numbers were no longer in general use, they were dropped from this edition. An individual library still wishing to class subject biography in CT using the earlier scheme should consult the second edition.

Currently, biography in specific subject areas is classed with the subject, for example:

PHYSICS

QC

	Biography
15	Collective
16	Individual, A-Z

Some of the earlier schedules contain alternative locations within subclasses for biography either by place or by period. For biography of artists, for instance, the Library of Congress prefers classification by place, with parenthesized numbers given under the period. The following example is found in Subclass NE.

NE	PRINT MEDIA
	Printmaking and engraving
	History of printmaking
501-794	Special countries.

******

	Biography
800	Collective
	Special countries, *see* NE501-794
(803)	Before 18th century
(805)	Unnamed masters, *see* NE468
	18th century
(810)	American
(812)	Other
	19th century and later
(815)	American
(817)	Other
	Special artists, *see* NE501-794

Parenthesized numbers, given as see references or "abandoned numbers," may be considered alternative numbers by other libraries for grouping all such biographies together.

Classical Philology and Classical Literature

At the Library of Congress, works on specific subjects from the classical period are classed with the appropriate subjects, rather than in Subclass PA Classical philology and literature. In Appendix A of Schedule PA, W. F. Koenig, who developed the subclass, suggests that such works may be brought together by affixing to the books "a small 'location' label PA in addition to their own class mark."[14] When the library wishes to place these works in their original classes, this can be accomplished, without reclassification, by simply removing these labels. Following are some of the alternative locations suggested by Koenig:

B	165-708	Greek and Roman philosophy
BL	700-820	Greek and Roman mythology and religion
DF	10-16,76-129	Greek antiquities
DG	11-16,75-143	Roman antiquities
G	82-87	Ancient geography
ML	167-169	Greek and Roman music
N	5605-5896	Greek and Roman art

In addition, Koenig also provided parenthesized numbers scattered throughout the subclass in cases of cross classification. For example,

PA   CLASSICAL LITERATURE
                       HISTORY
(3007)   Women authors. Literary relations of women, *see* PA 3067;
               PA 6015.
 3009   Relations to history, civilization, culture, etc.
               Cf. B 178; DE 71.

*****

 3016   Knowledge, and treatment, of countries, people, classes, etc.
               e.g. .S6 Slaves.
               .W7 Women.

*****

Drama.
3027   Tragedy.
          Prefer PA 3131-3136.
3028   Comedy.
          Prefer PA 3161-3166.

****

PA   GREEK LITERATURE
              ANCIENT (CLASSIC) TO CA 600 A. D.
                           HISTORY
          Literary history.
3067   Woman authors. Literary relations of women.
          Cf. PA 3016.W7 (Women in literature).
(3069)   Relations to history, civilization, culture (in general).
          Prefer PA 3009.

*****

          Comedy.
3161   General.
3163   Minor works. (Single) Lectures. Essays, etc.
          Special topics.
(3164)   Origin ("Comus"), *see* PA 3161.
(3165)   Sicilian (Dorian) comedy.
          For reference only; *see* PA 3161, or PA 3968 .E8
          (Epicharmus).

Fine Arts

Parenthesized numbers are also found in various Subclasses in Class N
Fine arts. For example:

NA   ARCHITECTURE
          History
            Medieval architecture
             Romanesque architecture
               Special countries, *see* NA701-1613
(395)   Austria
(397)   France
(400)   Germany

****

Norman architecture
423   General works
(425)   Normandy, *see* NA1049
(427)   Italy, Sicily, *see* NA1113, 1119

******

701-1613 Architecture of specific countries. Table IV.

A further example:

ND   PAINTING
    Watercolor painting
    History
    General works
(2133-2145)   Technical treatises, *see* ND2420-2440
   (2135)   Elements
   (2137)   Juvenile
   (2140)   General special
   (2145)   Miscellaneous

******

Techniques of watercolor painting. Materials and special
   media
2420   General works
    Transparent watercolor
2430   General works. Technical manuals
2435   Special elements of technique
2440   Minor technical. Juvenile

ALTERNATIVE CLASS NUMBERS IN LC MARC RECORDS

Alternative numbers are generally provided for subject bibliographies regularly classed in Z, for analytics in series or sets classed as a whole, for incunabula, and for microforms. On many LC MARC records one or more alternative class numbers are given in addition to the regular LC call number. Alternative subject class numbers appear in field 050 in LC MARC records. Coded as subfield "≠ a," it follows immediately the regular LC call numbers.

As a rule, the alternative number does not include the book or item number since it is not a valid LC call number. However, a Cutter number which forms a part of the class number, such as a topical or geographic Cutter number, is included.

Subject Bibliography

Recognizing the need for many libraries to collocate subject bibliographies with their appropriate subjects, the Library of Congress provides alternative class numbers for certain types of bibliographical materials.

Alternative class numbers are provided for all bibliographies, indexes, and book catalogs with LC call numbers falling within the following ranges of numbers:[15]

> Z1201-4980, National bibliography (except bibliographies having no topical focus)
> Z5051-7999, Subject bibliography
> Z8001-8999, Personal bibliography

Alternative numbers for special types of bibliographies are selected according to Table 1.[16]

Numbers from classes A-J, L, N-V, or Z1-1200 that most closely correspond to the topic of the bibliography are assigned as alternative numbers. Since there is generally no form subdivision for bibliographies in subject classes, the most general number for the subject (often with the caption "General works," "Treatises," or a variation thereof) is selected. Numbers for periodicals, directories, dictionaries, pictorial works, textbooks, etc., are not used, even if the items listed in the bibliography are limited to those forms.

Table 1: Alternative number for specific types of materials

TYPE OF MATERIAL	ALTERNATE NUMBER
Belles lettres	**General works** number under **History and criticism** in class P, as appropriate for the language, form, and period of the bibliography
Children's literature	PN1009, and numbers in specific **P** subclasses
Dissertations from a single institution	AS11 +
Dissertations from many institutions, not limited to a specific topic	None

TYPE OF MATERIAL	ALTERNATE NUMBER
Government publications, not limited to a specific topic or agency	Appropriate number in subclass **J**
Government publications on a specific topic or limited to a specific agency	Appropriate topical number
National bibliography with no topical focus, e.g., list of imprints of a specific country	None
Newspapers	PN4700+
Personal bibliography	Number for biographies of the person
Subject bibliography, including topical bibliographies classed in national bibliography numbers	**General works** number for the topic in classes A-J, L N-V, Z1-1200
University bibliography, i.e., publications issued by a university, not limited to a specific topic	AS11 +

Following are examples of alternative numbers for bibliographies:

Cultural anthropology of the Middle East: a bibliography/by Ruud Strijp. 1992-
    LC call number: Z3014.E85S77 1992
    Alternative number: GN640
    [Subclass GN Anthropology]

Tailless aircraft–an extensive bibliography for subsonic types/compiled and annotated by Serge Krauss, Jr. Cleveland Heights, Ohio: S. Krauss, 1992
    LC call number: Z5064.A25 K73 1992
    Alternative class number: TL158.60
    [Subclass TL Motor vehicles. Aeronautics. Astronautics]

Technology monitoring and evaluation in agroforestry projects: an annotated bibliography/compilers, E.U. Muller and S.J. Scherr. 1989
    LC call number: Z5074.A73M84 1989
    Alternative class number: S494.5.A45
    [Subclass S Agriculture (General). The Cutter number .A45, for Agroforestry, is part of the class number.]

Annotated bibliography: historical record of minority and women-owned business enterprises in public and private contracting in New Jersey: a report submitted to NJ TRANSIT and the Governor's Study Commission on Discrimination in Public Works Procurement and Contracts/by the Afro-American Studies Program, University of Maryland at College Park. College Park, MD. 1992
    LC call number: Z7165.U6 N3416 1992
    Alternative class number: HD2346.U52N52
        [Subclass HD Economic history and conditions. Both Cutter
        numbers, U52 and N52, meaning United States–New Jersey, are
        part of the class number]

Christopher Marlowe in the eighties: an annotated bibliography of Marlowe criticism from 1978 through 1989/Bruce E. Brandt. West Cornwall. 1992
    LC call number: Z8550.4 .B7 1992
    Alternative class number: PR2674
        [Subclass PR English literature]

Monographic Series and Sets

Many monographic series and multipart items are classified by the Library of Congress as collected sets, with the same call number assigned to all component parts of the series or collected set. Many of these are analyzed with a separate MARC record for each title within the series or set.[17]

A monographic series or set classed as a "collect" item may be analyzed in full, in part, or not analyzed. On the separate MARC record for each part in an analyzed series or set, an alternative class number appropriate for the content of the individual title is assigned in addition to the collected call number except when the collected number and the alternative number are the same or when the alternative class is Law. The alternative class number is carried out as far as needed to cover topical elements, including those represented by topical Cutter numbers. For example:

Solar eclipses, 1991-2000/by Alan D. Fiala, James A. DeYoung, and Marie R. Lukac. 1986 (United States Naval Observatory circular; no. 170)
    LC call number: QB4 .W34 no. 170
    Alternative class number: QB544

Handlist of the Glynne-Gladstone Mss in St. Deiniol's Library, Hawarden/ compiled by C.J. Williams. 1990 (Special series/List & Index Society; v. 24)
    LC call number: CD1042.A2 L56 vol. 24
    Alternative class number: CD1069.5.G59

Conservation research: studies of fifteenth-to nineteenth-century tapestry/edited by Lotus Stack. c1993. (Studies in the history of art (Washington, D.C.); v. 42)(Studies in the history of art (Washington, D.C.). Monograph series ; 2)
    LC call number: N386.U5 S78 vol. 42
    Alternative class number: NK2997

Les salines de Salins au XIIIème siècle: cartulaires et livre des rentiers/ René Locatelli, Denis Brun, Henri Dubois; préface de Jean Favier; avant-propos de Jean Courtieu. 1991. (Annales littéraires de l'Université de Besançon; 448)(Cahiers d'études comtoises; no. 47)
    LC call number: AS161 .B39 vol. 448
    Alternative class number: HD9213.F83S25
    [Both Cutter numbers belong to the class number]

On LC cataloging records, when a series containing a subseries is classed as a "collect" item, and the individual pieces of the subseries are analyzed, an alternative number is assigned to each piece and no alternative number is assigned to the subseries, for example,

New perspectives in early Greek art/edited by Diana Buitron-Oliver. 1991 (Studies in the history of art, 0091-7338; 32. Symposium papers; 16)
LC call number: N386.U5 S78 vol. 32
    Alternative class number: N5630

Autour de Victor Cousin: une politique de la philosophie/Jean Pierre Cotten. 1992 (Annales littéraires de l'Université de Besançon; no 469. Serie AGON; no 3)
    LC call number: AS161 .B39 vol.469
    Alternative class number: B2267

If the analytic is for a subseries that is not analyzed, an alternative number is assigned to the subseries. Alternative monographic class numbers are also provided for occasional numbers of periodicals or other series for which analytic records are provided.

Incunabula

At the Library of Congress, incunabula, i.e., books printed before 1501, are housed in the Rare Book Division, except those assigned to special collections such as the Law Library. Materials assigned to the incunabula collection in the Rare Book Division receive one of two broad classifications: "Incun. [date]" (used for entries which have definite imprint dates) or "Incun.X" (used when the precise date of publication is uncertain). A Cutter number based on the main entry is added to complete the call number.

For libraries that wish to classify incunabula in the regular manner, alternative numbers are provided on LC cataloging records. Following are examples of classifying incunabula.

> *Incipit tractatus de successionibus ab intestato*/Cino da Pistoia. 1472?
> LC call number: Incun. 1472 .C59
> Alternative class number: KJA2287

> *Iuuenalis familiare co[m]mentu[m]: cum Antonij Mancinelli viri eruditissimi explanatione: argumenta satyrarum Iuuenalis per Antonium Mancinellum* . . . [Lyon]: Impressum est hoc op[us] pro fido et bono bibliopola Stephano Gaynardo . . . arte et industria Nicolai Vvolf . . . ipso Asce[n]siovitio[rum] expu[n]ctore, anno Salutis Christiane 1498 ad decimu[m]quartu[m] K[a]l[endas] Dece[m]b[ris][i.e., 18 Nov.] [6], CXCVIII leaves; 25 cm. (4to)
> LC call number: Incun. 1498 .B25
> Alternative class number: PA6448.A15

> *Herodoti Halicarnasei libri nouem* . . . Venetiis: Impressa per Ioannem & Gregorium] de Gregoriis fratres, 1494 die viii Martii i.e., after 29 Mar.] 8], CXXXIIII leaves; 32 cm. (fol.)
> LC call number: Incun. 1494 .H46
> Alternative class number: PA4003.L38

Facsimiles of individual incunabula or excerpts from such facsimiles are treated as normal works and classed by subject. The class number Z241 is assigned only when it is clear that the publisher intends the work to serve as a specimen of early printing.

Microforms

Microfilms are arranged in the Library of Congress collection by accession numbers called "control numbers." The call number for a microfilm consists of three elements:

Microfilm
[control number]   (a sequential number)
([class letter(s)])   (based on the class or subclass)

For example,

> *Records and briefs of the United States Court of Appeals, Second Circuit* [microform].– [S.l.: s.n.], 1891-1975]
> LC call number: Microfilm 93/10002 (K)

The call number of the original, if available, is given in a note. For example,

> *Dante* [microform]/by T.S. Eliot. London: Faber & Faber, 1929. 69 p.; 20 cm. [Microfilm. Washington, D.C.: Library of Congress Photoduplication Service, 1987. 1 microfilm reel; 35 mm.]
> LC call number: Microfilm 87/5634 (P) <MicRR>
> Call number of original: PQ4390.E5 1929.

> *Platonis Res publica* [microform]/recognovit brevique adnotatione critica instruxit Ioannes Burnet. Oxonii: E Typographeo Clarendoniano, 1902 (Scriptorum classicorum bibliotheca Oxoniensis)
> LC call number: Microfilm 90/4730 (P) <MicRR>
> Call number of original: PA3405.S8P67 1902.

> *Socrates* [microform]: a translation of the Apology, Crito, and parts of the Phaedo of Plato. New York: C. Scribner's Sons, 1879, c1878. [Microfilm. Washington, D.C.: Library of Congress Photoduplication Service, 1983. 1 microfilm reel; 35 mm.]
> LC call number: Microfilm 83/6750 (B) <MicRR>
> Call number of original: B365.A5S3.

Many of the records for microform represent minimum level cataloging. Those representing full cataloging sometimes include entire class number rather than only the class letter as an alternate, for example,

> *The Pacific Northwest tribes missions collection of the Oregon Province Archives of the Society of Jesus* [microform]/edited by Robert C. Carriker and Eleanor R. Carriker.– Wilmington, DE: Scholarly Resources, c1987.
> LC call number: Microfilm 89/9004 (E) <MicRR>
> Alternative class number: E78 .N77

For libraries that wish to arrange microfilms by class numbers, the alternative numbers or the call numbers of the original with modification may be used.

Microfiche are classed in the same way as microfilms except for the label. A call number for a microfiche consists of the following elements:

Microfiche
[control number]
([class or subclass letter(s)])

For example,

Dictionary catalog of the library of the Freer Gallery of Art, Smithsonian Institution [microform].–2nd enl. ed. on microfiche.–Boston: G.K. Hall Micropublications, c1991.–252 Microfiches: negative.
LC call number: Microfiche 93/30 (z)
[formerly Z5961.A78 alternative class N7260]

The Alphabetical index of householders contained in the General valuation of rateable property in Ireland, County Waterford–1850 [microform]: also known by the short title Griffith's valuation of County Waterford. – Vienna, Va.: All-Ireland Heritage, c1988. – 6 microfiches: maps.
LC call number: Microfiche 93/18 (C)
    [formerly CS497.W3]

The A-IH computerized data base edition of the alphabetical index of householders contained in the General valuation of rateable property in Ireland, County Carlow–c. 1852 [microform]: also known by the short title Griffith's valuation of County Carlow. Dunn Loring, VA: All-Ireland Heritage, c1989. 3 microfiches: maps.
LC call number: Microfiche 93/13 (C)
    [formerly CS497.C32]

Early American history research reports [microform]. Alexandria, VA: Chadwyck-Healey, 1990-1992. ca. 1600 microfiches: ill., maps.
LC call number: Microfiche 93/249 (F)
    [formerly F234.W7]

ALTERNATIVE CLASSIFICATION

On many LC MARC records, class numbers based on other classification systems are given in addition to the Library of Congress Classification number. Such numbers may come from the Dewey Decimal Classification (DDC), the National Library of Medicine Classification (NLM), and the Superintendent of Documents Classification, as appropriate. In the USMARC format, specific fields are assigned for use with these class numbers:

050   Library of Congress Classification
060   National Library of Medicine Classification
082   Dewey Decimal Classification
086   Government Document Classification

Field 070 is designated for numbers assigned by the National Agricultural Library. Class numbers appearing in this field are based on LCC and are usually the same as the LC-assigned class numbers in field 050, with variations due to different Cutter numbers or different interpretation of content. Field 080 is defined for the Universal Decimal Classification but not implemented by the Library of Congress.

Dewey Decimal Classification

On many LC MARC records, DDC numbers are assigned in addition to LC call numbers. The DDC number does not include the Cutter or item number. For example,

The end of the Communist revolution/Robert V. Daniels. 1993
LC call number: HX311.5 .D36 1993
DDC class number: 320.5320947

This popular engine: New England newspapers during the American Revolution, 1775-1789/Carol Sue Humphrey. 1992
LC call number: PN4891.H86 1992
DDC class number: 071.4

Jews in Christian America: the pursuit of religious equality/Naomi W. Cohen. 1992
LC call number: E184.J5C619 1992
Alternative class number: 322.1089924073

Approximately two-thirds of all books cataloged by the Library of Congress receive DDC numbers. Books selected for coverage include those in major languages of interest to libraries using DDC: English, French, German, Italian, and Spanish.[18]

National Library of Medicine Classification

On many cataloging records for works in medicine produced through the cooperative cataloging program between the National Library of Medicine and the Library of Congress, alternative class numbers based on the NLM Classification are given in addition to the LC call numbers.

Currently, the cooperative program is limited to CIP (cataloging-in-publication) items. The National Library of Medicine prepares the descriptive cataloging data and assigns NLM call numbers and MeSH (Medical Subject Headings), while the Library of Congress is responsible for assigning the LC call number and LCSH (Library of Congress Subject Headings). The following examples illustrate the provision of alternative numbers for medical books on LC MARC records.

Brain mechanisms, attention-deficit, and related mental disorders: clinical and theoretical assessment of attention-deficit/by Jordan Joseph. 1992
   LC call number: RJ496.A863J68 1992
   NLM call number: WS 350.6 J83b

Rage, power, and aggression/edited by Robert A. Glick & Steve P. Roose. 1993
   LC call number: RC569.5.A533R34 1993
   NLM call number: BF 575.A5 R141

Conflict in intimate relationships/by Dudley D. Cahn. 1992
   LC call number: RC488.53.C325 1992
   NLM call number: BF 683 C132c

Practice and inquiry for nursing administration: solicited papers and proceedings of a conference, October 31-November 3, 1990, the Bishops Lodge, Santa Fe, New Mexico/edited by Beverly Henry, Jean M. Nagelkerk, Richard Heyden. 1992
   LC call number: RT89 .P72 1992
   NLM call number: WY 105 P8946 1990 (P)

Aerosols in medicine: principles, diagnosis, and therapy/edited by F. Moren . . . [et al.]. 2nd ed. 1993
   LC call number: RM161 .A38 1993
   NLM call number: WF 600 A252 1993 (P)

Principles of human anatomy/Gerard J. Tortora. 6th ed. c1992
   LC call number: QP34.53.T68 1992
   NLM call number: QS 4 T712pa

National Agricultural Library Call Numbers

On some LC MARC records, an alternative class number assigned by the National Agricultural Library (NAL) also appears. For example,

Biotechnology in agriculture, 1986-May 1992: citations from AGRI-COLA concerning diseases and other environmental considerations/ compiled and edited by Charles N. Bebee and United States Environmental Protection Agency, Office of Pesticide Programs. 1992 (Bibliographies and literature of agriculture; no. 119)
LC call number: Z5074.B543B43 1992
Alternative number assigned by LC: S494.5.B563
Alternative number assigned by NAL: Z5076.A1U54 no.119

Methylbromide and its alternatives as fumigants, 1979-May 1992: citations from AGRICOLA concerning diseases and other environmental considerations/compiled and edited by Charles N. Bebee and United States Environmental Protection Agency, Office of Pesticide Programs. 1992
LC call number: Z5074.P43B38 1992
Alternative class number: SB952.B75
Alternative number assigned by NAL: Z5076.A1U54 no.120

The NAL numbers are based on LCC. The differences between the LC and NAL numbers are mainly due to different interpretation of the content or shelf arrangement.

Superintendent of Documents Classification

The Superintendent of Documents Classification numbers appearing on LC MARC records for federal government publications are normally assigned by the Government Printing Office (GPO). These publications include books and nonbook materials. For example,

The Pacific Yew Act of 1991: joint hearing before the Subcommittee on Fisheries and Wildlife Conservation and the Environment of the Committee on Merchant Marine and Fisheries and the Subcommittee on Forests, Family Farms, and Energy of the Committee on Agriculture and the Subcommittee on National Parks and Public Lands of the Committee on Interior and Insular Affairs, House of Representatives, One Hundred Second Congress, second session . . . March 4, 1992. –

Washington: U.S. G.P.O.: For sale by the U.S. G.P.O., Supt. of Docs.,
Congressional Sales Office, 1992.
  LC call number: KF273.M447 1992i
  Alternative class number: Y 4.M 53:102-71

Azerbaijan/[Central Intelligence Agency]. 1992 {a map}
  LC call number: G7140 1992 .U5
  Alternative class number: PREX 3.10/4:AZ 2/3

CONCLUSION

Although LCC does not officially provide alternative or optional numbers, many parenthesized numbers are found where cross classification or
relocations occur. Such numbers may be used as alternative class numbers
by other libraries. The alternative class numbers indicating alternative
arrangement of certain categories of materials and those assigned from
other classification systems are provided as services to libraries not using
the Library of Congress Classification.

REFERENCES

1. Henry Evelyn Bliss, *The Organization of Knowledge in Libraries and the Subject-Approach to Books* (New York: H. W. Wilson Co., 1933), pp. 79-80.

2. Henry Evelyn Bliss, *A Bibliographic Classification, Extended by Systematic Auxiliary Schedules for Composite Specification and Notation* (New York: H. W. Wilson Co., 1940), vol. 1, p. 47.

3. J. Mills, *A Modern Outline of Library Classification* (London: Chapman & Hall, 1960), p. 34.

4. Arthur Maltby, *Sayers' Manual of Classification for Librarians,* 5th ed. (London: André Deutsch, 1975), p. 97.

5. Maltby, p. 97.

6. Bliss, *A Bibliographic Classification,* vol. 1, p. 23.

7. Leo E. LaMontagne, *American Library Classification with Special Reference to the Library of Congress* (Hamden, CT: Shoe String Press, 1961), p. 306.

8. LaMontagne, pp. 12-13.

9. LaMontagne, p. 308.

10. LaMontagne, p. 307.

11. LaMontagne, p. 318.

12. LaMontagne, p. 318.

13. Library of Congress, Subject Cataloging Division, *Library of Congress Classification: Classification, Class C: Auxiliary Sciences of History,* 3rd ed. (Washington: Library of Congress, 1975), p. 109.

14. Library of Congress, Subject Cataloging Division, *Classification: Class P: P-PA Philology, Linguistics, Classical Philology, Classical Literature* (with supplementary pages (Washington: Government Printing Office, 1928, reissued 1968), p. 417.

15. Library of Congress, Office for Subject Cataloging Policy, *Subject Cataloging Manual: Classification,* 1st ed. (Washington: Cataloging Distribution Service, Library of Congress, 1992), F150, p. 1.

16. Library of Congress, *Subject Cataloging Manual: Classification,* F150, p. 2.

17. Library of Congress, *Subject Cataloging Manual: Classification,* F130, p.1.

18. Barbara Bryant, " 'Numbers You Can Count On': Dewey Decimal Classification Is Maintained at LC," *Library of Congress Information Bulletin* 52(18): 373-374 (October 4, 1993).

Options in the Dewey Decimal Classification System: The Current Perspective

Joan S. Mitchell

SUMMARY. Options currently provided in the Dewey Decimal Classification system are reviewed. Options are an appropriate mechanism in a general purpose classification used by different kinds and sizes of libraries around the world. Dewey provides the universal option of close versus broad classification. Options also are provided to give emphasis to jurisdiction; racial, ethnic, or national group; language; topic; or other specific characteristics. Various devices are detailed or suggested to introduce options. Options may be an impediment to retrieval of information across systems. Options should not be introduced as a substitute for the appropriate placement of a topic in the Classification. Options help accommodate cultural differences in the Classification, and provide a mechanism for emphasizing topics of local importance.

The Dewey Decimal Classification (DDC) system is the most widely used library classification system in the world. In the United States, the

---

Joan S. Mitchell, BA, MLS, is Editor, Dewey Decimal Classification, OCLC Forest Press. Address correspondence to: Library of Congress, Decimal Classification Division, Washington, DC 20540-4330.

The author gratefully acknowledges the comments of the DDC editorial staff on earlier drafts. All opinions expressed and inadvertent errors remain the responsibility of the author.

[Haworth co-indexing entry note]: "Options in the Dewey Decimal Classification System: The Current Perspective." Mitchell, Joan S. Co-published simultaneously in *Cataloging & Classification Quarterly* (The Haworth Press, Inc.) Vol. 19, No. 3/4, 1995, pp. 89-103; and: *Classification: Options and Opportunities* (ed: Alan R. Thomas) The Haworth Press, Inc., 1995, pp. 89-103. Multiple copies of this article/chapter may be purchased from The Haworth Document Delivery Center [1-800-3-HA-WORTH; 9:00 a.m. - 5:00 p.m. (EST)].

Dewey Decimal Classification is used by 95% of all public and school libraries, 25% of all college and university libraries, and 20% of all special libraries. Around the world, Dewey is used by over 200,000 libraries in 135 countries, and has been translated into over 30 languages.[1]

The Dewey Decimal Classification is under constant development and revision in the editorial office located in the Decimal Classification Division at the Library of Congress. DDC numbers are applied to works acquired by the Library of Congress, and distributed in LC machine-readable cataloging (MARC) records. DDC numbers also are distributed in MARC records created in at least 12 other countries, including Australia, Canada, and the United Kingdom. The DDC is used in the national bibliographies of Australia, Canada, India, Indonesia, Italy, Jordan, Kenya, Pakistan, Papua New Guinea, the United Kingdom, Zimbabwe, and other countries.[2] DDC numbers appear in records contributed by national libraries and member libraries in various bibliographic utilities such as OCLC.

With such diverse usage by different types of libraries in different countries around the world, how can one general classification system meet the needs of its users? One way is through the use of options.

This paper reviews the options currently included in the Dewey Decimal Classification system, and the various devices used to introduce the options. The implications of using options and the future of options in the Classification are discussed.

PART I. USE OF OPTIONS

John Comaromi, editor of Edition 20 of the DDC, noted: "The provision of options in DDC is a long-standing tradition. Dewey's introduction to DDC 12 (1927), which was reprinted in later editions through the 18th, carried 'Suggested variations' that might be practicable in adjusting to special local requirements."[3] Benjamin Custer, editor of Editions 16 through 19, announced in the Introduction to Edition 17 a "full-scale attack" on Western bias through the introduction of various measures, including the use of optional letters and symbols.[4] The provision of options in Edition 20 is explained in the Introduction. "At a number of places in the Schedules, options are provided for libraries whose needs are not met by the standard provisions."[5]

Close versus Broad Classification

Libraries employ options to tailor the Classification to meet local needs. At the most basic level, Dewey provides the universal option of close versus broad classification. Libraries may use the notation to its fullest (close classification) or contract the notation (broad classification) to meet the needs of users. To aid in this process, the Library of Congress Decimal Classification Division provides segmentation marks in each DDC number assigned to indicate meaningful breaks in the number.

For example, a special library with a large engineering collection might wish to use the notation to its fullest for works in engineering, but would prefer a broader classification for the few works it owns on social services to young people. Here are two full DDC numbers with segmentation marks shown, one in engineering and one in social services:

> 621.39/814   Analog-to-digital and digital-to-analog converters
> Example: modems
>
> 362.7/12   Day care services

Given the hypothetical engineering library, the library would use the full engineering number for a work on engineering of modem hardware (621.39814), but might prefer to use 362.7 (the abridged number) instead of the full number 362.712 for a work on day care centers. The choice would be made on the basis that with a large engineering collection, the fullest representation of the subject is needed for proper collocation and retrieval. A more general classification might be preferred for the same library's small collection on social services to young people, since the broader number would collocate the few items at 362.7 Problems of and services to young people, instead of scattering them throughout the subdivisions of 362.7.

One might consider the Abridged Edition of Dewey[6] as a programmatic option of broad classification for libraries with collections of 20,000 volumes or less. Abridged Edition 12 is considered a true abridgment of the standard English-language edition, Edition 20. The first segmentation mark applied by the Library of Congress Decimal Classification Division represents the number in the Abridged Edition or the beginning of a standard subdivision.

> Edition 20:
> 621.39/814   Analog-to-digital and digital-to-analog converters
> Example: modems

Abridged Edition 12:
621.39   Computers

Numerous options are suggested throughout the Classification. Each provides a mechanism for emphasizing an aspect in the library's collection not given preferred treatment in Edition 20. In some cases, options also are suggested to provide shorter notation for the aspect.

Options are provided throughout the Classification to address one of the following needs:

Jurisdictional emphasis
Racial, ethnic, or national group emphasis
Language emphasis
Topical emphasis
Emphasis by other specific characteristics

Jurisdictional Emphasis

In several places in the Classification, options are provided to allow emphasis or subarrangement by jurisdiction. At 061 General organizations in North America, the option is suggested to use 061 to provide emphasis to organizations in a specific country other than the United States and Canada. A similar option is suggested at 071 for newspapers.

At 337.3-.9 Foreign economic policies and relations of specific jurisdictions and groups of jurisdictions, an option is provided to give priority in notation to the jurisdiction or group of jurisdictions requiring local emphasis instead of the jurisdiction or group of jurisdictions emphasized or coming first in the sequence of area notation. In several places in the 900s, a similar option is provided to place a war under the history of a country or area other than the one preferred in the Schedules. For example, an option is suggested to place the Livonian War under Swedish history in 948.502 instead of under Russian history in 947.043.

Several options are provided at 340 Law to give emphasis to a particular jurisdiction. In the standard version, law is arranged by branch of law, jurisdiction, and subordinate topic. One option (Option B) changes the citation order to give preference to jurisdiction over branch of law and subordinate topic.

Racial, Ethnic, or National Group Emphasis

Options are provided to allow emphasis or subarrangement by racial, ethnic, or national group. In DDC Table 5 (Racial, Ethnic, National Groups), options are detailed at–1-9 Specific racial, ethnic, national groups and at–1 North Americans to give local emphasis and a shorter number to a specific group. For example, an option is suggested at–1-9 to use a letter for a specific group (e.g., A for Arabs) to provide shorter notation and to emphasize the group by having it precede–1.

Language Emphasis

Options are suggested at several places in the Classification to provide local emphasis or shorter numbers to a particular language. At 031 American [encyclopedias], the option is given to class encyclopedias in a language other than English in 031, and then to class American English-language encyclopedias in 032 [Encyclopedias] In English. A similar option is given at 051 American [serials] and at 081 American [collections].

In 400 Language, several options are provided to give emphasis or a shorter number to a specific language. At 410 Linguistics, for example, an option is suggested to move linguistics to 400 and then use 41 as the base number for a specific language requiring local emphasis and a shorter number. Similarly, options are provided throughout 800 Literature to give preferred treatment or a shorter number to the literature of a specific language. Options for local emphasis and shorter numbers for specific languages are suggested in the introduction to DDC Table 6 (Languages) and at– 1 Indo-European languages in DDC Table 6.

Topical Emphasis

Some options are suggested in the Classification to emphasize a topic of local importance or collocate a topic in an alternative arrangement. Throughout 200 Religion, various options are provided to give preferred treatment or shorter numbers to religions other than Christianity. An optional number for topical geography, 910.1, is provided to gather topical geographic works in one place instead of scattering them by subject in 001-999.

Emphasis by Other Specific Characteristics

Sometimes within a given classification number, it is desirable to collocate items by name or some other identifying characteristic. Instead of detailing further subdivision of the class, an option is provided to allow the local library to collocate items by a specific characteristic, e.g., name, title, date, format. For example, alphabetical subarrangement by name of computer, name of programming language, and name of program is provided as an option at several places in 004-006 Computer science. Subarrangement by date is suggested for Olympic games at 796.48 and 796.98. Options also are provided to collocate items by format. In 780 Music, options are suggested to distinguish scores, miniature scores, and recordings in the same class number.

PART II. DEVICES FOR OPTIONS

There are several devices for introducing options. With the exception of alphabetical and chronological subarrangement, options are clearly labeled. Options described in notes appear in parentheses and begin with "Option:". Some optional numbers are enumerated in the Schedules and Tables and appear in parentheses in the number column. Descriptions of the various devices for implementing options follow.

1. Length of Notation

The universal option of shortening the notation when the fullest representation of the subject is not required by the library's collection has been discussed. There also are devices for creating more specific numbers than those provided in the Classification. These include options in number building, and alphabetical and chronological subarrangement.

1a. Options in Number Building

In several places in the Schedules and Tables, options are provided to extend the level of synthesis in built numbers. In DDC Table 1 (Standard Subdivisions) at–093-099, the option is provided to add to the geographic area the historical period notation from the period subdivisions of 930-990 instead of the general period notation from DDC Table 1. Use of this option could result in a more precise identification of the historical period in the DDC number. For example, the notation available in DDC Table 1 permits specification of the period to the level of the nineteenth century for a work set in the United States during the time of Reconstruction. The option for deriving period notation from 930-990 permits more specific identification of the period within the nineteenth century by using notation from 973.8 Reconstruction period, 1865-1901.

At 780 Music, an option is provided to allow synthesis beyond two concepts.

> 780   Music
>> In building numbers, do not add by use of 0 or 1 (alone or in combination) more than twice, e.g., history of rock protest songs 782.421661592 (not 782.42166159209)
>
> (Option: Add as many times as desired)

In language and literature, options are provided to allow further analysis for areas with limited treatment in the standard English-language edition. At 420-490 Specific languages, one may add 04 to the base number for a non-preferred group of languages, then add notation 01-86 from DDC Table 4 (Subdivisions of Individual Languages) to provide further analysis. At 810-890 Literature of specific languages, one may add 04 to the base number for any group of literatures and then add notation 01-89 from DDC Table 3-B (Subdivisions for Works by or about More than One Author) to provide further analysis. Such options provide additional topical emphasis beyond that provided in the standard English-language edition.

1b. Alphabetical Subarrangement

Alphabetical subarrangement is suggested at several places in the Classification where identification by specific name or other identifying characteristic may be desirable.

> 629.2222 Specific named passenger automobiles
>> Arrange alphabetically by name or make of car

Alphabetical subarrangement for serials is suggested at 051-059, for newspapers at 071-079, and for collections at 081-089. Alphabetical subarrangement by name of composer is suggested at optional number 789 Composers and traditions of music, and by name of people at optional number 970.3 Specific [North American] native peoples.

1c. Chronological Subarrangement

Chronological subarrangement is an option similar to alphabetical subarrangement. Chronological subarrangement of Olympic games is suggested as an option at 796.48 and 796.98.

796.48   Olympic games
Arrange specific games chronologically

2. Number Switching and Redefinition

Options frequently are introduced by switching the meaning of two numbers, or extending the meaning of a single number.[7] The option of switching two numbers to give prominence to organizations in a non-preferred country was mentioned earlier as an example of jurisdictional emphasis.

061   General organizations in North America
(Option B: To give local emphasis and a shorter number to organizations in a specific country other than the United States and Canada, class them in this number; in that case class organizations in North America in 068.7 . . .)

In the standard version, 068 represents General organizations in other geographical areas. "Other" refers to countries and areas not mentioned in 061-067. If the option at 061 is used for a country such as Namibia, then North America becomes an "other" area and is classed in 068.7 (068 plus the area notation from DDC Table 2 for North America, −7).

The number switching method may involve more than two numbers in a Schedule. In religion, an option is suggested to rearrange the topical emphasis throughout the 200s.

292-299 Religions other than Christianity
(Options: To give preferred treatment or shorter numbers to a specific religion, use one of the following:
(Option A: Class the religion in 230-280, its sources in 220, comprehensive works in 200; in that case class the Bible and Christianity in 298 . . .))

Options also are provided to redefine the meaning of a number. For example, an option is provided in DDC Table 2 (Geographic Areas, Periods, Persons) to collocate the ancient geographic area with the modern geographic area.

−62 Egypt and Sudan
(Option: Class here ancient Egypt; prefer−32)

Sometimes number switching and redefinition are combined. In DDC Table 5, an option is provided to give shorter and more prominent notation to a racial, ethnic, or national group not given emphasis in the standard notation.

> −1 North Americans
>> (Option: To give local emphasis and a shorter number to a specific group, e.g., Sinhalese, class it in this number; in that case class North Americans in−2 . . .)

In this option, the Sinhalese are moved into−1, and North Americans are merged with the British, English, and Anglo-Saxons in−2.

3. Change in Preference or Citation Order

An optional preference order is sometimes provided in the Schedules and Tables. This allows one to give preference to a topic not given preference in the standard edition. At 800 Literature, satire and humor appear last in the table of preference. An option is provided to give preference to satire and humor over all other forms.

Sometimes, an option will provide the means of switching the citation order within a number to give emphasis to another aspect. As described earlier, the following option at 340 Law allows one to emphasize jurisdiction ahead of branch of law.

> 340 Law
>> (Option B: To arrange by jurisdiction or area arrange the elements as follows:
>
> (1)   Base number 34
> (4)   Notation from Table 2, followed by a 0
> (2)   Notation for the branch of law
> (3)   Notation for the subordinate topic without the initial 0 . . .)

4. Optional Numbers

Optional numbers are provided in parentheses in several places in the Schedules and Tables.

4a. Optional Schedule Numbers

In 222-224 Books of the Old Testament, several optional numbers are provided for Apocryphal works. In music, 789 is provided as an optional number for composers and/or traditions of music. In 800 Literature, optional numbers are provided for the literatures and literary periods of non-preferred countries. Optional early history numbers are provided under individual countries in the 900s.

A special class of optional number, "permanently unassigned," is provided to allow local emphasis and shorter numbers for specific religions in the 200s, and for iconography of specific religions in 704.9481.

Several optional numbers are provided for individual and collected biography at 920. The optional class numbers 920.1-920.5, 920.9, and 921-928 all appear in parentheses for optional treatment of biography. In addition, 92 is identified as an optional number for biography in a note under 920, but is not listed separately in the number column. (Another option for biography, the letter B, is discussed under letters and symbols.)

4b. Optional Table Numbers

In DDC Table 1, optional standard subdivision –016 is provided to class bibliographies, catalogs, and indexes with the discipline or subject. For example, the standard number in Edition 20 for a bibliography on computer science is 016.004; the optional number would be 004.016. A similar option is provided for the classification of law of a specific discipline or subject with the discipline or subject through use of optional standard subdivision –026. In DDC Table 2, optional numbers are provided for specific states of the United States at –734-739.

5. Letters and Symbols

The use of letters or symbols to implement an option is suggested at numerous places in the Classification.

A letter representing the jurisdiction or language may precede the DDC number or be used in place of subsequent numbers to provide appropriate local emphasis. For example, the National Library of Canada uses C810 for Canadian literature in English. The use of the prefix C allows Canadian literature to file ahead of 810 American literature in English and be separated from other American literatures in English, notably that of the United States.

The use of a letter in the middle of a number to give prominence to a specific language is suggested at 420-490 Specific languages.

420-490 Specific languages
(Option B: To give local emphasis and a shorter number to a spe-

cific language, place it first by use of a letter or other symbol, e.g., Arabic language 4A0 [preceding 420], for which the base number is 4A . . .)

Use of the option for the Arabic language emphasizes Arabic at the beginning of the sequence of languages and provides a shorter number compared to the standard number for Arabic in Edition 20, 492.7.

A letter also may be used at the end of the number.

> 081-089 [General collections] In specific languages and language families
>
> (Option A: To give local emphasis and a shorter number to collections in a specific language, place them first by use of a letter or symbol, e.g., collections in Urdu 08U [preceding 081])

Letters are suggested as the mechanism for subarranging works by and about a literary author. The option is described at 822.33 with Shakespeare used as the model.

> 822.33 William Shakespeare
>
> (Option: Subarrange works about and by Shakespeare according to the following table, which may be adapted for use with any specific author:
>
> A   Authorship controversies
> B   Biography
> D   Critical appraisal
> .
> .
> .
> Z   Spurious and doubtful works)

In DDC Table 2, an option is suggested at –4-9 to use the DDC number for the continent coupled with a letter representing the country, further subdivided by notation for the city. In Edition 20, the standard number for Peshawar, Pakistan in DDC Table 2 is –549123. Using the option just described, this number could be shortened to –5P23:

> 5   Asia
> P   Pakistan
> 23   Part of the standard number for Peshawar

In DDC Table 5, the use of a letter (e.g., A for Arabs) is suggested as an alternative to numeric notation for racial, ethnic, or national groups. A similar option is provided for languages in Table 6. The use of the letter B for individual biography is suggested under 920 Biography, and under–092 in DDC Table 1.

An option at 780 Music describes a method of distinguishing scores and recordings by the addition of a letter or symbol to the beginning of the DDC number.

> 780 Music
>> (Option A: Prefix a letter or other symbol to the number for treatises, e.g., music for violin M787.2 or &787.2, violin recordings R787.2 or MR787.2; use a special prefix to distinguish miniature scores from other scores, MM787.2 . . .)

The use of alphabetical codes in place of, or in addition to, numeric notation for juvenile works is discussed in the Appendix to Edition 20.[8] The Children's Literature Team at the Library of Congress assigns E for easy books and Fic for fiction to juvenile works processed by the group.

6. Licensed Expansions and Adaptations

Sometimes, even with the optional devices provided, it is necessary for a country and/or language group to produce its own licensed expansion or adaptation of the Classification to provide for local needs. For example, none of the options in standard Dewey addresses the need for a fuller area table in a specific country. The standard English-language edition generally divides Western European countries to the first level administrative unit. In the recent Italian licensed translation and expansion, *Classificazione Decimale Dewey*,[9] the area table for Italy is much fuller than the table found in the standard Edition 20. In DDC Table 2 in the standard Edition 20, a single number is provided for the province of Bologna, –4541. In the Italian edition, a detailed breakdown of the Bologna region is provided in twenty-seven Table numbers from –4541 through –454158.

PART III. EVALUATION OF OPTIONS

It has been illustrated that options can provide a way of adapting the standard English-language edition of the Dewey Decimal Classification to provide emphasis to topics of local importance. The use of options in a standard classification system poses some questions:

Should the Classification include options?
What are the costs and benefits of options?
What is the future of options in the Classification?

Should the Classification Include Options?

While Dewey provides a good general organization of knowledge, libraries with a special focus not emphasized in the standard English-language edition may need to employ options. In recent editions, there has been a deliberate effort to reduce Western bias in the Classification. The editors are continuing this effort in the preparation of Edition 21, which is scheduled for publication in 1996. Nevertheless, libraries may find the need to adopt options to provide a preferred organization for subjects in disciplines more sensitive to cultural differences (e.g., history, language, literature, religion).

What Are the Costs and Benefits of Options?

Options provide a means of giving prominence to a topic of local importance. Given our earlier example of Arabic language, the optional number 4A0 is more prominent in the sequence of notation and shorter than 492.7. But adopting such an option comes at a cost. Going back to the same example, the position of the mixed notation in the hierarchy may not be understood by users. Also, Arabic will be separated from other languages in the Semitic language family. Furthermore, the number for Arabic has lost its meaning across library systems, at the very time when access to the holdings of multiple libraries has been extended through use of the Internet and bibliographic utilities.

In a paper on using options, Patricia Oyler observed: "A library must weigh its local needs against the advantages of following a standard notation available in bibliographic utilities and in many books. In this period of shrinking dollars, the library must decide if it can afford to maintain a local option when this means the cost of paying someone to apply it."[10] The use of options transfers the complete cost of classifying works to the local library, since central cataloging authorities seldom implement options. The only options assigned by the Library of Congress Decimal Classification Division are Option B at 340 Law and the letter B for biography. By agreement with the British Library, the Decimal Classification Division assigns the standard law numbers, and also numbers according to Option B to allow British libraries to arrange by jurisdiction first (see the earlier discussions of 340 Option B under jurisdictional emphasis and change in citation order). Likewise, the Division assigns the appropriate number for biography from the standard edition, and also the letter B. Some national libraries assign a few optional numbers, e.g., the National Library of Canada uses C810 for Canadian literature in English and C840 for Canadian literature in French. Most of the time, however, the responsibility for implementation of an option rests on the local library.

Once again, it should be noted that the most basic of Dewey options, close versus broad classification, is always available to the local library. One must be sure to abridge the DDC number at a meaningful break, and be willing to accept the resulting loss in subject specificity. Shortening the notation may provide a more helpful shelf arrangement, but also will eliminate some valuable subject information that could be of use in machine retrieval. As an alternative, Michael Gorman has suggested using abridged notation for shelf arrangement, but retaining the full notation in the electronic record to facilitate subject retrieval in online systems.[11]

WHAT IS THE FUTURE OF OPTIONS IN THE CLASSIFICATION?

At the beginning of this paper, the diversity of libraries and cultures using the Dewey Decimal Classification was described. Some devices are required to make the Classification serve needs beyond those represented in the standard English-language edition. The use of options can surmount cultural differences and make the Classification relevant for libraries where the bias of the standard edition may pose a problem. Sometimes options are not sufficient, and the requirement for local emphasis can be met only through licensed expansions and adaptations.

The problem of understanding optional numbers in different systems might be addressed in future online catalogs. The *USMARC Format for Classification Data*[12] provides coding in a control field (008/09) to indicate whether a number in the classification number field (153) is optional. Also, the format includes a note field (683) for description of the option. The integration of such information in an online catalog would explain the meaning of the optional number in the local system, and might facilitate switching between the optional number and a standard number in another system.

In a discussion of options at the 102nd meeting of the Decimal Classification Editorial Policy Committee (EPC) in May 1993, David Balatti, National Library of Canada, remarked: "Options should not be used as a substitute for a decision."[13] Caution should be exercised in allowing options to populate the Classification in place of a decision on citation order or the placement of the topic. Options have an important role to play, but only when cultural differences or specialized collections make it difficult to use the standard English-language edition of Dewey.

REFERENCES

1. Melvil Dewey, *Dewey Decimal Classification and Relative Index*, 20th ed., John P. Comaromi [and others], eds. (Albany, N.Y.: OCLC Forest Press, 1989), vol. 1, p. xxvi.

2. Ibid., vol. 1, p. xxvi.

3. Jeanne Osborn, *Dewey Decimal Classification, 20th Edition: A Study Manual*, rev. and ed. by John P. Comaromi (Englewood, Colo.: Libraries Unlimited, 1991), p. 24.

4. Melvil Dewey, *Dewey Decimal Classification and Relative Index*, 17th ed. (Lake Placid Club, N.Y.: Forest Press, 1965), vol. 1, p. 55.

5. Dewey, *Dewey Decimal Classification*, 20th ed., vol. 1, p. xlviii.

6. Melvil Dewey, *Abridged Dewey Decimal Classification and Relative Index*, 12th ed., John P. Comaromi [and others], eds. (Albany, N.Y.: OCLC Forest Press, 1990).

7. The author is indebted to Gregory R. New, assistant editor, Dewey Decimal Classification, for suggesting the name of this category.

8. Dewey, *Dewey Decimal Classification*, 20th ed., vol. 4, pp. 960-961.

9. Melvil Dewey, *Classificazione Decimale Dewey*, ideata da Melvil Dewey, 20th ed., edizione italiana diretta da Luigi Crocetti con la collaborazione di Daniele Danesi, 4 vols. (Rome: Associazione Italiana Biblioteche, 1993).

10. Patricia G. Oyler, "When and How to Use the Options," in *Dewey: Making it Work for You; DDC 20 Teaching Kit 1* (Albany, N.Y.: OCLC Forest Press, 1991).

11. Michael Gorman, "The longer the number, the smaller the spine; or, up and down with Melvil and Elsie," *American Libraries* 12, no. 8 (September 1981): 498-499.

12. Library of Congress. Network Development and MARC Standards Office, *USMARC Format for Classification Data; Including Guidelines for Content Designation* (Washington, D.C.: Library of Congress Cataloging Distribution Service, 1991).

13. Minutes of Decimal Classification Editorial Policy Committee, Meeting 102, May 13-15, 1993, EPC 103-3, p. 33.

Bliss Classification Update

Alan R. Thomas

SUMMARY. Development of the 2nd edition of the *Bliss Bibliographic Classification* (BC2) is outlined. The scope of the Introduction volume is described. Parts already issued, those ready for publication, and those awaiting completion are listed. The level of detail of the vocabulary is indicated. Four forms of synthesis are explained: addition of common subdivisions, facet combination including alternative combination patterns, array combination, and drawing marks from other parts of the system. Notational features which contribute to the relatively brief classmarks are identified. Different kinds of alternative location of subjects are discerned and examples provided. The potential feature of phenomenon-based classification is noted. Present use of the scheme is summarized and documented and its future application suggested.

The author thanks Jack Mills for reading the draft of this paper and making constructive suggestions.

[Haworth co-indexing entry note]: "Bliss Classification Update." Thomas, Alan R. Co-published simultaneously in *Cataloging & Classification Quarterly* (The Haworth Press, Inc.) Vol. 19, No. 3/4, 1995, pp. 105-117; and: *Classification: Options and Opportunities* (ed: Alan R. Thomas) The Haworth Press, Inc., 1995, pp. 105-117. Multiple copies of this article/chapter may be purchased from The Haworth Document Delivery Center [1-800-3-HAWORTH; 9:00 a.m. - 5:00 p.m. (EST)].

BLISS CLASSIFICATION UPDATE

Origins and Development

Henry Evelyn Bliss developed his own classification scheme at the library of the College of the City of New York. The full schedules of the first edition[1] completed publication in 1953. A good description of the scheme is provided by Mills,[2] while a variety of comments and observations by many different experts are included in Tauber and Wise.[3] The little known system evoked much professional response in Great Britain. The British Committee for the Bliss Classification was established in 1954, superseded by the Bliss Classification Association[4] in 1967.

Aided by members of the Classification Research Group the Association began the formidable and long-term task of revising the original classification. Most members of the BCA and its committee are experienced working librarians and such background has helped to provide a realistic foundation for the venture. It was the hope of editor Jack Mills that the result would be "the best ordered, the most comprehensive and up-to-date, and the easiest to use of any existing classifications."[5] The endeavors culminated in production and release of the 2nd edition of the Bliss Bibliographical Classification[6] (abbreviated to BC2).

PROGRESS OF BC2

Since 1991, all parts published bear the imprint of Bowker-Saur, the earlier volumes appearing under that of Butterworths. The *Bliss Classification Bulletin*[7] contains amendments to BC2, news items, and papers on the classification. Limited financial resources have delayed completion of the system though it is envisaged that all parts will have been issued by the turn of this century. Projected subject classes have been discussed in meetings of the Classification Research Group. Under supervision of the editor, subject specialists and working librarians have compiled or are now in the course of preparing particular schedules classes. Thus Chris Preddle has recently finished a revision of Class Q, Social Welfare, while Colin Ball is helping to finalize Class W, Arts and Recreation. Views of American information and library professionals on published volumes are welcomed as well as any suggestions and input for projected classes.

The *Introduction and Auxiliary Schedules*[8] volume contains material of interest to library and information professionals irrespective of the classification systems they may employ. Sections of general professional relevance include: Organising Information and the Role of Bibliographic

Classification, The Structure of a Bibliographic Classification, and a Glossary of fundamental terms in indexing and classification. The Introduction volume also contains analysis and description of the new edition, and provides advice on practical classing, the prerequisite concept analysis, the synthesis, and the final translation into notational classmarks. The auxiliary schedules themselves are lists of free-floating or frequently recurring subdivisions such as forms of presentation, kinds of relationships between subjects, geographic locations, ethnic groups, languages, and periods of time. The latter offers the classer/indexer a choice of three levels of detail: Schedule 4A is the recommended standard with medium provision for time specification; 4B is a shorter list; 4C permits the greatest detail. Special subject auxiliary schedules are provided in certain main classes, an example being auxiliary schedule AM1 (within Class A) which may be used to subdivide any mathematical system or applicable mathematical concept.

Each subject class volume features an introduction which includes consideration of class definition, scope, relations with other areas of knowledge, and alternatives. Each volume contains outline schedules, full detailed schedules, and an index. Building on the basic advice given in the Introduction volume, each published class explains the method of practical classing with special subject examples. A.G. Curwen has provided additional elementary practice through some twenty-two basic exercises and answers[9] as well as crossword puzzles[10] featuring BC2 notations.

AVAILABILITY OF BC2 FASCICLES

(a) Parts already published:

Introduction and Auxiliary Schedules 1977[8]

A/AL   Philosophy and Logic 1991
AM/AX Mathematics, Statistics, and Probability 1993
H   Anthropology, Human Biology, Health sciences 1980
          Includes medicine
I   Psychology and Psychiatry 1978
J   Education 1991 (Revision of the 1977 text)
K   Society 1984
          Includes social science, sociology, social anthropology, customs, folklore and mythology
P   Religion, the Occult, Morals and ethics 1977
          (When further revised this main class will be preferred in the humanities at Z)

Q	Social Welfare 1977
	Social Welfare and Criminology 1994
	(Revision of the 1977 text)
T	Economics, Management of economic enterprises 1987

(b) Parts completed and awaiting physical publication:

R	Politics, Public administration
S	Law

(c) Parts awaiting completion:

1/9	Generalia, Phenomena, Knowledge, Information science and technology
AY/B	General science and Physics
C	Chemistry
D	Astronomy and Earth sciences
E/GQ	Biological sciences
GR/GZ	Applied biology: Agriculture and Human ecology
L/O	History
	Includes area studies, travel and topography, and biography
U/V	Technology
	Includes household management and services
W	Arts and Recreation
	Includes music
X/Y	Philology, language and literature
Z	Religion, the Occult, Morals and ethics
	(When further revised, this main class of the humanities will be preferred here rather than at P).

BASIC VOCABULARY IN THE SCHEDULES

Basic terms have been isolated and selected after perusal of journals, abstracts, bibliographies, dictionaries, glossaries, classification systems and thesauri. The degree of specificity of simple terms exceeds that of the Dewey Decimal Classification and is usually greater than that within the Library of Congress Classification (although LCC alone does enumerate individual works in such classes as Literature, History, and Religion). The high level of detail in BC2 has varied somewhat from published class to class. Pressure from specialized libraries for depth provision has had to be tempered by fluctuating costs and time aspects of production. H, K, and T, as well as those classes currently being produced, are relatively much more detailed than the early schedules issued in 1977 and 1978.

RELATIVELY SLIM SCHEDULES

In order to accommodate the composite subject content of special subject literature, a comprehensive synthetic capability is provided which may be readily applied to terms in the basic listed vocabulary. A simple class or subject reflects only a single principle of division. The simple, elementary terms in each main class and in the auxiliary schedules have been formed into distinctive sets (facets), then terms in each facet are sorted into its several subsets (arrays). For the most part, BC2 term lists consist of simple, basic terms organized into sets. Its schedules are consequently much slimmer than those in a wholly or predominantly enumerative classification scheme for the same amount of specification. However slimming the schedules is not taken to unhelpful extremes. Sometimes a set of terms applicable to several classes (e.g., types of persons) may be presented rather differently in each case, the degree of detail and the internal order being customized to suit each special context. Again, compound subjects are occasionally enumerated during the compilation of the scheme by the editorial teams. This listing of compounds is done to show examples of the synthetic process, to gain shorter classmarks, or to relieve the library classer/indexer of pressure in difficult subject areas such as mathematics and law. In the latter, different legal structures and primary materials would render absolute facet synthesis by the working classer/indexer difficult and inconvenient.

In most cases terms from the clearly labelled facets and arrays will be combined by the classer/indexer to specify the subject content of incoming documents. Another manifestation of the analytico-synthetic structure may be seen in the separation of regular class schedules from the several common auxiliary schedules of free-floating or recurring subdivisions.

CONSTRUCTING PRECOORDINATED STRINGS AND THEIR CLASSMARKS

A postcoordinate approach can be employed for searching the file of bibliographic records: classmarks for the constituent terms are combined by the searcher using logical operators. In the *precoordinate* mode, BC2 classmarks are combined by the classer/indexer for arranging the document collection itself and/or the bibliographic records file in helpful order.

The scheme features several types of precoordination:

(i) Common Subdivisions Added to Regular Classmarks

Marks for recurring subdivisions are added to notations from the main scheme. Auxiliary Schedule 1 contains concepts (e.g., project design 6CN) and forms (e.g., serials 3G, select bibliographies 5WC). Auxiliary Schedule 2 lists places (e.g., Oklahoma YJ). In Class P, Religion, the regular schedule mark for Christian Science is PUC. Therefore a select bibliography of Christian Science is marked PUC 5WC. The subject "Christian Science in Oklahoma" is PUC 8YJ, while a select bibliography of this theme would receive the mark PUC 8YJ 5WC.

Auxiliary Schedule 1 also has capability for showing the kind of relationship between subjects as treated in a document. For example, the complex subject "influence of economic resources on social welfare" would be marked Q9J TK. Here Q stands for social welfare, TK for economic resources; and from the auxiliary schedule the influencing relationship is represented by 9J.

Terms from the other auxiliary schedules may be added to regular classmarks in similar fashion.

(ii) Facet Combination

A simple term in one facet may be combined with a simple term from another facet to form a compound subject and accorded a precise notational mark. A standard combination formula (citation order) obtains as far as appropriate. The first, primary facet in a string reflects the ultimate purpose or object of study, the end-product. Then follow Types, Parts, Processes, and Agents of the processes, Actions performed on the focus in the primary facet, and Agents of such actions. Properties of anything are subordinated to that thing in whatever facet to which it belongs. It will be seen that this formula moves from ends to means. Auxiliary schedules are usually the last to be added.

Once a classer/indexer or searcher grasps the principle behind the standard combination pattern, he/she can readily predict that "counseling the over-80's" is going to be located with the over-80's and not at counseling; that "Islamic prayer" is found at Islam and not at prayer; that "Christian Science missionary work" will not be found under missionary work but is collocated at Christian Science. In any event the combination formula for a particular subject is always the reverse of the way the facets are laid out in the schedules.

In Class Q, Social Welfare, the facets are listed as follows:

Auxiliary (recurring) subdivisions	Q2/Q9
Principles and management of social welfare	QA
Social work	QD
Social services	QE
Social security	QF
Persons in need, causes of need	QG/QM
Deviant persons	QN
Criminal persons	QO/QS

Terms from the facets involved are normally combined by proceeding upwards. The compound subject "counseling the over-80's" will be assembled to illustrate the procedure:

QEQ Counseling [a term within the Social Services facet, i.e., the *means*]

.

.

QLWS Over-80's [a term within the Persons in need facet, i.e., the *end-products*] Here the notation for the term in the lower set is augmented by the notation for the term in the higher set, dropping the letter common to both, and so producing QLW SEQ. A select bibliography of this compound secures the notation QLW SEQ 5WC.

In some subjects the standard, predictable pattern for combining the facets can be switched to reflect local needs. For instance, Class J, Education, includes these constituents:

JK Curriculum [Subject taught facet]

.

.

JN Secondary education [a term within the Educands facet]

The compound subject "secondary school curriculum" is assembled in the regular upwards direction to produce the classmark JNK (here the syntax pattern is secondary education divided by curriculum). Because the curriculum facet has a listed alternative location at JY, it is possible to synthesize this compound as JYA N (the syntax pattern is curriculum qualified by secondary education). The provision of alternative arrangements in Class I, Psychology and Psychiatry, have been examined critically by Curwen.[11]

Some libraries might wish to effect unauthorized changes in facet combinations where the schedules lacked choice for their special and perhaps unique requirements. Before embarking on any such course a classer/indexer would be well advised to contact BC2 editors on the implications for resultant order and notation. The Haddon Library[12] effected such alterations after consulting their teaching and research personnel. One fundamental change was reversal of the predictable BC2 combination order so that Processes (such as physiology, genetics) began the classmark while Parts and systems of the body were added at the end of the string. The Haddon librarian found this decision was "surprisingly easy to put into effect, owing to the clear facet structure of the scheme . . . "[13]

(iii) Array Combination

In large or specialized collections it is particularly serviceable to combine terms from different arrays or subsets of the *same* facet. Consider the multi-array subject "redeemable government securities." In Class T, T/TP encompasses Economics, and one of its facets is TGLR/TGX Kinds of securities. Terms within different arrays of this facet may be combined in the usual upwards direction as follows:

> TGQT Redeemable securities [a term in the Securities by redeemability array]

> .

> .

> TGV Government securities [a term in the Securities by borrower or issuer array]

The result is TGV QT, dropping not only the common main class letter but also the common facet letter.

(iv) Drawing Marks from Other Parts of the Scheme

Directions in the schedules show the classer/indexer where and how to amplify a particular classmark by notation transferred from elsewhere in the classification. In Class J, Education, career guides is denoted JKW which mark can be so extended. The subject "careers in law" is marked JKW S, the S being pulled from Class S, Law.

Sometimes there is direction to draw only from specified classes, for instance at JBH, Economics of education it is possible to add notation from TA/TP in the Economics class. Within TA/TP the mark for wage controls is TLS V. Therefore "wage controls in the economics of education" is specifiable at JBH LSV. Within the one published volume AM/AX, certain terms within Statistics and Probability may be qualified by others "imported" from nearby Mathematics.

At the cost of longer classmarks, precoordination can also be accomplished by simply stringing classmarks together without dropping any letters or figures and then inserting a dash or colon between them. This method facilitates both computer and human searching on the secondary or further facet or array and it paves the way for production of rotated multiple entries.

RELATIVE LENGTH OF CLASSMARKS

The literature of special subjects often requires the classer/indexer to synthesize highly specific elemental terms into compound and complex themes. Yet a reader is more likely to remember a brief classmark when using the library or searching files. In order to secure as short marks as possible, BC2 has adopted the devices of a wide notational base and ordinal notation. The base is 2/9, A/Z, that is a total range of 34 characters. This full span has been utilized by the editors wherever appropriate, as at AM2/AXZ Mathematics, Probability, and Statistics. In the case of ordinal notation, no attempt is made to show hierarchic relations between subjects. Consequently "we . . . can allow the notation to perform its fundamental job–i.e., to allow a user to locate a given subject accurately and quickly."[14] It will be seen that the increasingly specific links in the following logical chain all bear the same length marks:

PEX L   Holy Orders, ordination
PEX M   Vows
PEX S   Silence

To add a digit at each step of division would make two of these classmarks longer.

Sometimes, however, the notation *does* indicate a chain. This situation is found mainly at upper levels of hierarchy, for instance Q Social welfare and QD Social work reveal a main class and one of its facets. The hierarchy for all terms in BC2 schedules is always obvious to the classer/indexer because successively subordinate terms are always indented.

A decision which affects notational length is whether the classer/indexer prefers a slightly longer mark for multi-faceted combinations with a consequently briefer mark for multi-array combinations, or vice versa. If the literature and the readers' inquiries warrant frequent compounding of facets, for instance an educand combined with a teaching method as in "homework for the deaf," and warrant less frequent synthesis of arrays within one and the same facet, e.g., "deaf children," then the shorter mark would be given to the multi-faceted combination. It seems likely that a general library would adopt the editorial preference for shorter notation for the multi-faceted mix. Some special collections might profit from giving the briefer mark to the multi-array subject. This facility shows the subtle ability of the scheme to suit particular library circumstances.

ALTERNATIVE LOCATIONS PROVIDED
FOR THE CLASSER/INDEXER

Certain subjects can be transferred to a different main class. For instance, the editorial preference is to keep Educational psychology at JE within Class J, Education, but an official alternative permits insertion into Class I, Psychology, at IYJ. Mathematics of particular subjects may be either subordinated to those subjects or collocated at Mathematics in Class A.

In some cases it is possible to relocate a subject to a different section of the same main class. In Class H, Medicine, within HT/HW, the Parts, organs, and systems facet, the editorially preferred place for the diaphragm is at HWH X in the context of the respiratory system; the classer/indexer may, however, be more attracted to an alternative position provided at HWPL under the digestive system. Again, editorial preference is to locate Jewish philosophy at AIJ, Arabic philosophy at AIK, but the facility exists to have them at ADL and ADK respectively so as to include them in general medieval philosophy at ADJ/ADN.

In a special form of alternative location which Bliss originally termed *adaptation to nationality,* the concept value of an early position within certain arrays of terms is made variable. This prior place in an array may be used to denote a favourite country, language, or other focus in which a particular library specializes. For example, within Class J, Education, JNW is the starter notation for the subject of individual schools in the nation of choice, while JS9 represents higher education in the favoured state. In Class Q, Social Welfare, QFC/QFM is reserved for the social security of the appropriate motherland. The purpose is to bring the required material or bibliographic records to the front of the particular sequence. Using the favoured focus device, the subject "Aid to families with dependent children in the United States of America" could be assigned QFK B to gain an earlier position and a briefer mark; the regular mark would be QFQ Y3K B which necessitates using the auxiliary schedule of places.

Another kind of alternative location allows phenomenon-based classification. Because BC2 is primarily a discipline-based system it follows that material on any given topic (e.g., tomatoes; salt; petroleum) must be distributed among various disciplines. However, a novel provision[15] in BC2 will permit librarians and information scientists to group some or all of their material and/or bibliographic records around particular topics. This potentially useful "one place only" application awaits fuller clarification, directions, examples, and the publication of Classes 1/9 which will include the phenomenon schedules. These schedules are expected to provide for entities, artifacts, properties, and processes.

The relationships between main classes, disciplines, subdisciplines, and phenomena are broached in the Introduction volume;[16] Langridge[17] explores further these vexing though fundamental classificatory questions.

ADOPTIONS OF BC2

On completion of the entire set of volumes of the classification, general libraries will be able to make a full assessment of its suitability for their needs. Of the present 50 or so users in Britain, most are found within the category of special libraries and information centers, including several probation services. BC2 published and draft schedules are often consulted in respect of vocabulary and structure by compilers of other classifications and thesauri. As further, more attractively produced special subject volumes are issued then more such libraries are likely to consider parts pertinent to their collections. New special subject classes may also be utilized in varying degrees for thesaural use.

Because BC2 is not presently used within the United States, it is not yet possible to make investigative visits to libraries and information centers there to assess the impact and effectiveness of the scheme. However, reality-tested experience is readily available in the form of published reports of the adoption and application of the system in Great Britain. These include those of the Haddon Library,[12] the Tavistock Joint Library,[18] Dr. Barnardo's,[19] the Office of Population Censuses and Surveys,[20] the Central Council for Education and Training and Social Work,[21] the National Institute for Social Work,[22] the Supreme Court,[23] Queens' College, Cambridge,[24] King's College, Cambridge,[25,26] Chester College,[27] and Fitzwilliam College, Cambridge.[28] Sidney Sussex College, Cambridge, has very recently adjudged BC2 as the closest fit available for its tripos curricula and consequently begun work on reclassifying the stock. The classification has also been examined for its value in thesaurus construction;[29,30] specific applications include the *ECOT Thesaurus*[31] and the *DHSS-DATA Thesaurus.*[32]

NOTES

1. Henry Evelyn Bliss, *A Bibliographic Classification*, Volumes I-II. New York: Wilson,1952. Volume III, New York:Wilson, 1953.

2. Jack Mills, "Bibliographic Classification." In *Encyclopedia of library and information science*. New York: Dekker, 1969: Volume 2, 368-380.

3. Maurice F. Tauber and Edith Wise, *Classification systems*. New Brunswick: Graduate School of Library Service, Rutgers, the State University, 1961: 246-286.

4. Bliss Classification Association, The Library, Fitzwilliam College, Huntingdon Road, Cambridge, CB3 0DG, England.

5. Jack Mills, "Foreword," *Bliss Classification Bulletin* IV, no.3 (December 1969): 1-2, p.1.

6. *Bliss Bibliographic Classification*, 2nd edition. J.Mills and Vanda Broughton. London: Butterworths, 1977 (in progress).

7. *Bliss Classification Bulletin* (1954-to date) [This annual publication was issued by Wilson from 1954 until 1966 and thereafter by the Bliss Classification Association].

8. *Bliss Bibliographic Classification*, 2nd edition. Introduction and Auxiliary Schedules. J.Mills and Vanda Broughton, with the assistance of Valerie Lang. London: Butterworths, 1977.

9. A.G. Curwen, "Bliss for beginners: practical exercises in the application of the scheme," *Bliss Classification Bulletin* no. 31 (1989): 14-17. [These exercises involve use of the Introduction and Auxiliary Schedules and Classes J, P, and Q].

10. A.G. Curwen, "Blissword Puzzle." [Several puzzles and their solutions have appeared in issues of the *Bliss Classification Bulletin* since 1987].

11. A.G. Curwen, "The I's have it," *Bliss Classification Bulletin* no. 35 (1993): 16-18.

12. Susan Bury, "Comments on Class H and the Introductory volume," *Bliss Classification Bulletin* VII, no. 3 (1982): 14-18.

13. *Ibid* p. 17.

14. Jack Mills,"The new schedules," *Bliss Classification Bulletin* III, no.2 (December 1965): 2-5, p. 4.

15. Alan R.Thomas, "Options in the arrangement of library materials and the new edition of the Bliss Bibliographic Classification." In, Bella Hass Weinberg, ed. *Cataloging heresy: challenging the standard bibliographic product*. Medford: Learned Information, 1992, 197-211, p. 204-206.

16. As 6. pp. 36-37.

17. D.W. Langridge, "Bliss, the disciplines and the New Age," *Bliss Classification Bulletin* no. 34 (1992): 8-11.

18. Lindy Gill, "The Tavistock reclassification project." In, Arthur Maltby and Lindy Gill, *The case for Bliss: modern classification practice and principles in the context of the Bibliographic Classification*. London: Bingley, 1979: 109-120.

19. Chris Preddle, "The use of Bliss at Dr. Barnardo's Library," *Bliss Classification Bulletin* VII, no. 3 (1982): 10-12.

20. Chris Horsey, "The use of Bliss at OPCS," *Bliss Classification Bulletin* VIII, no. 4 (1983): 10-12.

21. Debbie Cowley, "The use of Bliss at CCETSW," *Bliss Classification Bulletin* no. 29 (1987): 8-10.

22. Giustina Ryan *and* Angela Upton, "The National Institute for Social Work," *Bliss Classification Bulletin* no. 33 (1991): 10-13.

23. Kenneth W. Best, "The Supreme Court Library," *Law Librarian* 10, no.1 (April 1979): 13-16.

24. Clare Sargent, "Classifying the undergraduate collection at Queens' College, Cambridge," *Bliss Classification Bulletin* no. 32 (1990): 10-12.

25. Elizabeth Russell and Julia Wilkinson, "Bliss is't to be in King's," *Bliss Classification Bulletin* VII, no. 4 (January 1979): 9-12.

26. Elizabeth M. Russell, "King's Bliss update," *Bliss Classification Bulletin* no. 29 (1987): 13-14.

27. Hilda Stoddard, "Reclassification by Bliss," *Catalogue & Index* no. 55 (Winter 1979): 4-5.

28. Marion MacClead, "BC2 and automation–some personal observations," *Bliss Classification Bulletin,* no. 36 (1994): 7-8.

29. Jean Aitchison, "Integration of thesauri in the social sciences," *International Classification* 8, no. 2 (1981): 75-85.

30. Jean Aitchison, "A classification as a source for a thesaurus: the Bibliographic Classification of H.E.Bliss as a source of thesaurus terms and structure," *Journal of Documentation* 42, no. 3 (September 1986): 160-181.

31. Jean Aitchison, *ECOT Thesaurus.* Milton Keynes: Open University, 1984. [Educational and Occupations Thesaurus]

32. Jean Aitchison et al., *DHSS-DATA Thesaurus.* London: DHSS, 1985. [United Kingdom Department of Health and Social Security]

Universal Decimal Classification Update

P. David Strachan
Frits M. H. Oomes

SUMMARY. The article gives an overview of recent developments in the organization and the policy of the Universal Decimal Classification. It describes the content and compilation of the Master Reference File, the database of the UDC that will be the starting point for future revision and enhancement of the classification. Some observations are added concerning the direction these developments will take.

Like the other principal classification schemes, the Universal Decimal Classification (UDC) is an aspect classification, arranging classes within major disciplines. The same subject (e.g., horses) may occur as a class in more than one discipline (e.g., zoology, transport, farming). The structure of the UDC is enumerative to a certain level, with a syntactical overlay

---

P. David Strachan, MA, DipLib, is a former staff member responsible for the maintenance of the UDC and for the implementation of the UDC policy with the International Federation for Information and Documentation (FID) and with the UDC Consortium.

Address correspondence to: 45 Willington Crescent, Templelogue, Dublin 6W, Ireland.

Drs. Frits M. H. Oomes studied General Linguistics and Classical Philology at the University of Nijmegen (Netherlands). He is a former lexicographer at the Thesaurus Linguae Latinae in Munich (Germany) and editor of reference works and services in printed and electronic form. He joined the UDC in October 1992.

Address correspondence to: UDC Consortium, P.O. Box 90407, 2509 LK, The Hague, Netherlands.

[Haworth co-indexing entry note]: "Universal Decimal Classification Update." Strachan, P. David, and Frits M. H. Oomes. Co-published simultaneously in *Cataloging & Classification Quarterly* (The Haworth Press, Inc.) Vol. 19, No. 3/4, 1995, pp. 119-131; and: *Classification: Options and Opportunities* (ed: Alan R. Thomas) The Haworth Press, Inc., 1995, pp. 119-131. Multiple copies of this article/chapter may be purchased from The Haworth Document Delivery Center [1-800-3-HAWORTH; 9:00 a.m. - 5:00 p.m. (EST)].

which permits the enumerated classes to be combined and qualified according to well-accepted principles. A very useful device is the colon (:) to express a concept by connecting two or more UDC numbers, as in:

17	Ethics
7	Art
17:7 or 7:17	Ethics in relation to art

There are further 'general auxiliary tables' applicable at all classes and each marked by its exclusive symbol.

Language	=	e.g	=111	English
Document form	(0 . . .)	e.g.	(038)	Dictionaries
Place	(1/9)	e.g.	(73)	United States of America

At various places in the tables 'special auxiliary subdivisions' occur which are applicable within a limited subject range and provide secondary facets within disciplines; e.g., in manufacturing the products are the main (primary) facet and raw materials, machinery, processes etc. are secondary facets. Special auxiliary subdivisions are marked by notational symbols such as .0 (point nought) or–(hyphen) and can therefore be distinguished clearly within numbers that are built with them, as in:

7	Art	7.01	Aesthetics and theory of art
72	Architecure	72.01	Aesthetics and theory of architecture
75	Painting	75.01	Aesthetics and theory of painting

These and other devices permit in the UDC the construction of compound numbers (synthesis) and the structural rationality is a feature quickly assimilated and much appreciated by the users who are able to tailor their practice to the particular needs of their system.[1]

HISTORICAL CONTEXT

The UDC began life around the turn of the century as an expansion of the Dewey Decimal Classification (DDC), then in its 5th edition. The Belgians, Paul Otlet and Henry LaFontaine, recognised in the DDC the basis of a powerful tool for systematizing their ambitious 'Répertoire Bibliographique Universel'–a card catalogue of all published information. They persuaded Melvil Dewey to allow them to adapt and extend the DDC for this purpose.

Soon, subject sections of this 'bibliographic decimal classification' were being issued by the Institut Internationale de Bibliographie (IIB) and the first complete edition appeared in French in 1905 as the 'Manuel du Répertoire Bibliographique Universel.' Thus, from the beginning, the UDC was an international responsibility and continued to be so after the IBB changed its name into Fédération International de Documentation, from 1986 International Federation for Information and Documentation (FID).

As well as expanding the DDC schedules, Otlet and LaFontaine converted what was then a purely enumerative classification by introducing common auxiliaries for place, time, language, etc.; special auxiliaries for certain subject fields, and methods for relating more than one class notationally, thus inventing the principles of analytico-synthetic classification.

In 1927-1933 the second edition appeared in four volumes, again in French, by which time the classification was well enough established to survive the demise of the Répertoire itself. Abridged editions quickly appeared in other European languages and an international system of revision based on the second edition gained strength with Dutch and German contributions increasingly frequent. The third full edition was published in German from 1934, with the seventh and final volume delayed by the war until 1948.

It was during the war that the English-language fourth full edition was begun, with sections for auxiliaries, class 0–Generalities and the whole of class 5–Mathematics and the Natural and Life Sciences being published by the British Standards Institution in 1943. Unlike the French and German editions which preceded it and most of the other language editions which followed, BSI decided to publish the UDC in a large number of separate subject sections (or "fascicles'). This practice may have contributed to the belief in Britain and the wider English-speaking world that the UDC was mainly for specialist information work.

The appearance of the UDC in more and more languages from the 1930s on was the result of the policy of the FID to give permission to organizations in each country or language area (e.g., BSI for English) to act as publisher and also as a focal point of UDC interest and activity. Representatives of these organizations also came to form the main controlling body of the UDC (the Central Classification Committee) under FID.

ORGANIZATIONAL DEVELOPMENT

In the decades up to the early 1980s, the central organization of the UDC had been based on a stable if complex system of committees, which was part of the larger FID committee structure. In short, there was the Central Classification Committee (CCC), made up of editors, classification experts and a range of international subject revision committees. In some countries this structure was reflected at a national level under the FID National Member organizations. Proposals submitted by revision committees or others would be examined centrally by the secretariat and the Proposals Committee of the CCC. Often after some necessary amendments requested by the Proposals Committee, the proposal would be widely distributed throughout the UDC community as a "P-Note," with normally four months for comment. Depending on the number, strength and variety of the comments, there would be a further round of communication (sometimes multilateral) resulting in an accepted version, a redrafted proposal or occasionally total rejection. The authorized changes were then published annually in 'Extension & Corrections to the UDC.' Proposals could be made and eventually authorized in English, French and/or German.

In the 1970s this complex structure was already showing signs of strain. This was partly, it must be said, because the expansion of the UDC into many more countries, and the rising number of FID member countries during the post-war decades were increasing the amount of participation but making the process more widely distributed and less effective. Geoffrey Lloyd, who from 1963 to 1976 was the head of FID's UDC Section, coined the word 'hyperdemocracy' for this state of affairs in FID's UDC structure. The introduction of a 'UDC Assembly,' electing a smaller CCC in 1979, resulted in some role conflict between these two bodies. FID finally commissioned an external management study from the British firm Alan Gilchrist & Partners. The initial remit concerned mainly the revision process, but came inevitably to encompass the manageability of the whole UDC operation and the need for product quality. On revision, the study concluded that the system of numerous revision committees varying greatly in size, subject scope and level of activity, was too dispersed and lacked coordination or strategic guidance. They tended to work in isolation, except in the case of the social sciences which had a coordinating committee. This led to an unbalanced programme of revision which was not set or controlled from the centre. It is worth remarking that the old international revision committees were not subcommittees to the CCC, but were independent FID committees. The study also recognized that the system based on international committees was grounded in the ethos of earlier decades, and that for financial reasons travel was becoming ever more difficult for experts working on UDC. On the central management and strategy level, the conclusion was that the organisational structure did not support effective management.

Out of these conclusions came recommendations, resulting in the UDC Assembly being discontinued and the CCC being replaced by a UDC Management Board at the end of 1986. The Board included a number of people from the more commercial areas of the information industry. A two-tier revision structure was recommended. The higher (strategic) level was embodied by five Coordinating Revision Committees (CRCs), each responsible for a range of subjects assigned to it by the UDC Management Board, and comprising a chairman and representatives of the lower level of specialist revision groups subordinate to the CRC. The new system devolved the main responsibility for revision policy and coordination away from the centre to the five CRC chairmen, who also had seats on the Management Board. The publishing organizations of the UDC language editions, whose representatives had formed the majority of the old CCC, were encouraged to form a 'Publishers' Consultative Group' independent of, but advisory to, the Management Board. This group also provided a forum for communication between publishers and editors of different editions, and it was not long before the chairman and one other member of the Publishers' Consultative Group were coopted onto the Management Board.

The Management Board was a fairly even mix of those who had some years of experience in UDC committees under the old system, and those who were coming to the UDC afresh. This was mainly beneficial, as it prevented the pursuit of misconceived ideas by both sides, and the Board took some valuable policy initiatives and got to grips with the organizational complexities.

The new devolved revision structure was less successful because it was founded largely on a rearrangement of the old subject committees, and the CRC chairmen were expected to achieve more than was realistically possible. In addition, some revision committees and groups had suspended further activity in the period of uncertainty following the consultant's report in 1984, and found their place in a devolved system less appealing.

The recommendations of the 1990 Task Force mentioned below contributed to the growing realisation, both in the Management Board and in the wider circles of FID that the hard judgements on the future development of the scheme and its exploitation are more likely to be made correctly by the publishers, who have the greatest interest in maximising demand and meeting users' requirements. This led inevitably to the conviction that the publishers should take the control of, and responsibility for, the UDC. After a series of meetings between FID and senior personnel from publishing organizations the formation of a UDC Consortium was agreed in principle in July 1991, and the Consortium came into existence on 1st January 1992. On the same date the rights in the UDC held by FID were transferred to the Consortium. Parties to the agreement, and founding 'executive members' of the Consortium, were the publishers of the UDC in Dutch, English, French, Japanese and Spanish, together with FID itself. The UDC Consortium (UDCC) is a nonprofit institution legally based in the Netherlands, where it is registered as a Dutch foundation. By agreement with the Dutch Royal Library, its small secretariat is accommodated in the Royal Library complex. The controlling organ is an Executive Committee, comprising one nominee from each 'Executive Member,' each with a single vote, and a chairman.

The 'executive membership' at present comprises the six founding organizations, but other organizations willing to make a commitment of financial resources and management effort in return for a say in the major policies and decisions may become 'executive members.' The UDC publishers who are not 'executive members' will have separate licence arrangements. The Executive Committee is also considering how best to link major users or user groups to the Consortium by encouraging the formation of 'user clubs' for users with similar interests or specialities.

DEVELOPMENT OF THE UDC

The 1984 management study criticised the revision process as being essentially reactive without enough attention being given to setting priorities centrally. This apparent lack of guidance in fact echoed the varying views throughout the UDC community on how the scheme should develop. The problem is the old one of stability versus renewal, and is faced by all large and well established information languages, whether they be classifications, thesauri or descriptor systems. In the latter half of the 1970s there had been much discussion about 'drastic development' into a fully faceted scheme, and some pilot studies had been mounted. These showed that a grandiose overhaul of the whole scheme was then unrealistic, and revision entered a pragmatic phase, with better faceting encouraged where major revision was contemplated.

In late 1988, the UDC Management Board decided to set up a Task Force on UDC System Development to make recommendations on the future development of the scheme. The scope of the task was:

> . . . to advise the UDC Management Board . . . concerning appropriate long-term, strategic development of the Universal Decimal Classification as in its entirety an effective, flexible and durable system for use in classifying recorded information and knowledge.

This was further defined as:

> To develop and recommend a strategy and supporting tactics for achieving the objectives: (a) To establish the UDC as–in its entirety, and at a predetermined depth or at predetermined depths–a classification scheme of high quality, easy applicability and international validity, for the full range of recorded information and knowledge; (b) To maintain the scheme at least at this level of quality, applicability and validity by means of continuing revision.

Membership of the Task Force was truly international, as well as representing the various categories of parties interested in the UDC.[2] The Task Force presented its final report to the Management Board in March 1990. During this period it sought and collected much detailed oral and written information on the UDC. It conducted a survey of a range of selected users by a combination of written and telephone contacts as well as personal visits wherever possible. It had access to the results of a questionnaire survey of users conducted by FID the previous year.

The main conclusions and recommendations of the Task Force regarding the direction in which the scheme should be developed can be summarized as follows:

* The survey showed a strong commitment to the UDC among existing users, and a willingness of the majority of them to accept a certain amount of radical renewal. Some had investigated changing to other systems (other classifications, descriptors) but had found no better alternative for their needs.
* Classifications will continue to be important for modern information systems and the UDC has a high potential to be applied for such purposes.
* However, to remain viable and to meet modern demands, a number of urgent changes in policy were needed.
* The sheer size of the full UDC, with the inertia this causes, has had an inhibiting effect on development in the past, and would continue to do so, especially in the key areas of revision and computerization. Most users would opt for a smaller, more manageable UDC.

It was therefore recommended that priority should be given to creating a core UDC of initially around 60,000 classes in machine-readable database format. This version should be the reference file on which centrally controlled subsequent revision would be based, and would be the basis for the published editions. In subject-fields where there was a demand from groups of users for more detailed subdivisions of classes, responsibility for these, including coordination with any revision of the core version, would be devolved to an institution or group. In this context one should realize that the UDC not only had been published in many language versions, but that every publishing institution made its own selections from the schedules. This resulted in the appearance of editions of various sizes using unclearly defined designations as 'full, medium, abridged' that were published at different times and therefore differed in the extent to which recently authorized changes had been incorporated.

This database would be the primary source for publishers in the preparation of their editions and other products. Once established the database would be simple to update, enabling the current version, in English at least, to be directly accessible to publishers as either a database file or a text file.

The Task Force also made recommendations on how the core database could be prepared, and how the revision process could be changed. The widespread distribution of proposals as P-Notes should be discontinued and replaced by more targeted evaluation involving selected institutions and the Consortium members. The annual *Extensions & Corrections to the UDC* would continue as the primary publication notifying changes to the scheme.

The Management Board accepted the principal recommendations of the Task Force and the first steps were taken in the latter half of 1990. A small panel of classification experts was set up to prepare guidelines for the compilation of the core version and for subsequent revision based on that version. The guidelines emphasise that the analytico-synthetic nature of the UDC should be maintained and strengthened, partly with a view to facilitating the use of the database by those working on knowledge-based systems. At the same time, a UDC computerization working party looked at several possible microcomputer database packages, and recommended that the initial preparation should use the Unesco software package Micro CDS/ISIS.

THE UDC MASTER REFERENCE FILE

Work on the database, named the UDC Master Reference File (MRF), started in 1991. The basic material came from the International Medium Edition (IME) published in 1985 by BSI Standards. This version was already available in machine-readable and its size was approximately 70% of the 60,000 class numbers recommended by the Task Force. To it modifications and supplements were added from:

1. Extensions and Corrections to the UDC, Series 10:1 (1978) up to 14:3 (1992).
2. Editions of around medium size published after the IME. This included the Japanese Medium Edition (1984) (especially science and technology), the Hungarian Large Abridged Edition (1991), the Serbo-Croatian Medium Edition (1991) and the French Medium Edition (first volume 1990).
3. Additions needed to fill gaps in hierarchies and arrays that resulted from the selective nature of medium editions but which did not match with the required consistency of the MRF.

Because various sources had to be used and compared, the compilation of the database was a highly complicated process. A special database design had to be developed for the administration of the sources and to keep track of the different phases of the compilation process.[3] Also, part of the materials had yet to be keyed in, and it was necessary to write software for converting the existing machine-readable sources into a suitable format for Micro CDS/ISIS.

The diagram of Figure 1 illustrates in a simplified way the different phases of the compilation process.

The IME-files contained the text of the International Medium Edition in a printing format that had to be converted for the database. EC13-files included updates from Extensions and Corrections, earlier than Series 13, that had to be keyed in; the contents of the EC13+files were the more recent updates that were already available in word-processed format.

The phase of final editing included the checking of references and the expansion of the IME in line with more recent editions and/or for reasons of consistency.

For practical reasons the UDC tables had been split up into around 30 separate databases of which the last one was completed in March 1993. In the final stage those were merged and converted to a new database structure leaving out the fields for the administration of the compilation and adding fields to account for the revision process.

The structure of the resulting MRF database is shown in Figure 2. The MRF will be licensed as basis for non-English language versions to be distributed in print, via a network or on disk; it also can be acquired for use on site or in a LAN, e.g., in combination with a local cataloguing or indexing system. By the end of 1993, licenses had been issued to the five executive members of the Consortium and to publishers and users in such diverse locations as Brazil, Croatia, Estonia, Iran, Poland, Portugal and Romania. Negotiations about a German version are at an advanced stage.

FIGURE 1. Compilation of the UDC Master Reference File.

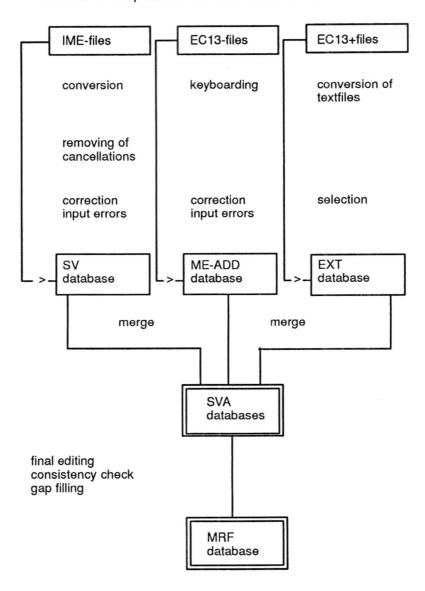

FIGURE 2. Record Structure in the MRF Database.

Descriptive fields

FIELD   FUNCTION AND EXPLANATION

1   UDC-number.
2   Table (codes).
     To allow for output in the correct sequence each of the Tables of
     the Common Auxiliaries and the Main Tables as a whole had to be
     individually coded.
3   Type of special auxiliary (if applicable) (codes).
     E.g., hyphen, point-nought, apostrophe, other (e.g. . . . .0/. . .9).
4   Combination type (codes).
     For composed notations this field should indicate the type of
     combination, e.g., with colon or with a certain type of special
     auxiliary.
5   If applicable, UDC number from which the number had been
     derived by parallel division.
11   If applicable, UDC number that is the source for parallel division of
     the number. With subfields for the notation and accompanying
     text.
12   Type of special auxiliary (coded) introduced by the parallel division.
13   Type of special auxiliary introduced by an application note (see
     field 111).

100 Description: definition.
     With subfields for language versions.
105 Description: verbal examples.
     With subfields for language versions.
110 Scope note.
     To explain the semantic content of the description.
     With subfields for language versions.
111 Application note.
     For technical details about the application (e. g., applicable spe-
     cial auxiliaries).
115 Combination examples.
     With subfields for the notation of the example, and language
     versions of its description, annotation and references.
120 Examples of the parallel division of field 11 with subfields for
     notation and language versions of its description.
125 References.
     With subfields for notation and language versions of accompany-
     ing text.

FIGURE 2 (continued)

Administrative fields

FIELD   FUNCTION AND EXPLANATION

901   Date of introduction.
903   Source of introduction.
904   Comments on introduction.
911   Date of cancellation.
912   Replacement(s).
913   Source for cancellation.
914   Comments on cancellation.
921   Date last revision.
922   Specification of revision indicated by number(s) of revised field(s).
923   Source for revision.
924   Comments on revision.
925   Revision history indicated by date and number of revised field.
951   Index only.
        Used for indexing UDC-numbers that are not covered by the selection tables defined for other fields.
952   Note concerning the use of special characters.
        In CDS/ISIS many diacritics and special signs have to be coded and this cannot be done in the description itself because this may disturb the searching facilities. Coding therefore has to be done in a special separate field.
955   Editorial annotations and comments.

FUTURE DEVELOPMENTS

The completion of the Master Reference File revived the discussion on its maintenance, especially in view of the use of the UDC in automated retrieval systems. The Consortium has committed itself to a continuing programme of review and revision and was aware of the need for a more systematic and structural approach. It decided in September 1993 to set up an Editorial Board to advise on the direction and the implementation of future development of the UDC and to overview the quality of the scheme. It also appointed Dr. la C. McIlwaine of University College London as Editor-in-Chief to take charge of the actual operations. Dr. McIlwaine has discussed the future of UDC in professional papers.[4,5] An overall design of revision priorities for the next six years has been submitted to the Executive Committee in the beginning of 1994.

The yearly publication of *Extensions and Corrections to the UDC* will continue, but in a slightly different form. While remaining the vehicle for authorizing changes in the UDC it will serve also as a medium for the exchange of information between users of the classification and between the users and the UDCC. The 15th issue, published in September 1993, already contained an article with fundamental recommendations by I.C. McIlwaine and N. Williamson about the direction the UDC should take in the future, and a proposal for restructuring Class 2–Religion. Theology into a more faceted and balanced scheme.[6]

It is self-evident that language independent mechanisms like classifications have great advantages especially in the exchange of information at international level. They also have specific advantages in an automated environment.[7]

The UDCC is aware of this and prepares itself to fulfil this function. In meeting this big challenge it prefers to see other systems and tools not as competitors, but rather as partners striving to the same goal who should cooperate and coordinate their activities to the benefit of their users.

NOTES

1. For a more detailed discussion of the features of the UDC see I. C. McIlwaine, *Guide to the Use of the UDC*. The Hague: FID, 1993 (FID 703).

2. The members of the Task Force were: Dr. I. C. McIlwaine (UK, chair), Ms. A-R. Haarala (Finland), Dr. H. Jobst (Austria), and Prof. N. Williamson (Canada). Drs. G. J. A. Riesthuis (Netherlands), A. Gilchrist and P. D. Strachan attended as observers.

3. Gerhard J. A. Riesthuis, "The Universal Decimal Classification as a CDS/ISIS Database," Proceedings of the First NISKO Conference, Bratislava, NISKO, Scientific Technical Society (1991): 116-124.

4. la C. McIlwaine, "UDC–Has it a future?" *Bliss Classification Bulletin* no. 35 (1993): 8-13.

5. la C. McIlwaine, "UDC: the present rates and future development," *International Cataloguing and Bibliographic Control* 23, no.2 (April-June 1994): 29-33.

6. *Extensions and Corrections to the UDC* Series 15, The Hague, September 1993.

7. See article by A. Buxton in I. C. McIlwaine, *Guide to the Use of the UDC*. The Hague: FID, 1993 (FID 703), p. 109 sqq.

The Classification Schemes
of The Research Libraries
# of The New York Public Library

Karen M. Hsu

SUMMARY. There are two unique classification schemes used by The Research Libraries of The New York Public Library. One is the Billings Classification, a broad subject classification created in the 1890's, the other is a fixed order scheme arranged by the size of books. This article describes the historical background of the schemes, how they have served the needs of The Research Libraries, and their possible suitability for other libraries.

Most university and research libraries nowadays use the Library of Congress Classification (LCC) and most public libraries use the Dewey Decimal Classification (DDC). However, within some large libraries, there are still special collections which use unique and locally devised classifications. Each of these local schemes has its own historical background, and the library using it has compelling reasons for doing so. What is unusual about The Research Libraries of The New York Public Library is that the whole library uses schemes which are not LCC, DDC, nor anything that has been used by any other libraries.

The Research Libraries of The New York Public Library will be

Karen M. Hsu is Assistant Director and Chief of Cataloging Division of The Research Libraries of The New York Public Library. She has worked for The Research Libraries for over 20 years.

[Haworth co-indexing entry note]: "The Classification Schemes of The Research Libraries of The New York Public Library." Hsu, Karen M. Co-published simultaneously in *Cataloging & Classification Quarterly* (The Haworth Press, Inc.) Vol. 19, No. 3/4, 1995, pp. 133-142; and: *Classification: Options and Opportunities* (ed: Alan R. Thomas) The Haworth Press, Inc., 1995, pp. 133-142. Multiple copies of this article/chapter may be purchased from The Haworth Document Delivery Center [1-800-3-HA-WORTH; 9:00 a.m. - 5:00 p.m. (EST)].

referred to in this paper in the singular form. It is a very special and unique library. It is one of the great libraries in the world, among the ranks of the Library of Congress, the British Library, and the Bibliothèque Nationale de France. It forms part of The New York Public Library (NYPL), but unlike The Branch Libraries, which comprises the other part of NYPL and is publicly funded, The Research Libraries (RL) is privately funded and is a closed stack, non-circulating research library. It generally collects one copy only of each title. The readers are not allowed to browse the stacks, and every item requested by readers is paged by the library staff. There are two classification schemes used by RL. One is called the Billings Classification, and the other is a fixed order scheme arranged by the size of items. These schemes may seem very unusual to most librarians, but they are the product of RL's unique history and characteristics.

BILLINGS CLASSIFICATION: GENERAL FEATURES

The Billings Classification was designed in the late 1890s by RL's first Director, Dr. John Shaw Billings. RL was formed in 1895 by the merger of three of the finest private collections at the time, namely, the Astor Library, the Lenox Library, and the Tilden Trust. RL's Board of Trustees enlisted Dr. Billings to be its founding director in 1895. He was a medical doctor to begin with and served in the Army as a surgeon during the Civil War. After the war, he worked at the Surgeon General's Office where he had the vision to establish a great medical library for medical research and where he also created an "Index Catalogue of the Surgeon General's Library."[1] It was this achievement, among others, that attracted the attention of RL's Board of Trustees. Dr. Billings served as the Library's Director for eighteen years; he died in 1913 at the age of 74, shortly before he was due to retire. He was buried with military honors in the National Cemetery at Arlington. Among the dignitaries that attended the memorial service held at the Library were Andrew Carnegie and R.R. Bowker.[2]

It was not an easy task for Dr. Billings to design a classification scheme that would consolidate the collections from the three originating libraries. At the time of the merger, there were altogether about 400,000 volumes and 70,000 pamphlets. No real subject classification had been applied to these collections. Most items belonged to various small special collections and had been shelved in specific physical areas of the three libraries to which they originally belonged. For instance, books relating to America in the Lenox Library were all shelved in the south gallery of the Lenox building, arranged chronologically by date of issue. A fixed location had also been used by the Lenox Library and the Astor Library by assigning a press number and a shelf letter. For example, such marks as 272B would indicate that an item was shelved on Shelf B in Press 272. While the processing arising from the merger of the three collections was proceeding, a new building was also being planned and constructed for RL. Many of the special collections would come to the special rooms in the new building. Dr. Billings, apparently a man of many talents, was also very much involved in the design of the building. Classifying or reclassifying 400,000 volumes and bringing them over to a new building was a daunting task. At this time during the 1890's, LCC did not exist yet. There were two classification systems available then, the DDC and the Cutter Expansive Classification. After much pondering, Dr. Billings decided that these two systems were designed for more universal collections and could not be fitted into the peculiarities of RL's collections. He set out to establish a new system for the Library, "basing it primarily upon the books he found before him."[3]

The Library of Congress (LC) had gone through similar developments as did RL. LC was established in 1800 but burned by British soldiers on August 24, 1814 and most of its books were destroyed in the fire. Thomas Jefferson offered to sell his personal library to the Congress, and the Congress paid $23,950 to purchase the Jefferson library of 6,487 books. This collection was classified according to Jefferson's own system, which was retained by LC until the 1890s. By then, the collection had grown from seven thousand books to nearly one million. The Jeffersonian system was no longer adequate. LC was also about to move to a new building in 1897. Here was an opportunity for LC to employ a new classification scheme which could accommodate its increasing needs. Interestingly enough, LC also decided to forgo both the DDC and Cutter system and to design its own. Thus was born the current Library of Congress Classification system.[4]

The first edition of Billings Classification was issued in 1899, and the second edition in 1955. The Billings Classification consists of two groups, the Main Groups (Table 1) and the Star Groups (Table 2). The Main Groups divide human knowledge into 16 Main classes, from Biography, History, Geography, Arts and Amusements, Literature, Science, to Philosophy and Religion. Under each Main class are sub-classes and sub-sub-classes. Each class consists of one to four letters, with most classes in three letters. For example, one of the Main classes is I (History of the United States). Under the I group, IB comprises the Constitution and Constitutional History, and IBD comprises the General Works on Constitutional History (Table 3).

TABLE 1. Main Groups.

Biography . . . . A

History . . . . B-I

Geography . . . . K-L

Arts. Amusements . . . . M

Literature . . . . N

Science. Mathematics. Astronomy . . . . O

Physics. Chemistry. Geology, etc. . . . . P

Biology. Natural History . . . . Q

Philology . . . . R

Sociology . . . . S

Economics . . . . T

Technology (Useful and Industrial Arts) V

Medicine . . . . W

Law X

Philosophy . . . . Y

Religion . . . . Z

The Star Groups of the Billings Classification consist of 19 classes. These Star classes designate special collections housed in special rooms. This was the result of carrying over the special collections from the Astor and Lenox Libraries into the new library building, which was completed in 1911. Some of these special collections have come to represent special formats such as Newspapers, Phonographs, and Microfilms. Some special collections are based on materials published in certain languages, e.g., Orientalia in the Oriental Division, Hebrew publications in the Jewish Division. Subject coverage by these divisions is not clear cut. For example, books on Oriental literature are classed in *O rather than in the N class where literature would normally be classed. Similarly, works on the Hebrew language are shelved in the *P class for the Jewish Division rather than in the general Philology class R.[5] What matters is to which special collection an item belongs. The same item going to different divisions will receive different class marks. For example, a book on Jews in Asia will have an *O class mark if collected by the Oriental Division and an *P class mark if collected by the Jewish Division.

TABLE 2. Star Groups.

Newspapers . . . . *A
General Collections . . . . *C
General Periodicals . . . . *D
Learned Societies . . . . *E
General Museums . . . . *F
Bibliography . . . . *G
Libraries . . . . *H
Book Arts . . . . *I
Incunabula. Rarities, etc. . . . . *K
Phonograph . . . . *L
Music . . . . *M
Literature: Special Collections . . . . *N
Orientalia . . . . *O
Jewish Collection . . . . *P
Slavonic Collection . . . . *Q
Public Documents . . . . *S
Patents . . . . *V
Bible . . . . *Y
Microfilms . . . . *Z

TABLE 3. History-America-United States.

United States: Bibliography, etc. I
   Periodicals and Society Publications . . . . IAA
   Dictionaries . . . . IAD
   General and Systematic Histories . . . . IAE
   School Histories, etc. . . . . IAF
   Collections. Essays. Miscellanies . . . . IAG
   Collected Works. Speeches of Statesmen . . . . IAW
   The Constitution and Constitutional History . . . . IB
      Commentaries . . . . IBC
      Constitutional History: General Works . . . . IBD

BILLINGS CLASSIFICATION: PROBLEMS

In a certain sense, the Billings Star classes serve also as location symbols. This feature has created problems for bibliographic control. Each time a title is transferred from one division to another, it has to be reclassified. And even though RL is a one-copy library, there are occasions when a reference book is held by several divisions. Then each copy will have a unique and different class mark. This is quite different from practices of most, if not all, other libraries, where one item would have one call number no matter how many copies a library holds. Furthermore, in today's automation environment, most systems are designed to handle the one-title one-call-number situation. Before going into a bibliographic utility or a vendor system, RL invariably has to do a great deal of system maneuvering in order to get all the class marks indexed properly, all the field data displayed properly, and all the shelflist cards printed properly.

If the Star classes are unusual in the Billings Classification, then the lack of a book number in a class mark is even more striking. Class marks from both the Main Groups and the Star Groups consisted of one to four letters only, and an * for the Star classes. There was no book number assigned to individual items within the same class. No distinct notations were added after the class marks. For instance, all items on the history of American Constitution had the same class mark–IBD. Shelving items within the same class is by the cataloging entry of the item, i.e., title if the main entry is title and author/title if the item has an author main entry.

Absence of book numbers in the Billings scheme incurred inordinate difficulty both in shelving and delivery of books. First of all, books must be labelled with their class marks and their full cataloging main entry. When a book had a corporate body/title entry in a foreign language, labelling was a laborious and time consuming process. In the old days before AACR2, RL used to recatalog serials under latest entry when there was a change in title. Relabelling of all the volumes to the latest title could involve a lot of relettering and reshelving of multiple volumes. Long strings of lettering on the spine of books also made it extremely difficult for a page to locate, shelve, or reshelve items. Furthermore, readers did not always copy the full entry on the call slip, causing the necessity to verify the entry and therefore a delay in delivery of the item.

These were the problems associated with the Billings Classification. But one must remember that when it was created, it had to take into consideration the state of the collections of the founding libraries. Many practical situations dictated that one could not have a perfect system. Dr. Billings himself put it wryly in regard to the classification that he created, " . . . that it is not logical so far as the succession of different departments in relation to the operations of the human mind is concerned; that it is not recommended for any other library, and that no librarian of another library would approve of it."[6] The scheme certainly has its own logic, and it has served RL's particular needs relatively well. Its applicability to other libraries is a different matter.

FIXED ORDER SCHEME

By the 1950s, many new subject fields had been developed, but it was very difficult to expand logically the Billings system due to its basic structure. For example, the class marks for the subject Mathematics cover Algebra, Arithmetic, Calculus and Geometry. It was impossible to squeeze in the subject Computer Science. One might wonder if it would have been a good opportunity for RL to switch to LCC. However, there were other factors that RL had to face. Most important among them was the acute shortage of space in RL. The collections had increased to such a scale that there was practically no room to shelve new acquisitions. RL estimated in 1956 that a fixed order scheme of shelving books according to size of an item would increase its stack capacity a minimum of 35%.[7] According to Hugo Alker, who reported in the May/June 1951 issue of the *Zentralblatt für Bibliothekswesen* on library practices in England, France and the Scandinavian countries, the subject classified arrangement of books incurred a loss of 20 to 50 percent of shelf space as compared to an arrangement in order of accession.[8]

In addition to space saving, a fixed order scheme offers other benefits. It eliminates the cost of repeated shifting of books to insert new accessions. It reduces the damage to books due to repeated shifting. In contrast to Billings, it provides a distinctive notation which facilitates shelving, simplifies preparation of call slips by readers, and expedites book deliveries. Therefore, in 1956, after a long period of wrenching deliberations and against strong objections from some staff librarians, RL made the decision to switch to a fixed order scheme for all its books shelved in the general stacks at that time. These books were assigned a fixed order class mark according to the size of the item. Books of the same size were shelved together regardless of their subject. This was a critical and unusual decision for a research library like RL. But then, RL is an unusual library. No readers are allowed in the stacks.

In 1972, a slightly different fixed order scheme replaced the older one. Instead of one fixed order scheme for all of the general stack items, each large division was assigned a scheme and thus was provided a divisional indication of the item. It is an alpha-numeric system (Table 4). The alpha part consists of three letters and the numerical part consists of the year of cataloging and a sequential number. The first letter is J, because that was one of the two letters not used in the Billings Classification. The second letter is a divisional designation, e.g., F for the Humanities and Social Sciences Division and S for the Science and Technology Division. The third letter indicates the size of the item, e.g., E for books of the size of 25 centimeters high. As shown in Table 4, the size of monographs is divided into eight groups from "Up to 17 cm." to "49 cm. and over," and the size of serials is divided into six groups from "Up to 22 cm." to "49 cm. and over." A class mark such as JFE 94-1234 signifies that it is a printed monograph belonging to the Humanities and Social Sciences Division and that it is of the size of 25 centimeters high and was cataloged in 1994.

TABLE 4. Fixed Order Class Marks for Humanities and Social Sciences.

Printed Monographs	Of Size Up to and Including
JFB	17 cm.
JFC	20
JFD	23
JFE	25
JFF	30
JFG	39
JFH	48
JFJ	49 cm. and over

Printed Serials	Of Size Up to and Including
JFK	22 cm.
JFL	25
JFM	30
JFN	39
JFP	48
JFR	49 cm. and over

The new fixed order schemes cover all the items cataloged for RL's three largest divisions, i.e., the Humanities and Social Sciences Division, the Economic and Public Affairs Division, and the Science and Technology Division. The other divisions continue to use the Billings Classification. Since 1972, however, instead of labelling the cataloging entries on the spine of materials to distinguish different titles within the same class, a numeric part consisting of the year of cataloging and a sequential number is added after the Billings class mark for these divisions. Thus, each class mark is unique and the lettering of the cataloging entry on the spine is eliminated.

In addition to the smaller divisions, all the open shelf reference collections also continued to use the Billings Classification. Then in 1992, the Economic and Public Affairs Division and the Science and Technology Division decided to reclassify their reference collections from Billings to LCC. They had a good reason for doing this: these two divisions were to be merged to form a new component library of RL called the Science, Industry and Business Library (SIBL). SIBL will be moved to a different location in a new building sometime in 1995. It will have a combined large open shelf reference collection. The Billings Classification would not be able to accommodate SIBL's need for providing a coherent and up to date subject approach for readers. Thus LCC has become RL's third classification scheme.

The problem with the fixed order scheme is, of course, the loss of subject grouping of materials on the shelf, and as a result, subject shelflisting is also no longer existent. This has not helped collection development staff in identifying the Library's holdings on specific subjects. The only way to do this is through subject access in RL's catalog. This is perhaps why RL has always paid such attention to subject analysis in cataloging its collections. It even had its own comprehensive subject list for decades until it decided to follow LC's subject headings in 1972 when it automated its cataloging. But then, that is another story.

CONCLUSION

RL's own two classification schemes are unique. Each of them was designed and adopted to address RL's particular needs at the time. The Billings system is hardly appropriate for any other library, yet the fixed order scheme may be useful elsewhere. It is quite true that nothing can replace the resulting loss from a fixed order scheme of subject grouping on the shelf and classified shelflisting. Nevertheless, a fixed order scheme may be good for storage of infrequently used materials. Non-browsable items such as video tapes and sound recordings could also be served adequately by it. When RL first adopted the fixed order scheme in 1956, space saving was the main if not the only reason. And in these days of cataloging simplification, a fixed order scheme dramatically reduces catalogers' time in classifying library materials.

NOTES

1. Harry Miller Lydenberg, *History of The New York Public Library, Astor, Lenox and Tilden Foundations.* (New York: The New York Public Library, 1923), 351.

2. Phyllis Dain. *The New York Public Library: A History of Its Founding and Early Years.* (New York: The New York Public Library, Astor, Lenox and Tilden Foundations, 1972), 361-362.

3. Lydenberg, *History of The New York Public Library, Astor, Lenox and Tilden Foundations,* 370-371.

4. Lois Mai Chan. *Immroth's Guide to the Library of Congress Classification.* Fourth Edition. (Englewood, CO: Libraries Unlimited, Inc., 1990), 1-15.

5. J. S. Billings. "Memorandum on Classification in the New York Public Library, January 1, 1899." In *The New York Public Library Classification Schedules for Printed, Microcopy and Phonorecord Materials in the Reference Department.* Second Edition. (New York: The New York Public Library, 1955), i-ii.

6. Billings, "Memorandum on Classification in the New York Public Library, January 1, 1899," iii-iv.

7. Rutherford D. Rogers, "Shelving Books by Size." *ALA Bulletin* 51:6(June 1957): 435-437.

8. Werner B. Ellinger. "Alker's Observation on European Library Practice." *Library of Congress Information Bulletin* 10:52 (Dec. 26, 1951):3.

Reader-Interest Classification:
The User-Friendly Schemes

Jacquelyn Sapiie

SUMMARY. A review of the current use of reader-interest classification since 1980 as an alternative arrangement of bookstock to traditional classification. Reader-interest classification is known by a variety of names and used in many countries. With a current trend to make libraries more accessible and user-friendly, librarians are experimenting with reader-interest classification. The paper discusses the reasons for using it, principles, catalog aspects, what it brings together and separates, implementation, arrangement and presentation of the bookstock, the kind and size of library where it is in use and the outlook for its continued use. Recent studies and surveys are also considered.

INTRODUCTION

Reader-interest is a "simple and broad classification intended to reflect the special interests of readers rather than the subject contents of books as such."[1] An early recorded use of reader-interest classification is found in the Detroit Public Library in 1945.[2] Recent literature since 1980 indicates that there is some variety of the schemes in use today in the United States, Britain and many other countries as an alternative to the major classification systems. Common to all who reorganize their collection using a read-

Jacquelyn Sapiie, BA, MLS is Librarian in the Queens Borough Public Library, New York, NY and a former middle school teacher.

[Haworth co-indexing entry note]: "Reader-Interest Classification: The User-Friendly Schemes." Sapiie, Jacquelyn. Co-published simultaneously in *Cataloging & Classification Quarterly* (The Haworth Press, Inc.) Vol. 19, No. 3/4, 1995, pp. 143-155; and: *Classification: Options and Opportunities* (ed: Alan R. Thomas) The Haworth Press, Inc., 1995, pp. 143-155. Multiple copies of this article/chapter may be purchased from The Haworth Document Delivery Center [1-800-3-HAWORTH; 9:00 a.m. - 5:00 p.m. (EST)].

er-interest classification plan is a desire to improve service for their patrons. By placing the reader at the center, reader-interest classification encourages self-service and promotes accessibility to the collection.

INSTANCES OF USE

This overview of the library literature published since 1980 hopes to synthesize the current interest in and implementation of reader-interest classification. Each library has devised an individualized plan to meet the perceived needs of the community served. Both the individual variations and the common threads of the plans will be explored.

There are nearly as many variations on the names given to reader-interest classification as there are instances of its use. Librarians in the U.S. have brought the plan into the modern age with the up-to-date terms of merchandising, marketing and bookstore arrangement. In Britain, such terms as reader interest categories, categories or categorization are favored, but broad interest groups or user orientation are also used. Librarians create centers of interest in France and special interest corners in Japan. In Germany, immediate concern areas or alternative arrangement is used; in The Netherlands, broad subject arrangement, reader interest categories or topics of current interest; and in South Africa, the plan is called reader's interest classification.

The majority of the documented cases reorganizing all or parts of their collection with reader-interest classification are public libraries and many of these are county or municipal systems with from two to sixty branch libraries. The size of these libraries is difficult to assess with accuracy as not all the reports include complete information. Overall, the libraries range in size from 2,500 volumes of adult fiction to 276,740 volumes of stock with annual issues ranging from 100,000 to 561,000. There are two instances reported in the literature of reader-interest classification in elementary and junior high school libraries.

Although no one plan or arrangement is universally used, the general plans and characteristics of the bookstock fall into six categories: reorganization of the paperback fiction only,[3] the adult fiction,[4,5] popular or general interest non-fiction and fiction,[6,7,8] non-fiction,[9] general interest non-fiction, fiction and juvenile stock,[10,11,12] entire collection,[13,14,15] and entire collection reorganized and integrated.[16]

REASONS FOR CHANGE

Local needs prompted librarians in all these situations to take a fresh look at their libraries in terms of stock, services, patrons and their communities. In-depth knowledge of the needs of the communities is evident throughout. In addition to working closely with patrons, in-house surveys were conducted by the library staff. The informal local survey supported by published surveys of public library use were considered. In at least one case, polls by a professional polling organization were commissioned.[17]

The reasons advanced for change can be grouped in four categories:

A Desire to Meet the Needs of the Users

Findings in the U.S. reveal that forty-nine percent of the library users browse for recreational materials[18] and similar studies in Britain confirm that from fifty-five percent of users in a central library to seventy-five percent or eighty percent in smaller branch libraries are browsers.[19] It appears that at least half of the library patrons are not focused purposive library users. Surveys also show that patrons find it difficult to find their way around even medium sized libraries[20] and experience information overload, the frustration and confusion encountered when an individual's capacity for processing information is exceeded. Browsers are more affected than the purposive user because of the unfocused nature of browsing. However, studies show varying results indicating at what point the size of the collection causes information overload[21] and separation becomes desirable.

A Stated Dissatisfaction with the Classification System

There was a growing criticism of the classification system which was seen as inadequate and an incomprehensible obstacle to the user. The Dewey Decimal Classification system was regarded as a disadvantage in a multicultural, inner-city school library. In all cases where the classification scheme in use was specified it was the Dewey Decimal Classification system. Instances from The Netherlands and Germany mention only use of the normal library classification or that provided by the National Bibliographic Service without naming a particular system.

As an Experiment

The reorganization of two school libraries was approached positively. In one instance marketing books were tried to determine if bookstore techniques would be effective,[22] and in another the decision to experiment with categorized stock was inspired by a library seminar.[23]

A Change in Circumstances Provides an Opportunity for a Fresh Look at the Library, Its Use and Services

Fires in two libraries prompted the staff to look at the stock differently, and although the initial aim was more relevant stock, surveys revealed the difficulties encountered by patrons locating material which inspired the more fundamental changes.[24] A move to new facilities provided the opportunity to consider new ideas and a decision was made for the book-store approach; success in one branch inspired change in additional branch libraries.[25]

DEVISING A PLAN

In all the reported situations except two, the Orange Free State Provincial Library Service, South Africa[26] and the Waterthorpe Library, Sheffield,[27] the professional librarians working in the library were responsible for drawing up a list of categories using reader interest patterns based on circulation statistics, requests and surveys. In a few instances, the local librarians formed a committee with librarians from the central library.

They relied on their own good judgment and experience in defining the categories, as the local needs do not necessarily match the published lists of fiction categories and genres or the most popular categories and genres of fiction often included in published surveys. It is recognized that intimate knowledge of the library community is required to define the categories and then to fill both fiction and non-fiction categories with books which match the readers' ideas of what belongs there.[28]

The Queens Borough Public Library, NY encourages staff members to participate in merchandising. In branch libraries, the librarians, clerks and pages are involved in this process from the determination of categories and selection of material to the display and maintenance of merchandised areas.

The number of categories varies according to local circumstances, such as how much of the collection is reorganized and which parts, fiction only or including non-fiction, adult stock only or including children's stock. The librarians state a desire to keep the number of categories simple, easy to understand and use and manageable in size.

Reports indicate the number of categories used is from as few as twelve to as many as thirty-four; however, the number used by most libraries is from twenty to twenty-six, e.g., the Cheshire County Public libraries use twenty-two categories. The means used for indicating the category on a spine label are equally divided among the use of two or three letter codes or graphics. The graphics are bold symbols printed on labels purchased from suppliers. The libraries which choose to use a two letter code, devise their own system as in the Cheshire County libraries which use FR (Romance), FT (Thriller) and FW (Western). Those which use a three letter code use the first three letters of the category name such as, ADV (Adventure) and THR (Thriller).

Although any concept or form can be used as a reader interest category for a shelf arrangement, there are two tests of a successful category: responsiveness to real reader interests and the unity of materials located in the same category.[29] The staff in the branch libraries of the Queens Borough Public Library system create their own merchandised areas to suit the needs of the immediate community.

Flexibility is one advantage of reader-interest classification acknowledged by several librarians. It allows for readjustments; new categories can be substituted for others,[30] and a book can be easily moved to another category, if it is not taken out in the first category.[31,32] Displays which do not attract borrowers can be changed or eliminated quickly.

IMPLEMENTATION

One of the expressed principles of reader-interest classification is that the arrangement of books by categories would be simple and self-explanatory and minimize the necessity to use the catalog or staff to find a specific book or subject.[33] Observations in libraries and bookstores reveal that users do not like to ask for directions or help;[34] therefore, the self-service nature of reader-interest classification encourages greater use.[35]

The physical arrangement which puts this principle into action is determined by local conditions, such as community needs and interests, physical size and layout of the building, and the size and nature of the collection. While not all of the literature provides a detailed account of how plans are executed, the following patterns emerge.

The majority of the libraries involved in converting their stock from a traditional classification system to a reader-interest classification system use interest categories to replace only part of their stock, retaining the Dewey Decimal Classification for the remainder. They also use both marks on all reorganized stock, spine labels denoting categories by color coding or symbols, and place books in random order within categories. A few libraries use the reader-interest categories to completely replace the classification system.[36,37]

Other plans use both marks on their old stock but new books bear only the category mark on the spine. There is one instance of classifying the new books by both systems, but displaying only the category mark on the spine and writing the Dewey class mark on the back of the title page. The Queens Borough Public Library displays the Dewey Classification mark on the spine of all books; the category code is written on a book's top edge when assigned to a merchandised area. Some of the libraries use the Dewey Classification numbers to keep order within the non-fiction interest categories.

One of the most refreshing aspects of these plans is the method of assigning categories to the books. This involves predicting the book's area of interest for the users or the category where users might expect to find it.[38] This belief is held so strongly that the task of categorization is not the responsibility of the cataloguing staff, but instead given to those responsible for selecting new stock. This change allows the library to assign categories to books at the time of selection and purchase[39,40] and to select books with the categories in mind, such as Mystery and Adventure, Animals, Making Money, and Parenting.

WHAT READER-INTEREST CLASSIFICATION BRINGS TOGETHER AND SEPARATES

The arrangements bring together different elements of the collection depending on the extent and aim of the reorganization. In the most far-reaching plans, the reader-interest classification brings together the entire adult collection plus the children's (12+ years) non-fiction in interest categories. For each category all adult books and children's (12+) non-fiction are merged and intershelved. This maximizes the use of the book stock. The older children's non-fiction may be used by the elderly, adult new readers, readers learning the language, young adults, and adults who all need a simplified approach on a topic without requiring a search in several different areas of the library.[41]

Another extensive arrangement brings together all non-fiction stock, including adults', children's (12+ years), reference, oversize materials and periodicals. The integration of the whole range of stock in categories brings together total resources on the topic usually separated by traditional classification schemes, as well as by function, or size.[42] A separate quick reference section is maintained with directories, encyclopedias and local information.

The most frequently used scheme reported in the literature is one which brings together books by subject by reorganizing the fiction and part of the non-fiction (usually the general-interest and popular topics) in categories. The fiction and non-fiction is sometimes intershelved and sometimes not.

An example of a frequently merged category is War. The intention is to bring together related subjects, such as Military history and World War history traditionally separated by a classification scheme.[43]

One variation is an arrangement where the fiction and non-fiction stock are categorized and the fiction is located next to the appropriate non-fiction category. This system brings the fiction and non-fiction together by subject and physically places them adjacent to each other but does not intershelve the two collections.

Reader-interest classification, while bringing some elements of a collection together, inevitably separates others. Where fiction is organized in broad interest groups, books written by the same author are often separated in two or even three places. An arrangement which categorizes the popular or general-interest non-fiction topics of the non-fiction collection separates this popular material from books for the purposive reader. None of the public libraries report categorizing children's (11 − years) books. They remain in the traditional sequences of easy reader, alphabetical author arrangement of fiction and classified non-fiction which are categories separated from the rest of the collection. An arrangement which presents only paperback books in general-interest categories separates those items from other books on the same subject and from works of fiction written by the same author.

PRESENTATION

The general approach is to shelve each reader-interest category in its own bay. The order within the categories is usually random, sometimes alphabetical author order and occasionally that of the Dewey Decimal Classification. The large categories are sub-divided by the use of shelf labeling.

The marketing principle that visibility is the key to selling[44] is generally applied by all libraries involved in reorganization. It governs where the categorized stock is located. The reader-interest categories are best shelved where they are most visible to entering patrons, as well as utilizing small displays or paper display cases called dumps located at key points near the entrance, the check out at the circulation counter or in the heavy traffic areas. Libraries employing merchandising principles prefer island and free standing shelving.

Related to this principle is how the books are placed on the shelves making them attractive and eyecatching. It is agreed that as many books as possible should be shelved facing out, rather than in the usual manner where only the spine is exposed. The books attract the most attention when shelved this way, as if on display.

Further creative techniques are employed. Books are concentrated on the shelves within the most accessible range, thirty-six to sixty inches from the floor.[45] The top and bottom shelves are used exclusively for books shelved face out. Sloping display shelves, either purchased or converted flat shelves, and the imaginative arrangement of books on the shelves with one-fourth face out or spread open are ideas also used.

As part of the user-friendly approach of Reader-interest classification, good shelf guiding and signs are considered essential and the key to the whole system. It is felt that patrons are more likely to look at a guiding system rather than a catalog, and since the books are not in a specific order, good shelf guiding is all the more important.[46] All libraries report giving considerable thought to the guiding system and all use shelf guiding, some with large display signs, posters, overhead signs, simple word signs (Novels, Travel) or header signs on free standing display shelves. The signs are often backlit or highlighted in some way, such as with spotlights.

In addition to shelf guiding and signs, spine labels and color coding are also considered an important element in a self-service system and are generally used except in one instance. Austin McCarthy regards any visual aid on the book as a hindrance to changing its location.[47] Most libraries use spine labels with some kind of symbol to represent the categories. Some use color coding or graphic symbols on the labels to represent the categories, e.g., a Stetson for Westerns. Other libraries use the first letter of the category name and others have devised a three letter code for the categories. Diagrams, detailed guides, leaflets and maps are also used to guide the library user around the arrangement.

READER-INTEREST CLASSIFICATION
AND THE LIBRARY CATALOG

A study of 334 large library systems in the U.S.[48] indicates that there are three principal methods used to denote types of fiction where fiction is separated by genres: separate shelf arrangement, spine labels and notation in the catalog. The findings show that sixty-seven percent of the libraries surveyed use notation in the catalog to specify the fiction categories assigned to specific books.

Forty-six percent of the libraries reporting in the recent literature update their catalogs by adding the new category marks to the existing entries. Thirty-eight percent of the libraries do not mention the catalog and only fifteen percent report not using the catalog after reorganization.

Whether there is a computerized catalog or a card catalog, the new categories are added to the existing entries; the old classification marks are retained. In several situations where the catalog does not reflect the changes that have been made in the reorganization, other tools are provided either for the library user or the staff. In one instance, a simple subject index and an index of authors and their assigned categories are available for patrons,[49] while in another library an alphabetical author index and an alphabetical title index are seen as more useful to the staff and the subject index is meant to be used as a guide to shelf order and is accessible to the users.[50] The catalog was abandoned in another library and an alphabetical author card file is used in its place mainly as a staff tool.[51] Another library reports that the class numbers in the union microfiche catalog cannot be relied on anymore. This is not a major drawback as it was used only by a small number of patrons and books should be easier to find by direct consultation of the shelves.[52]

One librarian acknowledges that innovations with stock arrangement have been restricted because of the work involved in altering the catalog records and that there has been a tendency to let these housekeeping routines take precedence over adapting services.[53]

REPORTED BENEFITS

Having implemented the reorganization of the bookstock with reader-interest classification to help their patrons use the collection and locate books more easily, librarians were pleasantly surprised to discover added benefits. It was found that the reader-interest classification was also useful for the meaningful collection of data and assessing and editing stock because it provides a visual means to determine the size of various collections, to identify low use or surplus stock and areas for future stock provision. The reorganization process provides an excellent opportunity for weeding stock.

Since the stock is physically divided into manageable groups, reader-interest classification provides an easy way to determine how many books of a particular genre a library owns. Future stock selection is facilitated because reader-interest classification gives a clear indication of reading preferences. An unexpected benefit was that less staff time is required for shelving books and tidying the shelves because many libraries do not maintain any specific order within the categories.

Increased circulation is reported in most instances. The study of major public library systems in the U.S. conducted in the mid-1980s indicates that circulation increased when fiction titles were classified into genre areas.[54] One library reports a thirty percent circulation increase of non-fiction in the first month of reorganization over the same period of the previous year.[55] Another library had a seventy percent increase in circulation.[56] A library system which reorganized large parts of their collection using merchandising principles reports that circulation grew more than 103 percent in seven years from 5,954,290 in 1980-81 to 12,138,604 in 1987-88.[57] Although many of the accounts do not indicate precise circulation statistics, most do report a steady increase in their circulation.

The users' responses, if any, were generally favorable. Some libraries conducted in-house surveys which vary from findings almost wholly favorable,[58] to seventy nine percent of patrons approving of the categorization.[59] One study of reader-interest classification showed that the children using the system became more independent library users.[60] Studies of large library systems suggest that the organization of fiction in categories has helped library patrons find the type of book wanted.[61] Others regard the increased numbers of patrons using the library, increased circulation issues and use of books previously underused as a measure of the reorganization's success and reader acceptance of the system.

CONCLUSION

The literature suggests librarians continue to experiment with reader-interest classification in their efforts to present their libraries and collections in a user-friendly manner. Arthur Maltby regards reader-interest classification as an interesting and imaginative idea for an alternative system. He suggests that if a challenger to the Dewey Decimal Classification could emerge for use in general libraries it would be based on reader-interest.[62]

In a time of budget cuts and financial restraints reader-interest classification schemes provide added value by maximizing the use of existing collections with creative arrangements and easier accessibility. It is evident from the literature that reader-interest classification suits the current trend for library orientation from the users' perspective and increased responsiveness to popular and changing needs.

REFERENCES

1. Ray Prytherch, *Harrod's Librarian's Glossary of Terms Used in Librarianship, Documentation and the Book Crafts,* 7th ed. Worcester, U.K.: Gower, 1990, p. 515.

2. Ralph Ulveling in Frank B.Woodford, *Parnassus on Main Street: A History of the Detroit Public Library.* Detroit: State Univ. Press, 1965, p. 119.

3. Mary Jo Langhorne, "Marketing Books in the School Library," *School Library Journal* 33, no. 5 (1987): 31-33.

4. Sharon L. Baker, "Fiction Classification, Schemes: An Experiment to Increase Use," *Public Libraries* 26, no. 3 (Spring 1988): 75-77.

5. Debra Kellum, "Fiction Separation," *The Unabashed Librarian* 71 (1989): 3-4.

6. Ian Moroson, Mike Perry, "Two-tier and Total: Stock Arrangement in Brent." In: *Alternative Arrangement in Approaches to Public Library Stock,* edited by Patricia Ainley, Barry Totterdell. London: Association of Assistant Librarians, 1982.

7. Petra Augenanger, "Der 'Nahbereich' aus Sicht des Benutzers, [The 'Immediate Concern' Area from the User's Point of View,] *Buch und Bibliotek* 33 (Jan. 1981): 46-48.

8. Kenneth G. Sivulich, "Merchandising Your Library," *Public Libraries* 28, no. 2 (March/April 1989): 97-100.

9. Hans Ban Wijland, "Toegankelijker Opstelling Van Informatie: di Duitse Dreigeteilte Bibliothek en de Britse Alternative Arrangement," [A More Accessible Arrangement of Information: the West German Tripartite Library and the British Alternative Arrangement,] *Bibliotheek en Samenleving* 13, no. 7/8 (July/August 1985): 133-238.

10. John Astin, "Cheshire: Alternative Arrangement and Beyond." In: *Alternative Arrangement: New Approaches to Public Library Stock,* edited by Patricia Ainley, Barry Totterdell. London: Association of Assistant Librarians, 1982.

11. Den Reader, "User Orientation in a Hertfordshire Branch." In: *Alternative Arrangement: New Approaches to Public Library Stock,* edited by Patricia Ainley, Barry Totterdell. London: Association of Assistant Librarians, 1982.

12. Austin McCarthy, "Burning Issues: Stock Appeal in Sunderland." In: *Alternative Arrangement: New Approaches to Public Library Stock,* edited by Patricia Ainley, Barry Totterdell. London: Association of Assistant Librarians, 1982.

13. Denis Chandler, "Self-Service Libraries: Providing for the Smaller Community in Cambridgeshire." In: *Alternative Arrangement: New Approaches to Public Library Stock,* edited by Patricia Ainley, Barry Totterdell. London: Association of Assistant Librarians, 1982.

14. Lyn Donbroski, "Categorisation at East Sussex County Library." In: *Alternative Arrangement: New Approaches to Public Library Stock,* edited by Patricia Ainley, Barry Totterdell. London: Association of Assistant Librarians, 1982.

15. Trude Venter, "'n Rangskikkingsmetode om die Gegruik Van Nie-fiksie in Openbare Biblioteke te Bevorder," [An Arrangement System to Stimulate the Use of Non-fiction in Public Libraries], *South African Journal for Librarianship and Information Science* 52, no.4 (December 1984): 110-112.

16. Douglas Betts, "Reader Interest Categories in Surrey." In: *Alternative Arrangement: New Approaches to Public Library Stock,* edited by Patricia Ainley, Barry Totterdell. London: Association of Assistant Librarians, 1982.

17. Sivulich, "Merchandising Your Library," p. 99.

18. Sivulich, "Merchandising Your Library," p. 99.

19. Patricia Ainley, Barry Totterdell. *Alternative Arrangement: New Approaches to Public Library Stock.* London: Association of Assistant Librarians, 1982, p. 10.

20. McCarthy, "Burning Issues: Stock Appeal in Sunderland," p. 89.

21. Sharon Baker, "Will Fiction Classification Schemes Increase Use?" *Reference Quarterly* 27, no. 3 (Spring 1988): 374-375.

22. Mary Jo Langhorne, "Marketing Books in the School Library," *School Library Journal* 33, no. 5 (January 1987): 31-33.

23. Donbroski, "Categorisation at East Sussex County Library," p. 78.

24. McCarthy, "Burning Issues: Stock Appeal in Sunderland," p. 89.

25. Denis Chandler, "Self-Service Libraries: Providing for the Smaller Community in Cambridgeshire." In: *Alternative Arrangement: New Approaches to Public Library Stock,* edited by Patricia Ainley, Barry Totterdell. London: Association of Assistant Librarians, 1982.

26. Venter, "An Arrangement System to Stimulate the use of Non-fiction in Public Libraries," p. 110-112.

27. Alan Woodis, Jr., "Categorizing Book Stock," *The Unabashed Librarian* 76 (1990): 5.

28. Gregg Sapp, "The Levels of Access: Subject Approaches to Fiction," *Reference Quarterly* 25 (Summer 1986): 488-497.

29. Sapp, "The Levels of Access: Subject Approaches to Fiction," p. 490.

30. Venter, "An Arrangement System to Stimulate the Use of Non-fiction," p. 112.

31. Venter, "An Arrangement System to Stimulate the Use of Non-fiction," p.112.

32. Lynn Sawbridge, Leo Favret, "The Mechanics and the Magic of Declassification," *Library Association Record* 84, no. 1 (November 1982): 385-386.

33. McCarthy, "Burning Issues: Stock Appeal in Sunderland," p. 90.

34. Sylvie A. Green, "Merchandising Techniques and Libraries," *School Library Journal* 28, no. 1 (September 1981): 35-39.

35. McCarthy, "Burning Issues: Stock Appeal in Sunderland," p. 90.

36. Sue Bridgwater, "Out of the Doldrums and into the Curriculum: De Beauvoir Junior School Library," *School Librarian* 38, no. 2 (May 1990): 53-54.

37. Lyn Donbroski, "Life Without Dewey," *Catalogue & Index* 57 (Spring 1980): 3-6.

39. Woodis, "Categorizing Book Stock," p. 5.

40. Donbroski, "Life Without Dewey," p. 4.

41. Ainley and Totterdell, *Alternative Arrangement,* p. 130.

42. Betts, "Reader Interest Categories in Surrey," pp. 66-67.

43. Moroson and Perry, "Two-Tier and Total: Stock Arrangement," p. 103.

44. Langhorne, "Marketing Books in Your School Library," p. 31.

45. Sivulich, "Merchandising Your Library," p. 99.

46. Donbroski, "Life Without Dewey," p. 4.

47. McCarthy, "Burning Issues: Stock Appeal in Sunderland," p. 64.

48. Gail Harrel, "The Classification and Organization of Adult Fiction in Large American Public Libraries," *Public Libraries* 24, no. 1 (Spring 1985): 13-14.

49. Chandler, "Self-Service Libraries," p. 51.

50. Bridgwater, "Out of the Doldrums and into the Curriculum," p. 54.

51. McCarthy, "Burning Issues: Stock Appeal in Sunderland," p. 90.

52. Moroson, "Two-Tier and Total: Stock Arrangement in Brent," p. 103.

53. McCarthy, "Burning Issues: Stock Appeal in Sunderland," p. 96.

54. Baker, "Fiction Classification Schemes: An Experiment to Increase Use," p. 76.

55. Sawbridge and Favret, "The Mechanics and the Magic of Declassification," p. 386.

56. Venter, "An Arrangement System to Stimulate the Use of Non-Fiction," p. 110.

57. Sivulich, "Merchandising Your Library," p. 97.

58. Betts, "Reader Interest Categories in Surrey," p. 71.

59. Reader, "User Orientation in a Hertfordshire Branch," p. 40.

60. Sharon L. Baker, "Designing Libraries to Meet the Needs of Browsers," *The Unabashed Librarian* 67(1988): 3-5.

61. Sharon L. Baker, Gay W. Shepherd, "Fiction Classification Schemes: The Principles Behind Them and Their Success," *Reference Quarterly* 27, no.2 (Winter 1987): pp. 245-251.

62. Arthur Maltby, *Sayer's Manual of Classification for Librarians,* 5th ed. London: Andre Deutsch, 1978, pp. 293-294.

COMBINATION PLATTERS AND RECLASSIFICATION

Intentional Use of Multiple Classification Schemes in United States Libraries

R. Conrad Winke

SUMMARY. Advantages and disadvantages of using more than one classification scheme are explored through a series of interviews with librarians currently employed at institutions that do so. These institutions can be categorized as falling into one of three major groups: (1) libraries that choose to shelve their government documents or technical reports by preassigned numbers, (2) libraries that retain DDC for some materials and LCC for other materials, and (3) libraries that implemented additional schemes when it became

R. Conrad Winke, Catalog Librarian, earned a BA in French Commercial Studies from the University of Illinois, Urbana, IL and a MALS from Rosary College, River Forest, IL.

Address correspondence to: Catalog Department, 1935 Sheridan Road, Northwestern University Library, Evanston, IL 60208.

The author wishes to thank those librarians, either mentioned or unmentioned, who graciously agreed to be interviewed for this paper.

[Haworth co-indexing entry note]: "Intentional Use of Multiple Classification Schemes in United States Libraries." Winke, R. Conrad. Co-published simultaneously in *Cataloging & Classification Quarterly* (The Haworth Press, Inc.) Vol. 19, No. 3/4, 1995, pp. 157-167; and: *Classification: Options and Opportunities* (ed: Alan R. Thomas) The Haworth Press, Inc., 1995, pp. 157-167. Multiple copies of this article/chapter may be purchased from The Haworth Document Delivery Center [1-800-3-HA-WORTH; 9:00 a.m. - 5:00 p.m. (EST)].

apparent that the existing classification scheme did not adequately cover their needs. Reasons behind the decisions leading to the use of multiple classification systems, the implications of these decisions for staff and user training, and the ongoing problems encountered by users are also explored.

INTRODUCTION

The purpose of the library is a determining factor in formulating policies of classification.[1]

No matter what scheme is chosen, or how large the library, the purpose of classification is to bring related items together in a helpful sequence from the general to the specific. Ease of access is especially important if the collection is heterogeneous.[2]

Libraries use classification systems and their attendant notations to assist in the organization and retrieval of the materials in their collections. Although it would seem that the use of a single classification system for all of the materials in a particular library would provide the best shelf arrangement for both staff and library users, this "ideal" situation is not necessarily typical in libraries, nor does it always represent the optimal use of a particular library's resources. There are, for example, libraries whose collections are split among different arrangement schemes, not as the result of any finding that this provides the greatest benefits, but because the expense of implementing a single system would impair the library's ability to perform more essential services. An example of this would be a library that switched from Dewey Decimal Classification (DDC) to Library of Congress Classification (LCC), and has not been able, for budgetary reasons, to reclassify older materials. This might be termed an "accidentally" split collection. There are also many libraries which, to facilitate the use of their collections, intentionally use two or more different classification schemes for their collections.

METHODOLOGY

This paper examines libraries where multiple classification schemes have been implemented intentionally. The advantages and disadvantages of using more than one scheme are explored through a series of interviews with librarians currently employed at such institutions, with the goal of determining the reasons behind the decisions leading to the use of multiple classification systems, the implications of these decisions for staff and user training, the ongoing problems encountered by users, and common threads found in the various types of libraries. In most cases, these librarians were not a part of the decision-making process that lead to the adoption of the multiple-scheme arrangement at their institution, but each was versed in the reasons behind the current arrangement.

Data for this paper were gathered in a series of interviews conducted between November 1993 and January 1994. Initial leads to libraries using more than one system of classification were gathered from an inquiry on AUTOCAT (an electronic cataloging discussion group accessible over the Internet) as well as from the author's personal knowledge and professional contacts within the library science field. This paper is an anecdotal introductory look into some of the reasons that multiple classification schemes have been used and the various situations which made the use of multiple schemes the most viable option. Given the method of information gathering utilized, this paper cannot claim to be a comprehensive study of the breadth of reasons why multiple classification schemes have been used or of the total number of libraries using multiple schemes. Also, because all of the librarians interviewed work in open-stack libraries in the United States, the situations described may not be relevant in other contexts.

SURVEY OF LIBRARIES
USING MULTIPLE CLASSIFICATION SCHEMES

The institutions that have intentionally adopted multiple classification schemes can be categorized as falling into one of three major groups. The first is composed of libraries that choose to shelve their government documents or technical reports by preassigned numbers. The second includes libraries that retain DDC for some materials, and LCC for other materials. The third category is comprised of libraries that implemented additional schemes when it became apparent that the existing classification scheme in use did not adequately cover the library's needs.

Libraries Using Government Documents or Report Numbers in Addition to Their Regular Classification Scheme

The most common instance of a secondary classification scheme found in many libraries in this country is a secondary shelf arrangement using preassigned government document numbers. Examples are Superintendent of Documents (SuDoc) numbers as well as state and local document numbers. While such shelf numbers are not a true classification scheme, they do allow for the arrangement of documents on the shelf by the agencies (or even the departments within the agencies) promulgating the works, and sometimes further divide by year of issuance and general topic.

Although the reasons for using a standard document number over the regular classification scheme are manifold, the case of the Drake Library at S.U.N.Y. College at Brockport, New York may be typical. According to Joyce Ogden, Senior Cataloger, the Drake Library is a depository library for both federal and state documents. All incoming documents are screened and those deemed of highest importance are placed in the regular classified collection. The remaining federal documents go directly to the shelves with SuDoc numbers. This system works well because documents are delivered with a shipping list which contains the SuDoc numbers for the accompanying documents, allowing library staff to mark and shelve the materials immediately. Library users access the documents collection using the Government Printing Office CD-Rom catalog, which includes the SuDoc numbers. Shelving by SuDoc number eliminates the need for patrons to use an intervening finding tool such as the regular catalog when doing known-item searches. An analogous situation exists for New York State documents. Because paper copies of documents are weeded over time, classifying by provided document numbers also saves staff the time and cost of classifying what is essentially a temporary collection. Both state and federal documents are also issued on microfiche that have the document number already printed in the header, obviating the need for staff to mark them prior to filing. The disadvantage of using document numbers, however, is that all materials owned by the library on a given subject will not sit next to each other on the shelf. The trade-offs are the savings made in staff time spent processing the materials, and the direct correspondence between document numbers listed for the materials in reference sources and the way they are filed on the library shelves.

Similar reasoning supported the decision to split the shelves between classification schemes at the Environmental Protection Agency Region 5 Library in Chicago, Illinois. When Lou W. Tilley was hired as the first Regional Librarian in 1972, she was confronted with stacks of books and documents that needed to be placed on shelves as quickly as possible. The easiest solution was to separate the documents by the report numbers that already appeared on the covers. This obviated the need to catalog each item immediately, yet provided access to the collection. This was also a distinct advantage over using SuDoc numbers that do not appear on the documents. Over time she has found that users, as well as librarians, tend to know the report numbers when searching for a known item, and that they tend to cite the report number more accurately than other bibliographic features such as title or author. Many of the report numbers (for example, those of the United States Environmental Protection Agency and Environment Canada) have breakdowns by issuing agency or sub-bodies thereof, year of publication, and general topics. While filing by report number does not permit optimal shelf browsing and does divide the collection, these disadvantages are again outweighed by the fact that items can be shelved immediately and located later through the online system.

Libraries Retaining DDC in a Collection Otherwise Classified in LCC or Vice Versa

Some libraries, while generally classified in LCC, have opted to keep a portion of their collections in DDC, often even after retrospective reclassification projects have been completed. An example of this is a library which has a juvenile and/or curriculum collection. The rationale of the William Peterson College Library in Wayne, New Jersey, as recounted by Amy Job, Head of Cataloging, proved typical of these types of institutions. These collections function as a working laboratory for education students. By classifying the collections in DDC (often an abridged edition), the students become familiar with the classification scheme they are most likely to encounter in actual school libraries. There are no obvious disadvantages in using both schemes, as only a certain portion of the users use the curriculum or juvenile collections, and these collections are shelved in separate areas of the library. None of the librarians interviewed from such libraries reported any difficulties with training staff to use two classification schemes.

The Graduate Library at the University of Michigan in Ann Arbor is another example of a largely LCC library with small pockets of its collection classed in DDC. According to Bonnie Dede, Head of Special Formats Cataloging, most of these pockets are remnants of a reclassification project begun years ago to move the collection from DDC to LCC. Certain heavily collected literatures (i.e., American, British, French, German, etc.) were not reclassified. The library had implemented DDC in a way that brought out neither the genre nor the time period of a given work of literature. For example, English language literature (that is, all English language works of imagination, irrespective of country of origin) was classified in 828 followed by a Cutter number. The library shelves were therefore strictly an alphabetical arrangement by author within a given language. This system appeared to suit the library users well. Although LCC, if implemented, would not have distinguished genres, it would have broken the given literatures into time periods, and for that reason this portion of the collection was not converted. For smaller literature collections (i.e., south Slavic literatures), however, the conversion was made to LCC. Dede feels that in general this system works well. Since the DDC numbers are so simple and so few, there is no problem in training the staff. Shelvers need special training, however, and students are occasionally confused by the two schemes.

The Transportation Library at Northwestern University (NUTL) in Evanston, Illinois is an example of the opposite of this situation. While the Main Library is classified in DDC, NUTL uses LCC for its collection. According to Mary McCreadie, Head of Technical Services and Assistant Department Head, the reason for this is simple. When founded in the late 1930s, NUTL was not a part of the Main Library, but was owned, funded, and operated by the Traffic Institute, and later by the Transportation Center, both institutions existing under the auspices of the University. From its inception, the collection has been classified using LCC. When the Transportation Center moved to a new building in 1972, it was determined that the new space would not accommodate the library, so the Institute offered the entire collection to the University Library, provided that the collection remain apart from the main collection and that separate staff would continue to run it. For this reason, the collection was neither reclassified to DDC nor physically merged into the general collection. McCreadie states that because NUTL has its own staff of catalogers and serves a specialized clientele, there are no significant drawbacks to using a different scheme from that in the main library, nor are there plans to reclassify the collection or to merge it into the main collection.

Libraries Which Implemented a Second (or More) Scheme when the First Did Not Adequately Cover Present Needs

Sometimes libraries are forced to implement a second scheme when their primary scheme does not adequately cover a certain field of knowledge. This group of libraries proved to be more diverse than those institutions falling into the previous two categories. The historical reasons why the original scheme no longer remained wholly adequate are varied. The long term level of satisfaction with the new scheme(s) has also varied considerably. Some librarians remain content with the split collections, while others feel that the more recently-implemented schemes may have served their purpose well in the past, but over time have become a hinderance to present day librarians and users, and are often retained more for historical or monetary, as opposed to philosophical, reasons.

A common example of this third group of libraries is that of the Library of Rush University (LRU) in Chicago, Illinois. This library was formed during the early 1950s by combining separate medical and nursing libraries which had variously been using LCC and DDC. At this time, it was decided to reclassify the newly created medical library using the National Library of Medicine classification (NLM). According to David Prochazka, Catalog Librarian at LRU, the library holdings in subject areas outside of medicine rendered NLM too restrictive for use throughout the entire collection. The solution was to use LCC for subject areas which could not fit into NLM. Prochazka feels that this is typical of most medical libraries and that because of the similarity between the appearance of NLM and LCC numbers, and the ability of the two schemes to integrate into each other on the library shelves, few problems are caused to the library users. He did not perceive any staff training problems caused by maintaining both schemes.

Another example of this situation is the "Benyon K" schedule developed by Elizabeth V. Benyon at the University of Chicago (UC) during the 1940s. At that time, the Library of Congress had yet to develop its Class K (law) schedules. Because the University of Chicago had already adopted LCC for the remainder of its collection, Benyon devised a LCC-like scheme for law materials using the reserved K notation of LCC and employing the general principles of that system, in addition to a similar arrangement of classes within the schedule and similar terminology. According to Julie R. Stauffer, Assistant to the Director of the D'Angelo Law Library at the University of Chicago, this provided a workable alternative to leaving the collection unclassified and waiting for LC to eventually publish its schedules. Over time, as LC published various portions of its K schedule, UC gradually migrated from the Benyon K scheme to the LCC K class. Currently, all secondary source materials, as well as some primary source materials, are classed in LCC. Because the library does not wish to separate older primary source materials for any one country from newer such works concerning that same country, and because funds have not become available to convert the remaining Benyon K primary source materials to LC, primary source collections have been retained in Benyon K.

Maintaining two systems simultaneously, however, has brought a host of disadvantages to the fore. In particular, similar numbers have different meanings in the two systems. For example, KF is United States law in LC, African law in Benyon K. In order to distinguish between identical class numbers in the two schemes, true LCC numbers are preceded by a double 'X.' This means the users must be trained to be aware of the double 'X,' and special maps and signs had to be made to direct them to appropriate areas in the stacks. It also means that class numbers assigned by the

Library of Congress cannot be used on materials being added to the Benyon K section of the collection, adding to staff time for the processing of materials. Further, the Benyon schedules are not being updated which creates problems in certain segments of the classification, especially in areas of political fluidity such as Eastern Europe. One advantage of Benyon K, and the reason that Stauffer believes it will be used indefinitely, is that, unlike LCC, which arranges legal periodicals in alphabetical order by main entry without regard to country treated in the periodical, Benyon K distinguishes by country in many instances.

The library at Princeton University in Princeton, New Jersey is another example of a library that continues to use a locally developed scheme. The Richardson Classification, created by Ernest Cushing Richardson around the turn of the century while he was employed as a librarian at Princeton, is a numeric scheme ranging from 0000-0999 and functioning akin to DDC. Richardson's scheme was initially adopted for the entire library, but over time, the majority of the collection was reclassified with the exception of the Near Eastern materials (and, until recently, classics materials). Today, according to David Johnson, Leader, Slavic/Germanic Cataloging Team, a select range of topics by Arab and Persian authors is still classified in Richardson classification. While the library would prefer that all materials were classified in one scheme, faculty involved in Near Eastern studies enjoy having materials in their discipline shelved together, so the Richardson classification will remain in use for the time being. Library administration was able to convince the classicists to allow the classical materials to be reclassified by agreeing to create a special location within the library for these works. Because there is only a select population using the materials still classed by the Richardson system, user training does not seem to be a problem. There are, however, problems of staff training in dealing with two classification schemes.

The Music Library of Northwestern University Library (NUML) is another example of a library adopting a second scheme because the one in place did not adequately serve the requirements of the library. As stated above, Northwestern University Library is primarily a DDC based collection. Such was also the case in the Music Library until Don Roberts, current head of the Music Library, accepted this position in the late 1960s. Along with many other librarians contemplating conversion from DDC to LCC at that time, he identified several problems created by DDC which adversely affected the music collection. Among these is the fact that DDC did not distinguish between printed books and musical scores. To circumvent this problem, catalogers had been adding an "M" to the beginning of the call numbers on scores and shelving them separately. Further, as applied at NUML, classification numbers could not adequately bring out the facets of geographic location and time period, resulting in works about music from different places and eras being shelved alongside each other. Finally, the class numbers in DDC (and the associated Cutter numbers) tend to grow to great lengths, making location of materials and maintenance of shelves extremely difficult as most scores are physically rather thin. In general, Roberts sees only positive results from this decision to switch to LCC. Since the Music Library had been housed apart from the main collection since it was established in 1945, conversion from one scheme to the other did not greatly affect the general collection. Incoming students are introduced to the Music Library in orientation tours and classes which are separate from those given by the main library. Because the material housed in NUML is by nature based on only one topic (and hence only in LCC class M), students do not seem to have trouble switching from the main collection's DDC numbers to the LCC numbers in the music collection. Initially, music cataloging staff needed to be trained in the new system, but since these catalogers work solely on this collection there are no training problems remaining.

Other libraries with music collections have taken even more radical approaches in finding the optimum shelf arrangement for their materials. The library at the State University of New York at Buffalo classifies its books in LCC and uses SuDoc numbers for their documents collection. The Music Library, however, classifies scores in the Dickinson Classification. This classification was developed by George Sherman Dickinson for the Vassar College Music Library. A typical call number consists of four lines. As explained by Carol Bradley, Associate Director of the Music Library, in her manual on this scheme:

> The scheme is mnemonic. In division 5, for instance, 52 is the number for string chamber music (5 denoting chamber music, 2 denoting strings); 53 is wind chamber music (5 for chamber music, 3 for winds). The system requires conventional titles, constant species title indications (i.e., su for suite throughout the classification), and constant Cutter numbers.
>
> The average call number consists of four lines. . . . The first is the division number; this denotes the original medium of the work. The second line consists of the composer's Cutter number. The third line describes the piece in hand: a species title indication, such as ov for overture; the first letter of the title, if distinctive; an opus or thematic catalog number. The fourth line is the first letter of the editor's or publisher's name.

Hence: 52   string chamber music
       B39-4   Beethoven Cutter number; 4 players
       (18/1)   opus 18, number 1
       B   Breitkopf & Härtel edition[3]

This gives the user a complete and concise description of the item without the need to examine it. According to Bradley, this classification scheme is superior to LCC for the classification of scores because it is strictly oriented toward musical compositions. There is only one place within the scheme into which any given score can go. Non-musical considerations, such as purchasing fund, place of publication, etc., are not considered. Bradley considers the scheme easy to learn for both employees and users, and because of its dissimilarity to LCC the numbers are rarely confused with each other.

A similar approach has been taken by the Paducah Community College Library in Paducah, Kentucky. Here, DDC is used for books, LCC for audio-visual materials, and ANSCR (Alpha-Numeric System for the Classification of Recordings) for sound recordings. According to Ken Bradshaw, Associate Librarian for Reference and Technical Services, it is possible that at some point in the future the book collection might be converted to LCC, but there are no immediate plans to do this. Initially, the audio-visual and sound recordings collections were shelved by accession number. When the library joined OCLC, however, it was decided to classify these collections as well. LCC was chosen for the audio-visual materials because it was felt that more copy on OCLC would contain LCC class numbers than DDC class numbers, and staff wished to take advantage of these ready-made call numbers. At the same time, it was decided that LCC was not detailed enough for use on the sound recordings. The solution was the adoption of ANSCR.

Similar to Dickinson in that it was developed with one specific medium in mind, ANSCR class numbers are also four lines long. The first line contains an alphabetical letter or letters representing a classification category, the second line contains the first four consecutive letters of a name or word, the third line contains the first letters of the first three key words of a title or the first three consecutive letters of a one word title, and the last line contains the first letter of a performer's surname followed by the last two digits of the recording's commercial record number. An example explained:

B   class number for opera
PUCC   first four letters of "Puccini"
ML   first letters of "Manon Lescaut"
T 17   first letter of "Tebaldi" (soprano on the recording) fol-

lowed by the last digits of the commercial record number
(London 1317)[4]

This system accommodates classical and popular music as well as spoken
word recordings. Bradshaw feels that the reality of using three schemes is
less complicated than it sounds. Because the different formats are all
shelved independently from each other, users must only deal with one
classification scheme per format. During user orientation sessions, all
three schemes are explained. Different catalogers handle the book and
non-book materials, so no one person must master all the schemes.

CONCLUSION

Given the informal method of information gathering used in the preparation of this paper, this discussion cannot be interpreted as being conclu-
sive with respect to the variety of libraries having intentionally implemented multiple classification schemes, nor the number of schemes
currently in use in the United States. What can be drawn from these
interviews, however, is that the use of multiple classification schemes is
not only a viable option but one that is routinely practiced. Further inves-
tigation into this topic would surely result in the identification of more
libraries using multiple schemes, more schemes than those mentioned
here, and more reasons for the use of multiple schemes.

NOTES

1. Margaret Mann, *Introduction to Cataloging and the Classification of Books*,
2nd ed. Chicago: American Library Association, 1943, p. 35.
2. Bohdan S. Wynar, *Introduction to Cataloging and Classification,* 8th ed.
Littleton: Libraries Unlimited, 1992, p. 317.
3. Carol June Bradley, *The Dickinson Classification.* Carlisle: Carlisle Books,
1968, pp. 47-48.
4. Caroline Saheb-Ettaba and Roger B. McFarland, *ANSCR: the Alpha-Numeric
System for Classification of Recordings.* Williamsport: Bro-Dart, 1969, p. 32.

The Reclassification Decision:
Dewey or Library of Congress?

June D. Chressanthis

SUMMARY. This paper describes various reasons why academic libraries have chosen to do or not to do reclassification projects from Dewey to Library of Congress. An historical perspective is provided to assist in making this decision. Arguments for and against both Dewey and Library of Congress are presented from this historical perspective along with modern interpretations. Issues important in planning a reclassification project such as cost, organization of the reclassification team, and the length of the project are also discussed. Implications and ramifications of a reclassification project for staff and patrons, such as disruptions in service and learning new book locations, are also highlighted.

INTRODUCTION

Many academic libraries today are continually evaluating their decisions whether or not to reclassify their Dewey Decimal Classification

June Chressanthis is Assistant Professor and Serials Cataloger at Mississippi State University. She is former Assistant Coordinator of the Reclassification Project at MSU. She holds an AMLS from the University of Michigan and a BS from Purdue University.

Address correspondence to: Mitchell Memorial Library, Mississippi State University, P.O. Box 5408, Mississippi State, MS 39762-5408.

The author gratefully acknowledges editorial assistance from Dr. George Chressanthis.

[Haworth co-indexing entry note]: "The Reclassification Decision: Dewey or Library of Congress?" Chressanthis, June D. Co-published simultaneously in *Cataloging & Classification Quarterly* (The Haworth Press, Inc.) Vol. 19, No. 3/4, 1995, pp. 169-182; and: *Classification: Options and Opportunities* (ed: Alan R. Thomas) The Haworth Press, Inc., 1995, pp. 169-182. Multiple copies of this article/chapter may be purchased from The Haworth Document Delivery Center [1-800-3-HAWORTH; 9:00 a.m. - 5:00 p.m. (EST)].

(DDC) collections into the Library of Congress Classification system (LCC) or to switch to LCC for new acquisitions. Some libraries are using DDC for all or part of their classification. Other libraries may have a split collection where DDC was used prior to a certain date and then LCC was started. This paper will highlight several reasons why libraries have chosen to do or not to do reclassification, the planning involved in such projects, and problems and ramifications encountered in staying with DDC or switching to LCC.

BACKGROUND

An historical review of the literature is necessary in order to gain an understanding of the current discussion involving reclassification projects. The few articles published in the 1950s dealt with the DDC and its various classification relocations and alterations.[1] The majority of libraries were using DDC, though the trend to LCC was gaining popularity by the mid-1950s. However, some librarians felt that LCC was unsuitable for small collections. Even so, small community college libraries and large academic research libraries operated with a combination of schemes depending on the existence or suitability of a LCC or DDC class amenable to each particular library.

The literature published in the 1960s presents a concentration of articles that dealt with reclassification decisions.[2] This prevalence of articles may have been due to librarians' dissatisfaction with the 1965 publication of the 17th edition of the DDC. This edition included some 700 relocations of numbers and a thorough alteration of the psychology schedule.

Fewer articles were published in the 1970s regarding reclassification.[3] However most of the articles reflected that libraries were still doing reclassification projects, though one brief article cited a library choosing to ignore a consultant's reclassification recommendations.[4]

More articles were written about retrospective conversion projects than reclassification projects during the 1980s.[5] These articles described the value of retrospective conversion projects and the problems encountered through the desire to implement an online catalog. A contribution by Dean describes a reclassification project in an automated environment.[6]

Articles written on reclassification projects are infrequent during the 1990s. This does not mean, however, that academic libraries are not implementing reclassification projects as the author has been in contact with librarians from around the country who have been or are in charge of such projects.[7] In addition, the issues of reclassification and classification in general have been discussed in recent years on AUTOCAT. AUTOCAT, available through Internet, is a discussion group in which issues pertaining to all aspects of cataloging are examined. Chressanthis described the steps involved in a reclassification project.[8]

All of the cited articles offer justification as to why an academic library should either stay with DDC or switch to LCC for new acquisitions. This rationale is carried further in explaining if a project is necessary to reclassify the remaining DDC collection. The next section will discuss various reasons by which librarians have based their reclassification decisions.

THE RECLASSIFICATION DECISION

In order to understand the justifications librarians use today, it may be useful to know why LCC was adopted or not adopted in the past. Many of the basic reasons employed since the 1950s concerning reclassification are still valid today. These reasons, along with contemporary interpretations, are presented below. They cannot be generalized to all libraries. Depending upon each library's unique situation some explanations may not be apropos to any one library. Also, what one library may argue as a reason to adopt LCC, another may use as a reason against LCC.

One major reason many librarians switched to LCC from DDC was the various classification relocations between new editions of DDC. The major relocations and alterations found in the 17th edition and succeeding editions of the DDC schedules resulted in the scattering of works on the same subject unless librarians reclassified them into the new number. To compensate for continuous relocations, many librarians developed local practices. These practices eventually resulted in problems with training new staff members on the unique in-house scheme, being unable to accept DDC call numbers from LC printed cards, and imprecision of notation leading to patron confusion.[9] Today, relocation problems continue to be an issue as DDC call numbers from LC-contributed records found in OCLC cannot be accepted without first conforming to the local practice. However, LCC has also relocated different class numbers to allow for the classification of new areas of knowledge, though to a lesser degree than DDC. This is not really a problem because "the subject divisions of LC can expand indefinitely without destroying any artificial philosophic organization of knowledge".[10]

The previously stated issues relate to another major complaint against DDC. Before the advent of the national bibliographic databases, academic libraries often took advantage of the printed cards available from the Library of Congress. The complete LCC call number appeared on 85-90% of the cards, while only 30-50% of the cards had DDC numbers. The DDC numbers were incomplete in that they lacked the cutter number and librarians often had to shorten them for local practices.[11] Today, this problem still exists using OCLC. Wajenberg relates that the University of Illinois at Urbana-Champaign, which is still a DDC library, "finds records for about 85% of our new acquisitions on OCLC. However, many of the records have LC call numbers rather than Dewey. In those cases, our staff must supply the Dewey classification. Much of the LC cataloging found in OCLC has Dewey numbers, but of course they are the complete class numbers. These often have to be shortened to match our local practices."[12] Stamm echoes this concern at Northwestern University. She states, "Our catalogers must take the time to create Dewey numbers for much of our collections. LC supplies suggested Dewey numbers for most of its cataloging (this was not always the case), but we must create Dewey numbers when we use OCLC copy or do original cataloging."[13]

This leads into another argument for LCC which ties the preceding two together. Many librarians have believed that the Library of Congress offered stabilization, standardization and efficiency in cataloging and classification practices. If the Library of Congress was accepted as the "authority" for entry and classification, then the individual library would not need to spend the time required to recatalog and reclassify every title.[14] The entire LCC call number appearing on 85-90% of the available cataloging records could be used without any checking in the shelflist as the likelihood of another title existing with the same call number was negligible. An exception, of course, could exist with the possible conflict of titles which had received local original cataloging. Accepting the LCC call number allowed materials to move through the cataloging department much faster and more economically than when using DDC. This point was especially valid as libraries enjoyed an increase in acquisition budgets during the 1960-70s.

Conversely however, this occurrence of increased acquisition budgets was also used as an argument against switching to LCC. Librarians felt that with an increase in materials coming through the cataloging department, there would be little time to reclassify older material if LCC were adopted for new acquisitions.[15] As a result a split collection would be developed which was felt to be a disservice to patrons and would require cataloging, reference, and circulation departments to run dual systems. "If LC is adopted for new acquisitions, the library may be unable to resolve economically the problems of reclassifying retrospective collections."[16]

Another view of this argument found some librarians stating that a reclassification project had to be done in order to bring about a unified collection "as a dual classification system seemed incompatible with one of the functions of a library, namely to present an organized collection, consistent in its ordering."[17] This would also allow the library to evaluate past cataloging practices and the collection. The savings in cost and time accrued due to processing new acquisitions with LCC could account for the time and money to do a reclassification project.[18] Taylor and Anderson state that during a two year period, while using LCC, a 15,000 volume backlog was eliminated while 45,000 new titles were cataloged and 27,000 items were reclassified.[19] Nevertheless, some librarians felt that the one-time cost of doing a reclassification project was too prohibitive.[20]

Still other arguments for adopting LCC included the notion that this scheme was more suitable for larger libraries because it was flexible, expandable, and had shorter class numbers. Smaller libraries reasoned that DDC's broader class scheme and mnemonic features lent itself to the smaller collection. Librarians also stated that the academic library should use the same scheme found in high school libraries so the beginning higher education student would be familiar with the scheme. The literature shows that these philosophies were followed, but there were also cases when larger academic libraries stayed with DDC and smaller libraries switched to LCC.

Other libraries have adopted LCC for a part of their collections or departmental libraries when it was felt DDC did not give proper coverage. Northwestern University started using LCC in the late 1960s for its Music Library. LCC was adopted for the Law and Transportation Libraries in the 1970s. The University of Illinois at Urbana-Champaign Library has used LCC to classify some of its departmental libraries: the "map collection (since the 1950's), Asian language material, printed music and sound recordings, new acquisitions of books about music (the publication of the 20th edition of DDC in 1989 completely revised the music classification so LCC was adopted then; older titles still remain in DDC), and the law library was reclassified as each of the law schedules was published." Wajenburg goes on to say that, "I feel our students and faculty are served better by our sticking with Dewey than they would be if we had a collection permanently divided into Dewey and LC sections. Also, in several subject areas, notably science and technology, I believe that Dewey provides a better classification than LC."[21] An opposing opinion was given by Varjabedian as she states, "We are a scientific and technical research library. Many of our patrons are scientists who had used LC-classed university libraries and were more familiar with LC. The LC classification scheme seemed more suited to our literature–a lot of scientific and technical fields are crunched into small areas in Dewey and you don't get a breakdown without using very long strings of decimals."[22]

Many libraries thought it a good idea to "join the bandwagon" and start using LCC when joining OCLC. "The economies produced by LC standardization were increased by the introduction of MARC tapes which were readily available in OCLC."[23] OCLC offered easy access to cataloging and classification decisions by the Library of Congress. "The OCLC record provided a cataloging record adaptable to local policies, further proving that standardization and centralization could streamline cataloging and classification functions."[24] The advent of such utilities and the continuous growth in the number of titles accessible allow many libraries to have easy access to LCC call numbers.

Many libraries started reclassification projects as part of a retrospective conversion project when holdings for older titles were added to OCLC. In the case of MSU, a reclassification project was not started until many years later due to a lack in staff and funds. Today, OCLC offers many services to assist the library in its reclassification project.[25] MSU contracted with OCLC to reclassify over 175,000 monographic DDC titles. Inks states that OCLC at one time was considering a pricing structure where a fee would be charged every time a record was examined. Inks further states that each record would have needed to be looked at twice, once to get the call number and the second time to call it back up again after the call number was checked in the shelflist and the number revised to fit into local practices. They decided to accept the LCC call number so only one charge would be incurred. This pricing structure was not adopted by OCLC at that time.[26] Today, however, OCLC does charge a fee for calling up the record each time. However, the extra charge can be eliminated by using OCLC's cataloging software CATME Plus. This software allows the user to capture the retrieved record from an OCLC search and store the record in another computer file. The file can then be used to access the record without garnering any additional searching fees.

Libraries may find themselves joining consortia or cooperative ventures where LCC is the favored classification scheme.[27] Again, the standardization offered by the Library of Congress in both its cataloging and classification can make these ventures very profitable in terms of efficient use of staff and time. A less frequently cited reason for libraries adopting LCC was by the recommendation of a consultant, an accrediting agency, or a task force. As mentioned earlier, the Los Angeles Public Library ignored a consultant's recommendation to change.[4] Purdue University decided to stay with DDC after a task force recommended a switch to LCC.[28] Still, another reason for switching to LCC may be merging two libraries together or the planning of branch or departmental libraries where classification and cataloging will be done at the main library as was the case at MSU.

Obviously, there were many arguments and justifications for adopting LCC. However, many librarians presented valid reasons for not switching to LCC. As mentioned earlier, LCC did present the classifier with relocations in various class numbers. This resulted in problems when accepting call numbers from the LC printed cards without first checking the updated LCC schedules. LC reprinted cards with obsolete call numbers until the card was revised for other reasons. This led to a scattering of books on the same subject.[29] Other concerns raised by librarians included a lack of a comprehensive guide to interpret the schedules and tables. Some catalogers also did not agree with LCC's rationale of cuttering and the arrangement of translations and other editions in relation to the original work. There was also a lack of cutter numbers in PZ3 and PZ4, and a frequent necessity to do original classification when LCC classed a title within a series.[30] The 1968 publication of Immroth's *A Guide to the Library of Congress Classification* addressed, at least in part, the issue of a lack of a comprehensive guide to the LCC schedules.[31] Many of the other concerns expressed by librarians were also addressed in Immroth's guide. As the individual schedules were developed and expanded, indexes were printed in each schedule. In addition, subject searches can be done on OCLC or in-house systems to locate titles on similar topics with the proper call number being devised from that point. The PZ schedules are no longer valid with titles in this area being reclassified to the proper literature schedule. Concerning the treatment of series, each library should establish a series authority file to handle this problem. No matter what classification scheme is used, some amount of original classification will need to take place.

ADDITIONAL CONSIDERATIONS

Obviously, there are many reasons for considering a reclassification project. Librarians should investigate and consider all available methods and their associated costs when conducting a reclassification project.[32] Finn suggests that for conversion projects, "the quantity of work, time frame for the project, type of materials and languages, a concept of local cataloging standards, and pertinent local data" be analyzed before a decision is made concerning whether a project can be done in-house or by a vendor.[33] These points will influence the cost of a project regardless of who does the reclassification.

Even if a vendor is employed, the library must still relabel, shift, and reshelve the reclassified volumes. The goal of the MSU project was to reclassify over 175,000 DDC titles. All the titles in the project had been cataloged prior to 1976, LCC was used for all classification after 1976, which probably meant previous cataloging would have to be updated to meet current in-house standards. MSU decided to use a vendor because of the size of the project and the age of the material involved. The existing technical services staff was too small to handle both daily cataloging functions and those of a special project. Moreover, the use of a vendor would allow for more efficient use of one-time funds.

Once the decision to reclassify the DDC collection has been made, a great deal of planning must take place. Understanding the decisions made in each library's past classification history and the present situation must be examined to develop and implement a sound project.

PLANNING

Planning is an integral part of any library project. Decisions must be made which will affect the entire library staff. In order for each department to feel a part of the project and to develop a good attitude about the project, a representative from each department should be involved in the planning who can report back to his/her unit. There should be one individual who acts as the Project Coordinator and as the contact person with the vendor.

Depending on what departments are involved, there will probably be individuals in charge of various phases of the project. During the reclassification project at MSU, one staff member of the Technical Services Department was in charge of the entire project except for weeding which was done by the Reference Department. Technical Services did all of the relabeling, shifting, and reshelving of the entire monographic DDC collection with the help of many library student assistants. A cataloger was placed in charge of relabeling, with another in charge of shifting, and another for pulling books to be relabeled. In other libraries, the Circulation Department or reference staff may be in charge of some of these activities, or, instead of the entire technical services staff being involved, the "Reclass Team" may be only a subset of the Cataloging Department.

Preliminary planning should include an inventory of the DDC collection. This step should be done before making the final reclassification decision. If the DDC collection is too large, then a reclassification project may not be feasible. This is a crucial step if a vendor bases its fees on the number of titles to convert and the labels that will need to be printed. The cost of the project should be based on the inventory count to determine a realistic figure. MSU's vendor printed spine labels for each copy and volume denoted on the shelflist card. During the inventory, any copies or volumes which were found to be missing or were to be withdrawn were marked accordingly on the shelflist card. The vendor would not make labels for any of these items. If all the copies/volumes were missing or withdrawn the shelflist card would not be sent to the vendor as it was undesirable to accrue charges for titles which were no longer in the collection.

Preliminary planning should also include the ordering of supplies. Such supplies could include label protectors, inventory flags, barcodes, and shipping supplies for sending shelflist cards to the vendor. Plans should take into consideration the length of time it takes to pull, relabel, and reshelve books so an estimate can be made on the number of student workers to hire. From MSU's experience, shifting and reshelving took much longer relative to pulling and relabeling books.

Regardless if public service staff are involved in the project, they must be kept informed of the progress of the project. They can provide assistance in planning the order of reclassifying the collection. MSU started with the Reference Collection as it was thought these titles were likely to be the most heavily used DDC titles. This would also give the reference librarians a chance to get used to these tools being shelved in a new location. Advice was given by reference librarians on the order of reclassification for the general collection. The reference staff kept the project coordinator advised of any class projects requiring use of a part of the collection. Plans could then be made accordingly as to when this section would be reclassified. The public service staff members need to know the progress of the reclassification project so they can assist patrons in the location of materials. Initially, the project began with reclassifying material from the 000's and moving forward. It was soon discovered that shifting could be facilitated if the project shifted to working with books in the 999's and moving backward. The LCC collection could then be shifted into the vacated shelves where the higher DDC class numbers had been shelved.

The staff in the Circulation Department was kept apprised of the project even though they were not directly involved in the project. The circulation staff was asked to route to the Cataloging Department any DDC books returned with call numbers in the DDC sections which had already been reclassified instead of reshelving them. The books would then be reclassified in a subroutine of the main workflow of the project and then reshelved in the LCC section.

The teaching faculty should also be kept apprised of the project. In the project at MSU, faculty were asked to review materials that had been marked for withdrawal during the weeding project. Faculty were also asked to return any DDC books that they may have checked out so these books could be reclassified.

Decisions should also be made as to the level of recataloging. If an outside vendor is used, these specifications will be written into the contract. Whether a vendor is used or not, a lot of recataloging of the bibliographic record will increase the cost of the project. MSU required their vendor to edit records to reflect their in-house cataloging practices. LCC call numbers were accepted without question from member and Library of Congress records. If the entire project is done in-house, a procedure will need to be established as to who will do the recataloging.

If the reclassified books need to be barcoded, an additional workflow will need to be implemented. The best time to barcode is probably when the books are being relabeled. However, this will lengthen the turn around time for getting the books back on the shelves. There should be two barcodes with the same number, one for the book and another for the shelflist card. The barcode on the shelflist card can then be used during the linking phase. MSU decided, perhaps unwisely, to postpone barcoding the reclassified collection until a later project because funding of the reclassification project did not include the added costs of personnel and time involved in barcoding. This created hardships for the circulation department as the reclassified books had to be checked out "on the fly."

RAMIFICATIONS

Despite all the planning done to implement a project of this magnitude, there are always unforeseen problems in the actual running of the project as well as impacts the project has on library staff and patrons. For example, circulation staff could be faced with barcoding at the time of checkout. In addition, MSU was switching to an online system at the time of reclassification. The circulation staff thus had to deal with both a manual and automated check out system. The DDC items were on the manual, but when the books were reclassified they were then in the online system. The staff also were on the receiving end of patron complaints concerning the dissarray of the collection during the reclassification project. These complaints were from faculty and students alike. Most faculty using the DDC collection knew where their materials were shelved, but faced a challenge in learning the new LCC locations. Naturally, the library staff also had to learn where everything was in the new LCC locations. Even the location of material in the LCC collection changes as books are shifted to make room for the reclassified titles.

The timeliness of getting the books relabeled when the new record appears in the online catalog is practically impossible. The online catalog provided the LCC call number for the patron, but the material was likely to still be in DDC. Every effort should be made to keep any disruption of service to a minimum but it cannot be avoided entirely. It is too time consuming to pull books to be relabeled and keep them in order so patrons can search by call number. MSU pulled the DDC books in order by the DDC shelflist. This made efficient use of time as the shelflist card and the corresponding book could be easily matched. The shelflist card with attached LCC spine labels were placed inside the front cover of each volume. The pulled books were stacked in random order on nearby shelves and the floor. The order of the books at this time was not important as the new LCC call number would result in an entirely different arrangement. However, efforts were made to keep multivolume sets and copies together. The books were then transported via booktruck to the relabeling areas as needed. Once the books were relabelled, student workers then put them in LCC call number order in a holding section of the stacks. Other student workers then reshelved from the holding area into the permanent LCC stacks.

Even the best plan cannot always successfully manage staff morale. As the project wears on, staff will begin to feel uncomfortable about giving less attention to their normal duties. Staff members who normally work well with each other can easily develop short tempers and lose their sense of humor while working in close quarters and performing fairly dull tasks. This can be partially handled with continuous demonstrations of appreciation for the work already done. The perceptive manager will gain respect from the team if the tense times can be lessened. Staff can be rewarded for beating deadlines or celebrating earmarks of the project.

CONCLUSION

Each library must evaluate the advantages and disadvantages in undertaking a reclassification project. The decision should be made based on the historical cataloging practices of that library and its mission for the future. If a collection is split between LCC and DDC, a reclassification project may be worthwhile. In the case of MSU, as an example presented in this paper, a significant split between LCC and DDC existed. The decision to pursue a reclassification project in this case was made to provide better service to patrons. While this decision by MSU was made with confidence, other libraries have reached the conclusion that DDC provides better access to their collections. At the same time other libraries successfully base their service on both LCC and DDC. Though this paper has not answered the question of whether a library should invest time and resources in a reclassification project, it is hoped that the trade-offs elaborated in this paper provide librarians some means to resolve this question.

NOTES

1. Eleanor Hungerford, "The 16th Edition: Meeting Consumer Demand," *Journal of Cataloging and Classification* 11, no. 3 (July 1955):145-152. Thelma Eaton, "Classification in College and University Libraries," *College and Research Libraries* 16, no. 2 (April 1955):168-175. John H. Moriarty, "Plea for Management Study of Partial Reclassification Problems," *Journal of Cataloging and Classification* 12, no. 1 (January 1956):32-35. Maurice F. Tauber, "Partial Reclassification," *Journal of Cataloging and Classification* 12, no. 4 (October 1956):221-225.

2. Daniel Gore, "The 50 cent Change to Library of Congress," *College & University Business* 44, no. 5 (May 1968):109-111. Howard Downey, "Dewey or LC?" *Library Journal* 89, no. 11 (June 1, 1965):2292-2293. Edward Evans, "Dewey: Necessity or Luxury?" *Library Journal* 91, no. 16 (September 15, 1966):4038-4046. Daniel Gore, "A Neglected Topic: The Cost of Classification," *Library Journal* 89, no. 11 (June 1, 1964):2287-2291. Desmond Taylor, "Reclassification: A Case for LC in the Academic Library," *PNLA Quarterly* 29 (July 1965):243-249. Richard M. Dougherty, "The Realities of Reclassification," *College & Research Libraries* 28, no. 4 (July 1967):258-262. William E. Connors, "Reclassification at the University of Maryland," *Library Resources & Technical Services* 11, no. 2 (Spring 1967):233-242. James E. Gaines, "Reclassification in the Libraries of the Great Lakes Colleges Association," *College & Research Libraries* 29, no. 4 (July 1968):292-296. Jean M. Perreault, ed., *Reclassification: Rationale and Problems, Proceedings of a Conference on Reclassification, April 4-6, 1968* (College Park, MD: School of Library and Information Services, University of Maryland, 1968). Theodore Samore, ed., *Problems in Library Classification: Dewey 17 and Conversion* (New York: R.R. Bowker, 1968).

3. Norman E. Tannis, "The Pros and Cons of Reclassifying to the Library of Congress System," *Kansas Library Bulletin* 39, no. 1 (1970):7-9. Doris R. Brown and Duane Mackie, "Putting the 'LC' in OCLC–Illinois Reclassification on OCLC," *Wilson Library Bulletin* 53, no. 8 (April 1979):570-573. Bert Phipps, "Reclassification: A Case for Conversion," *South Dakota Library Bulletin* 57, no. 4 (Special ed. 1971):257-271. Robert L. Mowery, "The 'Trend to LC' in College and University Libraries," *Library Resources & Technical Services* 19, no. 4 (Fall 1975):389-397. Gerry M. Taylor and James F. Anderson, "It Will Cost More Tomorrow," *Library Resources & Technical Services* 16, no. 1 (Winter 1972):82-92. Delia Mattison, "Library Classification Conversion," *Arkansas Libraries* 36, no. 2 (June 1979):14-15. Cleo Treadway, "Reclassification: The Tusculum Way," *Tennessee Libraries* 28 (Winter 1976):10-15.

4. "Reclassification at LAPL: Staff Says Thumbs Down," in "News" *Library Journal* 96, no. 3 (July 1971):2253.

5. Jon Drabenstott, ed., "Retrospective Conversion: Issues and Perspectives," *Library Hi Tech* 4 (Summer 1986):105-120. Carolyn A. Johnson, "Retrospective Conversion of Three Library Collections," *Information Technology and Libraries* 1, no. 2 (June 1982):133-139. Kathleen Joyce Kruger, "MARC Tags and Retrospective Conversion: The Editing Process," *Information Technology and Libraries* 4, no. 1 (March 1985):53-57. Richard Boss, "Retrospective Conversion: Investing in the Future," *Wilson Library Bulletin* 59, no. 3 (November 1984):173-178, 238. Richard E. Asher, "Retrospective Conversion of Bibliographic Records," *Catholic Library World* 54 (November 1982):155-161. Maureen D. Finn, "How to Prepare for Retrospective Conversion," *Bulletin of the American Society for Information Science* 13 (May 4, 1987):23-24.

6. Barbara C. Dean, "Reclassification in an Automated Environment," *Cataloging & Classification Quarterly* 52, no. 2 (Winter 1984):1-11.

7. Ling-Yuh W. Pattie, electronic mail (email) message to the author, 13 December 1993. Kathy Varjabedian, email message to the author, 20 December 1993. Gail A. Hitchcock, email message to the author, 15 December 1993 and 4 January 1994.

8. June D. Chressanthis, "The Mechanics of a Reclassification Project," *Technical Services Quarterly* 9, no. 4 (1992):19-28.

9. Dean, p.2. Conners, p. 233.

10. Taylor, p. 247.

11. Phipps, p. 258.

12. Arnold Wajenberg, email message to the author, 17 December 1993.

13. Andrea Stamm, email message to the author, 7 January 1994.

14. Conners, p. 233.

15. Taylor, p.2 43. Gaines, p. 296.

16. Dougherty, p. 259.

17. Elton E. Shell, "A Rationale for Using the Library of Congress System in Reclassification," in *Reclassification: Rationale and Problems, Proceedings of a Conference on Reclassification, University of Maryland College Park, April 4-6, 1968* (College Park, MD: School of Library and Information Services, University of Maryland, 1968):30-55.

18. Dougherty, p. 258. Gore, p. 109. Taylor, p. 244. Gaines, p. 293.

19. Taylor and Anderson, p. 83.

20. Eaton, p. 173. Downey, p. 2293.

21. Stamm, email message. Wajenberg, email message.

22. Varjabedian, email message.

23. Brown and Mackie, p. 571.

24. *Ibid.,* p. 572.

25. "Conversion and Contract Cataloging Services," *OCLC Newsletter* no. 205 (September/October 1993):9-20.

26. Cordelia Inks, email message to the author, 22 and 30 November 1993.

27. Treadway, p.10. Phipps, p.257.

28. Jan Addison, email message to the author, 28 December 1993.

29. James E. Gaines, "Moderator's Comments," in *Reclassification: Rationale and Problems, Proceedings of a Conference on Reclassification April 4-6, 1968* (College Park, MD: School of Library and Information Services, University of Maryland, 1968):112-115.

30. Gaines, "Reclassification," p. 295. Shell, p. 54.

31. John Phillip Immroth, *A Guide to the Library of Congress Classification* (Littleton, CO: Libraries Unlimited, 1968).

32. Gaines, "Reclassification," p.295.

33. Maureen Finn, "How to Plan Conversion and Contract Cataloging Projects," *OCLC Newsletter* 205 (September/October 1993):10-11.

Reclassification Revisited:
An Automated Approach

Ling-yuh W. (Miko) Pattie

SUMMARY. Many libraries undertook reclassification projects during the 1960s and 1970s, and some of them are still struggling to live with split collections due to lack of resources to complete their projects. The University of Kentucky Library is one that has reconciled itself to this predicament until plans begin to take shape for a new library building. An automated local system, NOTIS, presents new found capabilities to perform automated reclassification efficiently and cost-effectively. Retrospective conversion of all Dewey titles will precede reclassification. The paper describes how the decision was made, the planning that is in place, the method to be used, and the issues that need to be resolved before the project is implemented. It is hoped that other libraries may find this helpful should opportunities arise for a reclassification project.

INTRODUCTION

As one of the charter members of the Southeastern Library Network (SOLINET), the University of Kentucky Libraries began online cataloging using OCLC in 1974. Given the availability of LC MARC records and predominantly LC-classed member records on OCLC, the library decided to switch from the Dewey Decimal Classification (DDC) to the Library of

---

Ling-yuh W. (Miko) Pattie is Assistant Director for Technical Services, University of Kentucky Libraries, 301 King Library North, Lexington, KY 40506.

[Haworth co-indexing entry note]: "Reclassification Revisited: An Automated Approach." Pattie, Ling-yuh W. (Miko). Co-published simultaneously in *Cataloging & Classification Quarterly* (The Haworth Press, Inc.) Vol. 19, No. 3/4, 1995, pp. 183-193; and: *Classification: Options and Opportunities* (ed: Alan R. Thomas) The Haworth Press, Inc., 1995, pp. 183-193. Multiple copies of this article/chapter may be purchased from The Haworth Document Delivery Center [1-800-3-HAWORTH; 9:00 a.m. - 5:00 p.m. (EST)].

183

Congress Classification (LCC) beginning June 21, 1978. Not unlike other libraries that have undertaken reclassification projects during 1960s and 1970s, the library looked to LCC for a more efficient way of processing the rapidly-growing collection (as validated by Joe Hewitt's Survey of OCLC members[1]) and a better alignment with other ARL counterparts to facilitate interlibrary cooperation. With the funding of $200,000 for a small-scale reclassification project, the library decided to tackle the reference collection first and then reclassify the rest of the collection whenever more funding materialized. The project was implemented in 1978. It was realized that the library would have split collections, and it was believed that library users would become adjusted to shelf-browsing in both DDC and LCC collections.

During these past fifteen years, the staff in Technical Services had attempted to integrate reclassification into the retrospective conversion process as there remains a sizable collection not reflected in our local bibliographic database. Yet this limited reclassification activity had to be halted due to the compacted stack area and the inability to conduct major shifting in a very cramped building. Both library users and staff seem reconciled to the fact that split collections are here to stay.

RECLASSIFICATION DECISION

In 1991, when the new university President, Dr. Charles T. Wethington, took office and announced that a new library building would be his top priority, the academic community was gratified and rallied to this cause. With an effective fund raising campaign, Dr. Wethington was able to convince the Kentucky legislature in 1992 to authorize the university to undertake the design stage with the private funds already raised. Now that the design of the new library building has been completed, the President is poised to work with the legislature this spring to obtain state funding for the construction of the building.

Exulted over the new-found status of being the center of attention, the library initiated a planning process to incorporate state-of-the-art information technology and client-centered service components into the new building. Ever cognizant of the significance of user input, our library director, Paul A. Willis, conducted a series of forums for faculty and students on the building. Much to our surprise, the issue of reclassification and conversion came up consistently and caught the administration's attention. Coupled with strong support from the Vice-President for Information Systems, Gene Williams, to whom the library reports, the library was able to include a combined retrospective conversion and reclassification project as one of the top priority items to be funded in the 1994-96 biennium budget. The objective is to be able to move into the new building with a complete bibliographic database and a single, coherent classification system.

TARGET COLLECTIONS

The University of Kentucky Library has been a NOTIS library since 1991, having migrated from the LS/2000 system. Prior to implementing the LS/2000 system, the library contracted with OCLC for a major conversion project and ended with approximately 84,000 titles marked as problems. These DDC titles contain mostly foreign language and special collections material, and some items with incomplete bibliographic data. In addition, we estimated there were around 25,000 serials to be converted. They are either dead, cancelled, or linked to current receipts and were not qualified to be included in previous serial conversion grants. These 109,000 titles, the 84,000 problem titles and the 25,000 serials, comprise the target collection for conversion.

The attempt to arrive at an estimate for the entire DDC collection for reclassification purposes was more problematic than for the conversion. As not all items are contained in NOTIS, we took a snapshot on March 16, 1993 of NOTIS copy statements and came up with 479,348 copies with classification code "D" (DDC titles). With volume estimates for both the stacks and periodicals area, balanced with NOTIS DDC copy statements and unconverted titles, we came up with a total of 720,000 volumes as the target collection for reclassification.

RESEARCH

In reviewing what has been done in other libraries for a reclassification project, we failed to find any that utilized a local online system's capability to perform such a task. As Barbara C. Dean so aptly observed in 1984:

> –one project that replaced reclassification in popularity, automation, may in time lead us back to an interest in reclassification because projects involving changes in bibliographic records can be done so much more cheaply and quickly when working with an electronic record than with cards.[2]

The most recent published report by Suzanne Massonneau from the University of Vermont of a two-year computer-based reclassification project[3] provided a detailed description of how a library seized a unique opportunity to barcode and reclassify the collection prior to the implementation of an automated system. We learned from their experience about the use of a printed shelflist to aid local LC call number assignment, the need for the supervisor to be a traffic manager, and the type of problems encountered in reclassifying from DDC to LCC. Yet we were still in search of a library that had tapped the online capabilities of an automated system to perform the reclassification tasks. As usual, I turned to the net for answers. A call for help titled "Reclassification–Shortcut" was sent out to AUTOCAT, an online listserv for catalogers, and NOTIS-L, an online listserv for NOTIS users, on January 28, 1993. I specifically asked for feedback on a scenario that I have envisioned, i.e., to pull DDC titles out using NOTIS copy statements that are coded "D" (classification code for DDC titles), flip it to "L" (classification code for LCC titles) by grabbing the LCC call number from the bibliographic record, and generate spine label information from the flipped records. It was my assumption that out there on the net, someone, especially one of the NOTIS programmers, was ready to let me know that this would never work. No one came forward to stop me. Judging from the responses I received, reclassification is still a very popular topic in the field.

In addition to the usual requests for more information on our project, I did receive information on three projects that were of interest to us. The Australian National University Law Library completed a project for 40,000 items reclassifying from DDC to LCC and Moys (for K collection) classification.[4] It involved contracting out to a vendor to have new call numbers keyed into the classification field of bibliographic records and writing a local program to move the new call numbers into item records and to produce labels. It was very encouraging to hear of their success using such a similar process even if they used a different local system– URICA. The second project from the University of Oregon involved the retrospective conversion and reclassification of 240,000 DDC titles.[5] By using a vendor to do conversion and produce label sets, the library staff barcoded and relabeled the items as reclassified records were loaded into the local database. For the 20,000 DDC titles that are already in their INNOPAC database, the staff are currently working on reclassifying them as a separate mini-project. The third project came from Occidental College Library.[6] They extracted records from the INNOPAC system and sent them to a vendor to generate spine labels and wide labels containing both DDC and LCC call numbers for item matching. The system vendor, Innovative Interfaces, then did the call number flipping changing from the 092 field (DDC) to the 090 field (LCC) based on the original list generated on the INNOPAC. In concluding our findings so far, we realized we were in uncharted waters yet confident that the NOTIS system would be capable of facilitating such an undertaking more quickly and cheaply.

TEST RUN

When the library director requested to have a proposal ready by May of 1993, a series of meetings were held among the Associate Director for Public Services and Systems, Systems Librarian, NOTIS Tech. 1 (programmer) and the staff in Technical Services. It was decided to have a test run in order to determine if this methodology were feasible and, if so, what the cost would be to undertake such a project. The course of action was as follows:

1. Extract copy statements with code "D" in classification type in the "LM" processing center. The other processing center "MC" is for the Medical Center Library that uses National Library of Medicine Classification and thus is not affected by reclassification. Report the total.
2. Extract records with 050 field (LC-assigned LC call number). Report on the total and generate a sample printout containing OCLC control number, NOTIS record number, LCC and DDC call numbers.
3. Extract records with 090 field (member-library-assigned LCC call number) without the presence of 050 field. Report the total and generate a sample printout as above.
4. Extract records without 050 field and 090 field. Report on the total and generate a sample printout as above.
5. Write the program to replace the DDC call number in copy statement with the LCC call number in either 050 field or 090 field of the bibliographic record,
6. Run the program on test file to see if all goes as planned.

During the months of March and April, the programmer worked closely with us in generating statistics critical to defining the scope of the project. We knew as of March 16, 1993, that there were 1,256,496 copies in our NOTIS database, of which 479,348 copies were coded as DDC titles. Among these DDC copies, 325,468 copies (67.89%) contained 050 field;

94,755 (19.76%) contained 090 field without 050 field; and, 59,125 copies (12.35%) had no LCC call numbers at all. Cognizant of the quirks of 050 fields, we also requested that the following statistics be run and a printout of randomly selected records be generated:

1. Monographic series and sets: 26,180 copies
   A traditional coding of analyzed series and sets classed together in our online records enabled us to obtain this total. Because of the inconsistent LC treatment of series on both cataloging and classification decisions, we will have to review these titles one by one based on our central series file in order to come up with valid call numbers.

2. PZ3 and PZ4 (literary works): 3,112 copies
   Since we do not use these two class numbers, we will need to complete the alternative call number or to assign one if no alternative class number is available on the record.

3. Z1001–(bibliographies): 6,520 copies
   Our local practice requires us to assign call numbers based on subjects covered for all collections except for the Reference Collection, the only holding library opting for the Z class for all bibliographies. We will need to complete the alternative call number or assign one if no alternative call number is available on the record.

In order to ensure having unique call numbers when using 090 fields in those 94,755 member copies, we requested to have a program written to add a zero to the last cutter, a practice the library uses to identify locally-assigned LCC numbers. In addition, we also asked to have the small "x," a work mark used by many member libraries for locally-assigned LCC numbers, deleted from either the last cutter or the date before the zero is inserted. This complicated program unexpectedly tested out well.

The final test run on the call number flipping based on a sample file in our test database came out successfully. The output file for labels proved to be an easy follow-up task. At last, the project as envisioned was confirmed to be feasible.

METHODOLOGY

Given the thrust to perform reclassification in an online environment utilizing NOTIS capabilities, the inclusion of all unconverted titles in the local database will have to be the first task for this project. When the conversion of 109,000 titles is completed, the reclassification then will follow to include all DDC titles in the NOTIS database. The planned process is to be as follows:

1. To contract a vendor for the conversion of 109,000 titles.
2. To make certain there is a valid LCC call number on each bibliographic record for all DDC copies, including the newly loaded converted records: This involves verifying all titles in analyzed series and sets, PZ3, PZ4, and, Z1001–a total of 33,012 copies plus an estimated 7,957 titles from the conversion bucket, and either completing or assigning LCC call numbers. For those 59,125 DDC copies plus an estimated 13,625 titles from the conversion bucket that do not have 050 or 090 fields, original LCC call numbers will have to be assigned.
3. To use SAS programs to retrieve DDC copies (Coded "D" in NOTIS copy statements) and flip them to code "L" based on valid LC call numbers on bibliographic records. This includes the deletion of small "x" and the insertion of zero at the end of the last cutter in 090 fields.
4. To generate an output file containing label and matching information from NOTIS of all the DDC copies that have been flipped.
5. To produce spine label sets via vendor contract.
6. To match spine label sets against physical items.
   Multi-volume sets and serials will have to be matched and flagged for in-house label production.

COSTS

There is a common realization among all involved in this project that this will be once-in-a-lifetime opportunity. In the past, the library has made frequent funding requests for conversion and has garnered some understanding and support from the university administration. The obstacle has always been the dollar amount attached to these requests. Cost estimates have been high because our contention was that only in-house conversion could tackle these more difficult-to-convert problem titles. During the initial planning for this project, we searched a sample set of records from these "problem" shelflist drawers against the OCLC database, and were pleasantly surprised to find a hit rate of 60%. This finding, along with the firm deadline of completing this project by the fall of 1996, led us to determine that a vendor contract for the conversion part would be the most economical and efficient alternative. Following a series of phone calls with various vendors, we estimated a cost of $297,483 for the conversion of 109,000 titles. An in-house project team composed of 2 librarians, 2 technicians and 2 graduate assistants plus appropriate equipment and supplies made the total cost for conversion $490,028.

Estimating the cost of the reclassification of 720,000 volumes proved to be more complicated. A review of the average cost per volume among published reclassification projects yielded the following:

University of Maryland[7]	1963-66	$1.96/volume
Arkansas State University[8]	1966-70	$ .93/volume
McMurry College[9]	1968	$ .50/volume
Tusculum College[10]	1973-74	$ .95/volume
University of Vermont[3]	1987-89	$1.54/volume

While the University of Vermont's cost contained barcoding, University of Maryland's involved recataloging, and McMurry's included only volumes processed without problems, these cost figures did provide us with a framework for comparison purpose. As the SAS programming was absorbed as one of the tasks for the NOTIS Tech. 1, this cost had been excluded. For the validating and assigning of LC call numbers, we had a dry run using a library science student trained in LC call number assignment and arrived at an average of 20 titles an hour. A similar test was done with a technician assigning cutter numbers for those PZ and Z records containing alternative class numbers. An average of 30 titles an hour was arrived at. Based on these two personnel costs, we calculated the total cost of assigning LC call numbers at $60,594. For the spine label sets, we estimated the cost at $33,555 based on phone inquiries with vendors. As for the cost of matching and retrieving items we again relied on a dry run using students and came up with $33,954. In case of multi-volumes and serials that required in-house generation of spine labels, our costing was based on our label stock and average production for a total of $28,701. The last cost item was for the labelling of 720,000 volumes and the estimate was $64,701. Thus we have the total cost for reclassification of 720,000 volumes at $221,505, i.e., $.31 per volume. It should be interesting to validate this cost estimate upon the completion of this project. There are simply so many variables that are unpredictable at this planning stage but will likely affect the total cost. However, if all goes as planned we will be very proud to claim in 1996 to have completed the most inexpensive reclassification project.

PLANNING

Owing to the scale and complexity of this recon/reclass project, the director appointed a planning committee composed of staff from Preservation, Collection Development, Circulation, Serials, Reference, Systems, Building Planning, Medical Center, Special Collections, Agriculture Library and Technical Services to address planning issues and lay the groundwork for implementation in July of 1994, provided that the project gets funded. During its initial meeting in September, 1993, the committee decided to form subgroups to grapple with the following issues:

1. Vendor Contract for Conversion:
   This includes writing a set of specifications for conversion, releasing bids, evaluating vendor responses, negotiating and signing the contract before July 1, 1994.
2. Vendor contract for label sets:
   This includes writing a set of specifications for label sets, releasing bids, evaluating vendor responses, and negotiating and signing the vendor contract. The timing for this task is more flexible as reclassification will not occur until after conversion is completed.
3. Personnel:
   This includes job descriptions, interviews and selection of the project staff. Organizational structure, workflow, and procedures will also be addressed by this group.
4. Collection Evaluation:
   This contains systematic weeding of the DDC collection prior to the initiation of the project and establishment of non-intrusive alternatives for project staff to weed the deteriorating DDC titles.
5. Equipment:
   This calls for the purchase of workstations, network connections, printer, labelling station, and a setup to equip workstations with tuggling capability for both OCLC and NOTIS.
6. Reclass Synchronization:
   This comprises the timing and sequential alternatives for call number flipping, labelling, shifting, and moving to the new building. This has proven to be the most complicated issue and requires extraordinary efforts to come up with an alternative that will be feasible, cost-effective, least disruptive to users, and, in the meantime, will facilitate the move to the new building.

These monthly committee meetings provide us opportunities to deliberate on issues brought up by subgroups and to develop into a cohesive group in an attempt to chart a course for this immense task. Even with such a representative group, we are preparing to conduct library-wide forums to solicit staff input hoping to get as many good ideas as we can.

CONCLUSION

The University of Kentucky Library is in a unique position to implement a second-generation reclassification project utilizing NOTIS, an automated local system. An impending move to a new building, user frustration with split collections, the availability of a most cost-effective automated alternative, and strong administrative support all contributed to the decision. The unique local programming to flip call numbers and generate label information makes this project less cost-prohibitive than other reclassification projects. Retrospective conversion of all DDC titles is to precede the reclassification phase. Our long-awaited goal of including all cataloged items in the NOTIS database will thus be achieved. In preparation for the implementation, a representative planning group is grappling with issues of vendor contracts, personnel, equipment, weeding, and timing/sequencing of reclassification. The planning for this intricate project invigorates the staff and presents us with a challenge to stay on target, under budget, and on time.

It is our hope that, given our cost data and methodology, other libraries might reexamine their priorities and give reclassification a second chance. Through the implementation of this reclassification project we hope to be able to enhance not only stack browsing for those users that visit the library but also online call number browsing for those users that access our virtual library. As Robert S. Taylor explained in comparing these two styles of browsing:

> –the listing of items in the order that they are parked may be more useful than stack browsing, because it will also show those books that are in circulation, frequently the best and the most recent books.[11]

REFERENCES

1. Joe A. Hewitt, "The Impact of OCLC," *American Libraries*, (May 1976): 268-275.

2. Barbara C. Dean, "Reclassification in an automated environment," *Cataloging & Classification Quarterly*, 5:2 (Winter 1984): 1-11.

3. Suzanne Massonneau, "Reclassification and barcoding: a unique opportunity," *Collection Management*, 13:1/2 (1990):15-37.

4. Communication with Judy Churches, senior librarian, Bibliographic Records, Library, Australian National University via email on Feb. 1 & March 10, 1993.

5. Communication with Alice Allen, Assistant University Librarian for Technical Services, University of Oregon via email on Jan. 29, 1993.

6. AUTOCAT Posting from Gail A Hitchcock, Cataloging Librarian, Occidental College on Jan. 29, 1993.

7. William E. Connors, "Reclassification at the University of Maryland," *Library Resources & Technical Services*, 11:2 (Spring 1967):233-242.

8. Gerry M. Taylor and James Anderson, "It will cost more tomorrow," *Library Resources & Technical Services*, 16:1 (Winter 1972):82-92.

9. Daniel Gore, "The 50 cent change to Library of Congress," *College & University Business* 44, no. 5 (May 1968): 109-111.

10. Cleo Treadway, "Reclassification: the Tusculum way," *Tennessee Librarian*, 28 (Winter 1976):10-15.

11. Robert S. Taylor, Value-added processes in information systems (Norwood, NJ: Ablex Publishing Corp., 1986), p. 80.

CLASSIFICATION
AND THE NEW TECHNOLOGY

Options in Classification Available
Through Modern Technology

Gertrude S. Koh

SUMMARY. Options in classification available through modern information technologies are explored and discussed in terms of system design options and user searching options. The integrated subject tool will give options for the simultaneous presentation of the types of catalogs desired–dictionary, divided, or classified, as well as the concurrent consultation of multiple classification systems. The problems of electronic union catalogs, including a "virtual union catalog" in particular, are considered and enhancements made possible through classification are explored. The combined system of subject headings and classification is presented as the model of the integrated subject searching tool, which will meet individualized learning styles and user responsive vocabulary. The integrated subject tool box (including classification) for an effective modern sub-

Gertrude S. Koh, PhD, CAS, MLS, is Associate Professor, Rosary College, Graduate School of Library and Information Science, River Forest, IL.

[Haworth co-indexing entry note]: "Options in Classification Available Through Modern Technology." Koh, Gertrude S. Co-published simultaneously in *Cataloging & Classification Quarterly* (The Haworth Press, Inc.) Vol. 19, No. 3/4, 1995, pp. 195-211; and: *Classification: Options and Opportunities* (ed: Alan R. Thomas) The Haworth Press, Inc., 1995, pp. 195-211. Multiple copies of this article/chapter may be purchased from The Haworth Document Delivery Center [1-800-3-HAWORTH; 9:00 a.m. - 5:00 p.m. (EST)].

195

ject system is discussed in particular as a searching tool to assist "shelf browsing" of virtual reality (VR) objects.

CLASSIFICATION AND INFORMATION TECHNOLOGY (IT)

The advent of the computer age in libraries has opened the door to hitherto unimaginable avenues of access to bibliographic records. The fundamental changes in the way information is gathered and organized for use are evident everywhere today when the power of computer technology is indorsed by its companion twin ultrahigh technologies, storage and telecommunications. In the past, the linear and sequential recording by manual means, such as card catalogs and paper based documents, has yielded the one-dimensional pattern for information representation and organization. The arrival of the "Three Musketeers" of companion information technologies (i.e., computing, telecommunications, and storage) has changed this dramatically.

Today information technologies enable organizing and using the multidimensional and dynamic nature of information and knowledge. However, in this process of making information powerfully and multi-facetedly available, one area which has not yet been implemented adequately but which has been researched, thought about, written about, and probably dreamt about, is the use of library classification systems as an online subject searching retrieval tool.

However, classification in online systems must demonstrate workability *and* cost effectiveness.[1] This paper discusses such use of classification systems and explores other options in classification available through modern technology, including online searching aspects and system design options available to libraries. The critical importance of classification systems for searching at the output stage (as distinct from the input stage of cataloging) is emphasized. The paper further extrapolates how these options which serve to demonstrate advantages of classification systems can meet individualized learning styles and user responsive searching vocabulary.

A. User-Driven Catalog with Multiple Classification Systems

The user of any of the online databases today determines the type of searches desired and thus the type of divided catalog desired. For instance, when qualifiers such as *DE* for subject descriptors are specified, a subject file results. The same user may limit his search by using *AU* for authors' names, thus creating another divided catalog by a different subset of files, while the use of *YR* for the publication date desired or *TI* for titles of works can be used to limit the search results. This creation of the particular type of a catalog the user desires is an easily available subset of any alphabetically arranged dictionary catalog. A dictionary catalog is the default option when the user does not limit the search type.

All OPACs should provide the same option of user-engineered construction of a classified catalog. Provision of a classified catalog in an OPAC is relatively simple, since the same bibliographic records in MARC formats contain classification information as well as descriptors, authors and titles. A simple link between all the fields for classification and call numbers and electronic classification systems like *Electronic Dewey*[2] should provide a classified catalog. To achieve the full power and capability of subject collocation, catalogs should use terms in the classification schedules and indexes as well as the class mark notations. The classification schedule structure with notations will prove a powerful subject tool when all such online features as keyword searches, boolean operators, truncations, limit specifications, nestings, and neighboring techniques are employed fully.

As advances in information technologies take hold in the construction of catalogs, a single library will be able to use multiple classification systems per item/work for different purposes. Technological advancement will inevitably enable the use of classification as the "marking and parking" device (i.e., *"book"* retrieval) plus the retrieval of subject *"information"* contained in those documents. These two retrieval purposes will converge effectively if a collection uses more than one classification system. The same library may use two very different classification systems per item/work simultaneously, one for the physical item retrieval and the other for subject retrieval. The same library may use a 3rd classification system, (for instance, Class W, the NLM classification for medicine) which is designed for one special subject or discipline. The optimum subject retrieval can be met best by this scenario of using more than one classification system.

This option of using more than one classification scheme in a library can be further extended as multi-cultural and multi-national boundaries converge. Analogous to multiple languages across national and cultural boundaries, modern information technologies support this scenario of one collection using multiple classification systems, which together contain diverse linguistic, ethnic, and cultural idiosyncracies. As a first step in achieving this development, various culturally based classification systems must be converted into machine readable forms.

B. Integrated Subject Tool: A Combined System of Classification and Subject Headings

Librarians must focus on turning the online catalog into a true classified catalog.[3] This is important for its potential of introducing a logical structure to subject searching. A classified-system is by its nature a more systematic and logical outline of knowledge than any alphabetical list of subject headings. However, the *deep* structure of a subject heading list is classificatory. For instance, a recast with thesaural symbols[4] of a subject heading, *Dogs,* in its authority record from *Sears (15th ed.),*[5] is more expressive of its subject relationship than symbols used in earlier editions as contrasted below.

Dogs   **599.74; 636.7**
   UF   Dog
   SA   types of dogs, e.g. **Guide dogs***;*
          and names of specific breeds of dogs, to be added as needed
   BT   **Domestic animals**
          Mammals
          Pets
   NT   **Collies**
          Guide dogs
          Hearing ear dogs
          Puppies
          [subject heading record in Sears, 15th ed.]

Dogs 599.74; 636.7
See also **classes of dogs, e.g., Guide dogs; Hearing ear**
      dogs; etc.; also names of specific breeds,
      e.g., Collies; etc.
   x   **Dog; Puppies**
   xx   **Pets**
          [subject heading record in Sears, 14th ed.]

The depth of semantic context of this subject heading is further revealed in a different presentation of the same heading, *Dogs* and its references. The kinds of subject relationships are better clarified and distinguished by use of BT and NT (Broader Term, Narrower Term). Clarified subject relationships of terms provide a re-defined role of a subject heading list–its transformation to a searcher's tool at the interactive searching stage, not only for librarians but also for users. Subject relationships of terms are fundamentally classificatory as demonstrated in the structural recast of the same heading, *Dogs*, below:

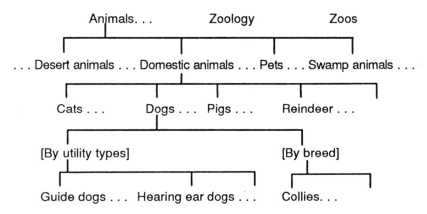

[classificatory recast of subject heading relationships]

Using subject headings as index terms to get to individual members contained in a classification will be a logical step for optimum subject access. One must attempt to preserve the fundamental essence of structural components of each subject method; purposefully structured and designed integration of subject headings and classification. Authority control as the underpinning core of the subject heading structure results in a user responsive vocabulary system, including both subject headings and cross references. The logical grouping as the underlying nature of classification structure facilitates user navigation for semantic context. However, the advancement of modern technologies will provide a transparent user responsive system with all the deep structures hidden from the users.[6]

Today's technologies will support the advantages of both alphabetic and classified catalogs by incorporating user responsive *open ended* terminology and everyday vocabulary in one integrated subject tool. For example, if a user prefers *canine*, a term which is not even a see reference, the system should respond to such an unpreferred access vocabulary term just as directly and fully as in *dogs,* the preferred subject heading.

C. Individual Learning Styles

One of the important available options in classification is to assist users in online subject searching. An online subject searcher has two principal tasks: first, he/she must identify his/her information needs, and second, he/she must express or articulate his/her information needs to the system in terms which match those indexed in the system. Users are frequently unable to match their query terms exactly with subject headings in the system, unless appropriate cross references are provided by the authority control. Responsive authority control should provide venues for user input and incorporating user supplied data. Otherwise, users often retrieve nothing when using subject headings. In contrast, keyword searching (with Boolean operators) of multiple fields often produces large retrieval sets, but a keyword search is insensitive to the syntactic, semantic, and logical aspects of natural language. The result is that such retrieval sets often contain many items not relevant to a user's information needs. Therefore, users may frequently experience search failure by retrieving no items, by retrieving too many irrelevant items, or by retrieving too few relevant items.[7]

It is not surprising, therefore, that consideration is being given to the use of classification for online subject access. In a sea of full-text information which is automatically indexed and which is keyword searchable, classification serves as a *logical window* for subjects. This window of concept maps helps humans identify focused experience and helps them associate thoughts and things. Classification as a systematic window serves as a complementary tool to full-text natural language terms. It is thought that systematic outlines of subjects from classification schedules can assist a user in retrieving items which he/she would be unlikely to retrieve by using conventional subject heading or keyword search methods.

The integrated subject tool online can accommodate individual learning styles of users by combining classification with authority controlled subject headings as an index to the classification. Human brains learn and remember information by categorization and by association, not by alphabetic means. Users look for unknown subjects by associations and by grouping like things together. Classification provides clues to unknown subjects.

Placing what is sought in any predefined and predetermined structured frame such as a classification system is inadequate unless there is an entry term which serves as a lead. The initial step to any search is naming the search object. An alphabetic list of every member in the classification is therefore necessary. The individual learning styles, often idiosyncratic, and the diverse vocabulary terms of particular users may be best supported, accommodated, predicted, and met by a true classified catalog combining alphabetic and systematic arrangements of information in one integrated subject tool online.

In designing the integrated subject tool, which is purposefully to meet the individualized styles of learning in mind, the main question is how to link class numbers and subject headings in an online system. Svenonius states that "an argument can be made that the effective use of classification in online retrieval will ultimately depend upon the existence of adequate indexes to the classification."[8] Such indexes would presumably include subject headings. Clearly, class numbers and subject headings can be linked indirectly through bibliographic records where MARC fields contain both. For example, a user conducting a subject heading search can retrieve bibliographic records and then use the class numbers appearing in those records for an extended search. Conversely, a user can conduct a class or call number search, retrieve bibliographic records, and use the subject headings appearing in those records for an extended search. Svenonius indicates that the method of indexing has not been resolved:

> . . . probablistic methods and strategies that seek to predict class numbers using combined information from a variety of sources (not subject headings alone) deserve exploration. . . The feasibility of chain indexing needs re-examination . . . [9]

Resolution of indexing problems might provide a response to the criticisms of Crawford[10] and Gorman[11] to the use of classification online based on the fact that an enumerative classification does not generally reveal secondary subject aspects.

D. User Navigation

Conventional systems place the burden upon the user to select query terms that match the system's index terms. But one cannot always assume that the user knows precisely what he/she needs to investigate, or that the user is able to express needs in the system language.[12] Bates indicates that "In effect, people do not naturally have 'queries;' rather they have . . . an 'anomalous state of knowledge.' . . . "[13] Though users are aware that a gap or anomaly exists in their knowledge, they are at the same time unaware of and cannot specify the nature of their missing knowledge. Hildreth refers to the "fundamental paradox of information retrieval: the need to describe that which you do not know in order to find it."[14] Further, we cannot expect even those users who have identified their information needs to be able to formulate a reasonably well-articulated expression of those needs. They may lack sufficient "domain knowledge," i.e., knowledge of substantive concepts in a given subject field and the relationships between those concepts.[15]

In addition, users will generally express their information needs to the system in natural language terms. But any natural language term has no inherent meaning, or has different meanings or may acquire different meanings through its use in different subject fields or contexts. Hildreth indicates that the use of a term within a narrow or "well-defined" field or context may result in the reduction of possible ambiguity in its meaning, or "disambiguation" of its meaning. He also suggests, however, that this disambiguation is unlikely in the case of an indexed term in a library catalog, which contains records "from many different subject areas, each likely to include many different aspects from a variety of different perspectives."[16] Conventional online catalogs may offer users little assistance in this regard. For instance, an alphabetic browsing list of subject headings provides little contextual aid to users unless it displays various term relationships.[17] A keyword search in multiple fields is conducted outside of any subject context. If any context exists it is a product of the relationship between search terms created through the use of Boolean operators. Similarly, browsing of call number displays does not necessarily make their "underlying structural logic" explicit to users.[18]

The use of an online classification scheme can mitigate these problems. Liu and Svenonius observed that:

> Classifications, however, go beyond thesauri by semantically structuring not only the vocabulary associated with concepts but also the concepts themselves. Classifications have sometimes been likened to semantic nets, in which concepts are linked by meaning relationships. They have also been likened to knowledge trees, in which each concept is comparable to every other concept, in the sense that its position in the scheme is defined with respect to every other position. While thesauri consist of . . . term clusters, classifications attempt to integrate these clusters into meaningful monolithic wholes . . . [19]

By consulting a classification structure, a user is more likely to identify and to position the topic of interest within a given knowledge domain. Use of a classification scheme can therefore serve to assist a user in articulating and focusing a search query.[20] In a classification scheme such as DDC, terms are displayed in hierarchical relationships in which all attributes of a superordinate term belong to, or are inherited by a subordinate term.[21] A user's topic of interest, when positioned within a hierarchy, is contextualized by its relationship to superordinate terms, and/or by its relationship to subordinate terms. A user who browses the hierarchy should be assisted in transforming an otherwise indefinite query to one that is specific and conceptually bound.

Classification schemes not only assist a user in locating his topic of interest within a hierarchy or cluster, but also help that user identify his topic of interest from different perspectives. An enumerative classification scheme such as DDC divides the knowledge base into broad disciplines. Each discipline may present a different aspect or perspective by which a given subject may be viewed.[22] Svenonius argues that an online system can collocate effectively "distributed relatives" of a subject and present the user with a "map" of the various hierarchies within which the subject appears. Therefore, a user who can use the system to browse across concept hierarchies should more readily identify the topic of interest in various perspectives. This capability should also assist a user in contextualizing the desired topic, especially in the case of homonymous terms which participate in more than one hierarchy.[23] Svenonius envisages a system/user dialogue wherein the system presents the user various perspectives of a given term and allows the user to successively choose perspective(s) in which he/she is interested.[24]

Williamson is confident that " . . . computer-based catalogues can be designed to transcend the problem of interdisciplinarity and multi-dimensionality of subjects, as well as the physical scatter of documents."[25] Markey and Demeyer suggest that the use of a classification scheme enhances searching vocabulary and results in the retrieval of those records which in a conventional system would not be retrieved.[26]

E. Catalog Browsing and Shelf Browsing at the Catalog

The facilitation of browsing at the catalog is the most obvious advantageous option of using a classification system in an online searching mechanism. Svenonius stated in 1981, well over a decade ago:

> The main use of classification, at least in the United States, has been to facilitate browsing of books on the shelves. A possible future use might be to facilitate the browsing of machine-readable bibliographic records at a computer terminal.[27]

However, as discussed by the profession so far, browsing at the computer terminal means little more than the perusal of bibliographic records by users. In fact, browsing at a computer terminal is more advantageous than browsing shelves, even without considering the savings in time and physical effort involved. First, the total holdings of a library can be browsed by their bibliographic records without regard to the absentee items on shelves due to circulation and without regard to the problems of intershelving odd shaped packages such as slides, microfiche, CD-ROMs, magnetic tapes, etc., along with books and periodicals. The total holdings of multi-media can be best browsed if they have been classified.

More than one classification number should be assigned to each bibliographic item, as discussed earlier, for the purposes of subject searching as opposed to shelf location, so that an item can be accessible under all of its aspects. If the entire classification system (similar to the *Electronic Dewey* in CD-ROM)[28] is appropriately linked to the bibliographic records and indexed, a user may key in a search term in natural language,[29] and call up a list of items in shelf list order. Subsequently the user could then browse up or down the list (which in DDC will make the search broader or narrower, respectively), and can then browse through *full-text* of items–not just brief catalog records representing those items–in a *systematic* fashion.[30] If he/she so desires, the user may obtain more records and fuller information on the coverage of a specific topic.

A modern subject system design should present one integrated *subject resource,* instead of the conventional two step approach to effective subject searching. The conventional first process is finding a call number by consulting subject headings in the catalog of bibliographic records. The second step, in open stack collections, is browsing at the shelf. Subject searching is enhanced by shelf browsing guided by classification, the first basic component of a call number. Each process retrieves items not retrieved by the other, and used together they result in more productive searching. Finni and Paulson support this statement when they discussed Markey's study of classification as an enhancement to subject searching:

> A key conclusion of the study was that, while the two methods of searching were relatively equal in precision, recall, and search time, each method retrieved different relevant bibliographic items from the same database.[31]

The possibility of a virtual reality (VR) representation of the information resource in constructing catalogs underscores the importance of shelf browsing at the catalog. The option of using classification as an object (or resource) browsing tool will redefine the catalog. In a VR world of information, a shelf full of VR information packages like "books" will be invoked by pointing (or touching) bibliographic elements such as physical description of pages and illustrations. This invocation of the physical object, when the subject is first searched at the catalog, should further facilitate users' browsing of the table of contents or index as desired. The dynamic and multi-dimensional use of information is inevitable through this option of invoking VR objects by classification in the catalog.

Use of classification for the VR "books" at the shelves becomes vital because information is increasingly packaged in electronic forms. Packaged information has expanded from printed pages to video cassettes and electronic publishing of various types such as CD-ROMs, electronic newsletters, etc., all media which cannot be browsed easily on conventional library shelves.

The VR browsing option proposed here, linked to an electronic classification system, uses much more sophisticated techniques than mere call number searching as now offered by numerous online public access catalogs. The major drawback with most call number searching alternatives is that the user must know the exact number of the item desired. Few users know this, or have any idea of how to determine it. Although a searcher could cull a class number from a bibliographic record retrieved through other techniques, few people go to the trouble; and if the searcher did this, all that would be retrieved might be a short list of slightly related book titles. A similar list of somewhat related titles might result when selecting the choice, "View nearby items on shelf," in many of the OPACS through Internet, for instance.

Even more sophisticated call number searching capabilities, such as the ability to truncate,[32] are of minimal use. First, the searcher must know the subject matter represented by the classification number in order to use it effectively, unless the system already includes an index, and few do.[33] Moreover, the related display of specific citations is seldom in shelflist order, so that browsing is impossible; and the bibliographic records themselves usually must be examined to determine their subject content.[34] As a result, call number searching tends to be the least used option in automated library catalogs even by those knowledgeable.[35] In view of the prospects of a VR representation in the catalog, the option of object browsing by means of the classification scheme imbedded in call numbers must be studied seriously to ensure its effective incorporation into catalog design. The link between the bibliographic record and an electronic classification system, as discussed earlier in the sections *A* and *B* (user-driven multiple classification systems and the integrated subject tool), overcomes these concerns over the utility of call numbers.

F. *"Virtual Union Catalog" and Its Environment*

Nowhere is this need for invoking VR "books" more true than in the networking of catalogs. In the context of various union catalogs such as OCLC (Online Computer Library Center) or IO (ILLINET Online), the majority of collections are *closed* to off-site users. Incorporation of VR information packages in a catalog allows off-site users to replicate their subject searching experience by "shelf browsing" as if in open stack collections. Increasing applications of telecommunication technologies create a complex context of union catalogs.

The explosive advancement of telecommunications technology during the last five years made real the linking of virtually all electronic packages, textual, audio and visual, in a seamless manner and over remote distances. Emerging new packages of information make conventional shelf browsing impossible, calling for another new solution. Increasing connectivity of electronic union catalogs present a complex environment in which the notion of conventional shelf browsing by opening and examining "books" may be impossible to preserve. Yet the salutary practice for self learning and self discovery of further knowledge by shelf browsing is undeniable. Considering that remote users experience different sets of problems to a local OPAC and that one of the difficult unsolved problems is subject searching,[36] the magnitude of subject access problems in a union catalog is immeasurable. Incorporating VR information objects, the union catalog should provide not only *access* to the physical items but also the physical items or *resources* themselves.

Today, in addition to a single union catalog constructed in one automated system environment (e.g., OCLC), there is a networked environment of many union catalogs. These catalogs stem from many automated systems and make shelf browsing by classification more critically important than ever before. Union catalogs based on many automated and interconnected systems present the most difficult and complex problems in subject access.

An ever growing number of users on the Internet plus more libraries looking for local automated systems with Z39.50 platform compliance suggest that users will soon encounter all the OPACs on a continuum as "one" big catalog, i.e., a *"virtual union catalog."* In principle, the holdings of many libraries can be browsed at once, as if one huge library contained all the volumes. This virtual union catalog will make subject searching increasingly frustrating and difficult for an ordinary user. In each of these libraries there is an underlying complexity of subject problems. The complexity is at each local OPAC level, because the local catalog records may be juxtaposed with files of many producer-sources, externally created. Examples are A & I services as well as primary information packages like encyclopedias, dictionaries, etc., which may already be in multi-media forms.

Adding a cautionary note concerning online classification number access, Hill concludes that:

> Online subject searching by classification number would offer an approach to information well beyond the capabilities of card catalogs, and it is undoubtedly worth aiming for. Providing this avenue of access should form a part of our long-term speculations and plans,

but it presents complex problems of programming, funding, bibliographic instruction, and more.[37]

G. Integrated Tools at the Workstation: Librarians and Users

Modern technological advancement facilitates the integration of all the tools used by librarians, both reference and catalog librarians. The notion of integrated resources applies not only to users' subject tools which give access to physical items and provide those physical items (information resources) themselves but also to the series of resource tools used by catalogers in their construction of the catalog. There are numerous cataloging tools such as *AACR2R, LCSH, US MARC, DDC,* etc., each developed and maintained separately. These catalogers' integrated resource tools must incorporate cataloging and classification standards as well as search and retrieval protocols. The integrated tool box should be used from the time bibliographic elements are identified and entered, through the stages of assigning cataloging and classification standards, to the point for assigning search and retrieval protocols. The first example of this type of a bundled tool box is the recent CD-ROM, *Cataloger's Desktop,* by LC.[38] Indexing tools as well as access to the non-bibliographic information content should also be provided in this integrated tool box, as stated by Dunsire.[39]

The integrated resource tool at a single computer will impact librarians' work, their knowledge bases and the organizational structure of a library. Classification is central to the integrated resource tool box. At a workstation with the integrated resource tool, a librarian may perform an entire series of tasks, instead of compartmentalized and specialized tasks such as reference work or cataloging. Organizing and retrieving information will be the most crucial and essential job for this breed of holistic librarians. Retrieval of information will be accomplished best by organizing user queries in the manner of cataloging or indexing. Conceptualizing user queries in classificatory maps will optimize subject retrieval. This conceptualization by categorizing user queries presupposes understanding of classification. Optimal effectiveness will derive from their knowledge bases for classification. The context of networking today eliminates the necessity for librarians to be in the same building with their workstations. The virtual library promoted by librarians' integrated resource tools at their workstations is a harbinger of what may develop in the organizational structure of libraries. Its ultimate impact will be a redefinition of libraries, librarians, and education for librarianship.

CONCLUSION

Studies on OPACs found that subject searches are the type most frequently used but are less likely than any other types to be successful.[40] Theoretically and technologically there are good options available for the use of a classification scheme online in effective information system design and in conjunction with subject heading and keyword searching. Using an online classification system as a subject searching tool can turn the catalog into both a classified catalog[41] and a dictionary catalog, and thus the library can have the best of both worlds.[42] This supports the recent emerging consensus that the most powerful retrieval method is a combination of controlled alphabetical vocabulary, classification, and uncontrolled keywords. Options discussed here go beyond Markey's conclusion that:

> Instead of placing the burden of subject searching on library patrons, online public access catalogs must be enhanced with online user aids to assist in the selection of subject vocabulary, facilitating browsing, and provide additional information for making relevant assessments.[43]

The more intractable problems involve human factors as found in both library user and librarian. Classification is pivotal in solving the human problems.

REFERENCES

1. Janet Hill, "Things are Taking a Little Longer Than That: A Response to Dewey Decimal Classification in the Online Environment," *Cataloging & Classification Quarterly* 11, no. 1 (1990): 59-69. John P. Comaromi, "Summation of Classification as an Enhancement of Intellectual Access to Information in an Online Environment," *Cataloging & Classification Quarterly* 11, no. 2 (1990): 100.

2. *Electronic Dewey: DDC20*. Dublin, Ohio: OCLC, 1993. (The DDC Schedules, Tables, Manual and Relative Index, including the LCSH.)

3. Gertrude Soonja Koh, *The Semantic Problems of Translated Subject Headings*. Seoul, Korea: SooMoon SeoKwan, 1978: p. 263.

4. *Library of Congress Subject Headings*. 17th ed. Washington, DC: Library of Congress, 1994. (The first use of thesaural symbols in the 11th ed., 1988.)

5. *Sears List of Subject Headings,* ed. by Joseph Miller, 15th ed. New York: H. W. Wilson, 1994: p. 211.

6. Robert R. Freeman and Pauline Atherton, *File Organization and Search Strategy Using the Universal Decimal Classification in Mechanized Reference Retrieval Systems*. New York: American Institute of Physics, 1967.

7. Carole Weiss Moore, "User Reactions to Online Catalogs: An Exploratory Study," *College and Research Libraries* 42 (July 1981): 295-302. Karen Markey,

"Thus Spake the OPAC User," *Information Technology and Libraries* 2, no. 4 (December 1983): 381-387. Thomas Mann, *Library Research Models: A Guide to Classification, Cataloging, and Computers.* New York: Oxford University Press, 1993, pp. 113-150.

8. Elaine Svenonius, "Bibliographic Control." In *Academic Libraries Research Perspectives,* ed. Mary Jo Lynch, Chicago: American Library Association, 1990: 49.

9. Ibid., p. 48:

10. Walt Crawford, *Patron Access: Issues for Online Catalogs.* Boston: G.K. Hall, 1987: 25.

11. Michael Gorman, "The Longer the Number, the Smaller the Spine . . . " *American Libraries* 12 (September 1981): 499.

12. Charles R. Hildreth, "Beyond Boolean: Designing the Next Generation of Online Catalogs." *Library Trends* 35, no. 4 (Spring 1987): 653.

13. Marcia J. Bates, "Subject Access in Online Catalogs: A Design Model. *Journal of the American Society for Information Science* 37, no. 6 (November 1986): 361.

14. Charles R. Hildreth, "Beyond Boolean: Designing the Next Generation of Online Catalogs": 653.

15. Kamran Parsaye, Mark Chignell, Setrag Khoshafian, and Harry Wong, *Intelligent Databases: Object-Oriented, Deductive Hypermedia Technologies.* New York: Wiley, 1989: 307.

16. Charles R. Hildreth, *Intelligent Interfaces and Retrieval Methods.* Washington, D.C.: Library of Congress, 1989: 84.

17. Karen Markey and Ann H. Demeyer, *Dewey Decimal Classification Online Project: Evaluation of a Library Schedule and Index Integrated into the Subject Searching Capabilities of an Online Catalog.* Dublin, Ohio: OCLC, 1986: 249.

18. Carol A. Mandel, "A Computer Age Classification: Implications for Library Practice." *Classification Theory in the Computer Age: Conversations Across the Disciplines: Proceedings from the Conference,* Albany, November 18-19, 1988. Albany: State University of New York, 1989: 89.

19. Sonqiao Liu and Elaine Svenonius, "DORS: DDC Online Retrieval System." *Library Resources & Technical Services* 35, no. 4 (October 1991): 360.

20. Elaine Svenonius, "Use of Classification in Online Retrieval." *Library Resources and Technical Services* 27, no. 1 (January/March 1983): 79. Winfred Godert and Silke Horny, "The Design of Subject Access Elements in Online Public Access Catalogs." *International Classification* 17, no. 2 (1990): 68. Lois Mai Chan, "The Library of Congress Classification System in an Online Environment." *Cataloging & Classification Quarterly* 11, no. 1 (1990): 7-25.

21. Elaine Svenonius, "An Ideal Classification for an Online Catalog." *Classification Theory in the Computer Age: Conversations Across the Disciplines: Proceedings from the Conference,* Albany, November 18-19, 1988. Albany: State University of New York, 1989: 38. Rao Aluri, D. Alasdair Kemp, and John J. Boll, *Subject Analysis in Online Catalogs.* Englewood, Colorado: Libraries Unlimited, 1991: 119.

22. Elaine Svenonius, "An Ideal Classification for an Online Catalog,": 37.

23. Sonqiao Liu and Elaine Svenonius, "DORS: DDC Online Retrieval System," :360.

24. Elaine Svenonius, "An Ideal Classification for an Online Catalog," :See a dissenting view as expressed by F.W. Lancaster and Tschera Harkness Connell, Nancy Bishop, and Sherry McCowan, "Identifying Barriers to Effective Subject Access in Library Catalogs." *Library Resources & Technical Services* 35, no. 4 (October 1991): 384.

25. Nancy J. Williamson, "The Library of Congress Classification: Problems and Prospects in Online Retrieval." *International Cataloging* 15, no. 4 (January/March 1986): 45-48.

26. Karen Markey and Ann H. Demeyer, *Dewey Decimal Classification Online Project:* XXXIX.

27. Elaine Svenonius, "Directions for Research in Indexing, Classification, and Cataloging," *Library Resources & Technical Services* 25, no. 1 (January/March 1981): 94.

28. *Electronic Dewey: DDC20.*

29. Pauline A. Cochrane and Karen Markey, "Preparing for the Use of Classification in Online Cataloging Systems and in Online Catalogs," *Information Technology and Libraries* 4, no. 2 (June 1985): 109.

30. Thomas Mann, *Library Research Models: A Guide to Classification, Cataloging, and Computers.* New York: Oxford University Press, 1993, p. 15. Lois Mai Chan and Theodora Hodges, "Subject Cataloging and Classification: The Late 1980s and Beyond." In *Technical Services Today and Tomorrow,* ed. Michael Gorman, Englewood, Col.: Libraries Unlimited, Inc, 1990, 82.

31. John Finni and Peter J. Paulson, "The Dewey Decimal Classification Enters the Computer Age: Developing the DDC Database and Editorial Support System," *International Cataloguing* 16, no. 4 (October/December): 47.

32. (i.e., a right truncation to retrieve all records whose DDC number begins with, for example, 37* to retrieve everything on education, or 378* to narrow to everything on higher education; or retrieve all records whose DDC number has a middle truncation, e.g., 8*2 for all drama, regardless of language)

33. Elaine Broadbent, "The Online Catalog: Dictionary, Classified, or Both?" *Cataloging & Classification Quarterly* 10, nos. 1/2 (1989): 107.

34. Pauline A. Cochrane and Karen Markey, "Preparing for the Use of Classification in Online Cataloging Systems and in Online Catalogs": 98.

35. Elaine Broadbent, "The Online Catalog: Dictionary, Classified, or Both?," 108.

36. Karen Markey and Ann H. Demeyer, *Dewey Decimal Classification Online Project: Evaluation of a Library Schedule and Index Integrated into the Subject Searching Capabilities of an Online Catalog.* Dublin, Ohio: OCLC, 1986: XXXIX.

37. Janet Hill, "Online Classification Number Access: Some Practical Considerations," *Journal of Academic Librarianship* 10, no. 1 (March 1984): 22.

38. Library of Congress, *Cataloger's Desktop: Windows CD-ROM*. Washington, DC: Library of Congress, Cataloging Distribution Service, 1994.

39. Gordon Dunsire, "Sex, Lies and Catalogue Cards," *Catalogue & Index,* 109 (Autumn 1993): 2.

40. David W. Lewis, "Research on the Use of Online Catalogs and its Implications for Library Practice," *Journal of Academic Librarianship* 13, no. 3 (July 1987): 154.

41. Lois Mai Chan and Theodora Hodges, "Subject Cataloging and Classification: The Late 1980s and Beyond,": 80

42. Elaine Broadbent, "The Online Catalog: Dictionary, Classified, or Both?,": 107. Lois Mai Chan, "Subject Analysis Tools Online: The Challenge Ahead," *Information Technology and Libraries* 9, no. 3 (September 1990): 260.

43. Karen Markey, "Subject-Searching Experiences and Needs of Online Catalog Users: Implications for Library Classification," *Library Resources & Technical Services* 29, no. 1 (January/March 1985): 40.

Electronic Dewey:
The CD-ROM Version
of the Dewey Decimal Classification

Ross Trotter

SUMMARY. This paper describes the features of Electronic Dewey bringing out the ways in which it differs from the printed version of the Classification. The various search techniques available are discussed and the use of the DDC functions is considered. The paper concludes that while improvements could be made the CD-ROM heralds the electronic age of classification.

Electronic Dewey, as the CD-ROM version of the Dewey Decimal Classification is called, was first issued as a commercial product by OCLC Forest Press, the owners and distributors of the Classification, in 1993, after extensive testing of pilot versions during the preceding two years. This is very much a "first," since it is the first time that a general classification scheme has been offered in this format, or in machine readable form. As with all innovations it represents a big step forward, but also leaves room for improvement in later releases–which assuredly there will be.

Ross Trotter, BA, ALA, is Project Officer, Director's Office, Acquisitions Processing & Cataloguing, British Library.

Address correspondence to: British Library, Boston Spa, Wetherby, West Yorkshire, LS23 7BQ, United Kingdom.

All Electronic Dewey screens used in this article were reproduced with the permission of OCLC Online Computer Library Center, which holds the copyright.

[Haworth co-indexing entry note]: "Electronic Dewey: The CD-ROM Version of the Dewey Decimal Classification." Trotter, Ross. Co-published simultaneously in *Cataloging & Classification Quarterly* (The Haworth Press, Inc.) Vol. 19, No. 3/4, 1995, pp. 213-234; and: *Classification: Options and Opportunities* (ed: Alan R. Thomas) The Haworth Press, Inc., 1995, pp. 213-234. Multiple copies of this article/chapter may be purchased from The Haworth Document Delivery Center [1-800-3-HAWORTH; 9:00 a.m. - 5:00 p.m. (EST)].

Before discussing ways in which the product could be improved it is first necessary to describe exactly what the CD-ROM version of Dewey, which I shall refer to as EDDC, has to offer the user, and how it differs from, adds to or even subtracts from the printed version. It contains the full text of both the schedules and tables of DDC20, published in 1989, plus all the amendments to these subsequently issued in *Decimal Classification Additions Notes and Decisions* (*DC&*), which has been regularly published in March of each year. Consequently it includes the amendments found in the DC& of March 1993.

EDDC also includes all the Manual entries found in Volume 4 of the printed edition, and these are interfiled as search results with the numbers that they relate to, as will be seen shortly. What EDDC does not contain is the Editor's Introduction, the lists of relocations and reductions, and the comparative and equivalence tables. Instead EDDC is accompanied by a user guide giving instructions on how to use the product. This guide also contains the maps, flowcharts and glossary from the printed version.

It will already be seen from the description above that the presentation of EDDC is, as might be expected, very different from that of the printed text. The latter can obviously only present its data in a single linear fashion while the machine readable version enables far greater flexibility in the way access to this data is gained. The screen for EDDC is divided into three parts (see Figure 1). At the top left is the results window, which shows the number of records retrieved by the current search, the number marked (this will be explained later), and the record in the set which is currently being viewed or highlighted. At the top right is the query window in which searches are entered and previous searches stored. The ways in which previous searches can be reused will be looked at later on. The largest window is the view window which is below the other two, in which the results of the search can be viewed. This displays various things according to the type of search or command that has been issued.

You obviously always start by entering something in the query window, which can be a word, phrase or number. If you enter a query without specifying a particular index the search will be carried out by default on the basic index–which searches all the following fields: captions, notes, index entries and class numbers. If there is more than one hit a record list in class number order will be displayed with the highlight on the first record. Figure 1 shows the start of the record list for a search on the term "Time" in the basic index with the highlight moved down to the tenth record. Note the way Manual entries, identified by an M, are interfiled. You can view an individual record by pressing Enter. As the basic index searches notes and index entries as well as captions it does generate some noise and needs to be used with care. It will be seen from Figure 1 that the search for "Time" has retrieved "003 Systems." Figure 2 displays the record itself which shows why this is so–the word "time" occurs in the note as part of "control of discrete-time linear systems."

Numbers as well as words can be searched using the default basic index, and will again retrieve every occurrence of that number in a note as well as a class number. Thus Figure 3 shows the start of the record list following a search of the basic index for "599," for which the result is 350 hits. And Figure 4 shows that 338.372 is retrieved because 599 is part of the first note. However, it is very easy to make sure that extraneous detail is omitted by using what are called Index Labels. A list of these is shown in Figure 5. Note how the list is on a pop-up menu over the record list, and how the query entry point has moved as a result. It will be seen from this list that captions, index terms and subject heading terms–taken from the LCSH associated with each class number entry–can be searched as both keywords and phrases. Performing the same searches for "Time" and "599" as before, but this time using the Index Labels cn for Caption keyword and dd for Dewey number, shows how the use of these labels narrows the search. The results are displayed in Figures 6 and 7–the number of hits for "Time" has been reduced from 110 to 37, and for "599" from 350 to 2!

This already indicates how much more flexible the search procedure is using EDDC than is possible with the printed edition. And of course all the usual aids to on-line searching are present as well, such as Boolean operators, truncation and wild cards. And the normal Boolean AND, OR, NOT are expanded to include WITH and ADJn. The difference between AND and WITH is that the first means that both terms are present somewhere in the record, whereas WITH means they both occur in the same field, be it caption, notes, or index term field. How useful this distinction might be is debatable. For instance "computer and programming" results in 25 hits, while "computer with programming" results in 24. The extra hit is the number 005.43 as in the notes to that number "computer" happens not to appear in the singular, only in the plural. The ADJn command enables you to search for two terms within a certain degree of adjacency. The default is ADJ0, so if you search for "computer programming" it will search for any records in which those terms appear next to each other–the result is 10 hits. Increasing the number above zero will obviously increase the possible number of hits. Thus "computer adj2 programming" increases the hits to 12, as it also retrieves, e.g., the index term "Interpreters (computer science)–programming languages." You can follow ADJ by any number up to 25, but it is difficult to see just what value this facility has–in what

FIGURE 1

```
Database: EDEWEY
                        2>time
RETRIEVED: 110          3>
    Marked:   0         F2=Indexes    F3=Index Labels    F4=History
    Record:  10

            DDC Number        Caption

            003               Systems
            003.7             Kinds of systems
            003.8             Systems distinguished in relation to time
            003.83            Discrete-time systems
        M   004.11-004.16     Digital computers
            004.32            Multiprogramming
            004.33            Real-time processing
        M   005.369           Specific programs
            115               Time
  >>        116               Change
        M   140 vs. 180-190   Specific philosophical schools and viewpoints vs.
            152.3             Movements and motor functions
            152.8             Quantitative threshold, discrimination, reaction-
            152.83            Reaction-time studies
    F7=Print                     ↑↓ Select    Ins/Del=Mark/Unmark    ↵View Record |
    Alt+D=DDC Functions
    Electronic Dewey  v1.00                      F1 Help  F8 Databases  F10 End
```

FIGURE 2

```
Database: EDEWEY
                        2>time
RETRIEVED: 110          3>
    Marked:   0         F2=Indexes    F3=Index Labels    F4=History
    Record:   1         Ctrl+F3=Pull On/Off

        CLASS NUMBER:    003

            CAPTION:     Systems

              NOTES:     Class here operations research [formerly 001.424];
                         systems theory, analysis, design, optimization; models
                         (simulation) applied to real-world systems

                         Unless other instructions are given, class complex
                         subjects with aspects in two or more subdivisions of 003
                         in the one coming last, e.g., control of discrete-time
                         linear systems 003.830115 (not 003.5 or 003.74)

                         Class simulation in education in 371.397; systems in a
                         specific subject or discipline with the subject or
                         discipline, using notation T1--011 from Table 1, e.g.,
    F5=Previous  F6=Next  F7=Print                Use ↑↓ PgUp PgDn to view text.
    Alt+D=DDC Functions
    Electronic Dewey  v1.00    ESC Record List   F1 Help  F8 Databases  F10 End
```

FIGURE 3

```
Database: EDEWEY
┌──────────────────┐ ┌─ 3>599
│ RETRIEVED: 350   │ │  4>
│    Marked:    0  │ │  F2=Indexes     F3=Index Labels     F4=History
│    Record:    1  │ │
└──────────────────┘ └─
```

	DDC Number	Caption
>>	338.372	Products of fishing, whaling, hunting, trapping
	380.1432-380.1439	Products of fishing, whaling, hunting, trapping
	398.2452	Real
	398.369	Animals
	591	Zoology
M	591	Zoology
M	591 vs. 610	Zoology vs. Medical sciences Medicine
C	592-599	Specific animals and groups of animals
	593.1	*Protozoa *Plasmodroma
	593.11	*Sarcodina
	593.113	*Proteomyxida
	593.115	*Mycetozoa
	593.117	*Amoebida
	593.118	*Testacea (Arcellinida)

```
 F7=Print                     ↑↓ Select   Ins/Del=Mark/Unmark   ⏎View Record |
 Alt+D=DDC Functions
 Electronic Dewey  v1.00                    F1 Help  F8 Databases  F10 End
```

FIGURE 4

```
Database: EDEWEY
┌──────────────────┐ ┌─ 3>599
│ RETRIEVED: 350   │ │  4>
│    Marked:    0  │ │  F2=Indexes     F3=Index Labels     F4=History
│    Record:    1  │ │  Ctrl+F3=Pull On/Off
└──────────────────┘ └─
```

CLASS NUMBER:	338.372
CAPTION:	Products of fishing, whaling, hunting, trapping
NOTES:	Add to base number 338.372 the numbers following 59 in 592-599, e.g., sponges 338.37234
	Class the culture of invertebrates and cold-blooded vertebrates in 338.371
	See Manual at 338.372
LCSH TERMS:	Aquaculture
	Fishery resources

```
 F5=Previous  F6=Next  F7=Print
 Alt+D=DDC Functions
 Electronic Dewey  v1.00     ESC Record List    F1 Help  F8 Databases  F10 End
```

FIGURE 5

```
Database: EDEWEY ┌──────────────────────────────────────── Index Labels ─
                 │ Use Index Labels to limit a search to a specific field.
┌──────────────┐ │
│RETRIEVED: 350│ │
│  Marked:   0 │ │ Index  Fields                              Search
│  Record:   1 │ │ Label                                      Example
├──────────────┤ │
│   DDC Numb   │ │ bi:    Captions, Notes, DDC Index          bi:nursing
├──────────────┤ │        Terms, Class Numbers (keyword)
│>>   338.372  │ │ cn:    Captions (keyword)                  cn:botany
│     380.1432 │ │ cp:    Captions (phrase)                   cp:"public health"
│     398.2452 │ │ dd:    DDC Number (keyword)                dd:610.73
│     398.369  │ │ it:    DDC Index Terms (keyword)           it:library networks
│     591      │ │ ip:    DDC Index Terms (phrase)            ip:"sacred music*"
│   M 591      │ │ su:    Subject Heading Terms (keyword)     su:indoor games
│   M 591 vs.  │ │ sp:    Subject Heading Terms (phrase)      sp:"global warming"
│   C 592-599  │ │ nt:    Notes (keyword)                     nt:holidays
│     593.1    │ │
│     593.11   │ │ Use Restrictor Index Labels to limit a search to a DDC
│     593.113  │ │ discipline or table number.
│     593.115  │ ├──────────────────────────────────────────────────────
│     593.117  │ │
│     593.118  │ │ 4>
└──────────────┘ │ ESC=Cancel

  Electronic Dewey  v1.00                      F1 Help           F10 End
```

FIGURE 6

```
Database: EDEWEY ┌──────────────────────────────────────────────────────
                 │ 4>cn:time
┌──────────────┐ │ 5>
│RETRIEVED:  37│ │ F2=Indexes    F3=Index Labels    F4=History
│  Marked:   0 │ └
│  Record:   1 │
├──────────────┴────────────────────────────────────────────────
│      DDC Number          Caption
├────────────────────────────────────────────────────────────────
│ >>    003.8              Systems distinguished in relation to time
│       003.83             Discrete-time systems
│       004.33             Real-time processing
│       115                Time
│       152.8              Quantitative threshold, discrimination, reaction-
│       152.83             Reaction-time studies
│       153.753            Time and rhythm perception
│       281.1              Apostolic Church to the time of the great schism,
│       304.23             Geographical, space, time factors
│       331.2162           Time payments
│       389.17             Time systems and standards [formerly 529.75]
│       519.55             Time-series analysis
│       529.2              Intervals of time
│       529[.75]           Time systems and standards
│ F7=Print                 ↑↓ Select   Ins/Del=Mark/Unmark   ⏎View Record │
└ Alt+D=DDC Functions
  Electronic Dewey  v1.00                      F1 Help  F8 Databases  F10 End
```

circumstances would anyone want to search for two terms within, say, fourteen words of each other in an entry? These are certainly things you cannot do when using the printed edition, but their presence seems to suggest a determination to include things that are possible with a machine readable file without fully considering whether they are necessary. Anyone wanting to search for two terms in the same field would surely be more likely to use an Index Label rather than the operator WITH.

There are two wild cards–? representing a single character or none (so that "g?psy" will retrieve "gipsy" or "gypsy" and "h?at" will retrieve "hat" or "heat") and * representing an unspecified number of characters or none. * can only be used at the end of a term and is therefore the truncation symbol. Truncation is a well established technique in on-line searching so needs no explanation, but the circumstances in which the * has to be used with EDDC most certainly do, and this leads to a discussion of the Index Labels for phrase searching.

As will be seen from Figure 5 there are three phrase Index Labels–cp for captions, ip for DDC index terms and sp for LCSH phrases. One peculiarity is that all searches using these labels must be enclosed in quotation marks. There is no obvious reason for this. Omission of them will generate an error message. Also, as with most phrase searching, you need to know exactly the form of the complete entry to avoid getting a zero response. Figure 8 shows an unsuccessful search for cp: "computer programming" and Figure 9 shows how the same search performed with a truncation symbol is successful because no caption consists of solely the two words searched for. (Incidentally there are a number of shortcut key combinations to ease repeated searches like those two–Alt + R puts the last search on the query line where it can be edited.) However, when you use ip to search phrases in the index you *must* use the truncation symbol as well as the quotation marks–even a legitimate search without it will fail, as Figures 10 and 11 for ip: "physics" illustrate. There would seem to be no logical reason why the truncation symbol in ip searches is mandatory while it is optional for cp and sp searches, but the high failure rate of any phrase search without it suggests there would be benefits in making it mandatory in every case.

Nor is this the end to the mysteries of searching EDDC. The previous searches have all been carried out by entering the Index Labels on the query line to produce a record list. However there is an alternative search approach, which is to use F2 to select the Index menu, highlight a particular Index Label, and then type the term or phrase with or without a truncation symbol. In this case the quotation marks are not required. Pressing Enter gives the user a browse display with the sought term, or the nearest

FIGURE 7

```
Database: EDEWEY ┌─────────────────────────────────────────────────────────
                 │ 5>dd:599
RETRIEVED:    2  │ 6>
   Marked:    0  │ F2=Indexes    F3=Index Labels    F4=History
   Record:    2  └
──────────────────────────────────────────────────────────────────────
         DDC Number          Caption
──────────────────────────────────────────────────────────────────────
    C  592-599           Specific animals and groups of animals
 >>    599               Mammalia (Mammals)




  F7=Print                     ↑↓ Select    Ins/Del=Mark/Unmark    ┘View Record │
  Alt+D=DDC Functions
  Electronic Dewey  v1.00                    F1 Help  F8 Databases  F10 End
```

FIGURE 8

```
Database: EDEWEY ┌─────────────────────────────────────────────────────────
                 │ 6>cp:"computer programming"
RETRIEVED:    0  │ 7>
   Marked:       │ F2=Indexes    F3=Index Labels    F4=History
   Record:       └
──────────────────────────────────────────────────────────────────────

              No Records Found - Try a New Query.



                              NOTE
              You can use the Indexes to check how often
              a term occurs in the database. To do this,
              press <F2> and enter the term you want to look up.
──────────────────────────────────────────────────────────────────────
   Electronic Dewey  v1.00                    F1 Help  F8 Databases  F10 End
```

FIGURE 9

```
Database: EDEWEY ┌─────────────────────────────────────────────────
                 │    7>cp:"computer programming*"
┌──────────────┐ │    8>
│RETRIEVED:   4│ │    F2=Indexes    F3=Index Labels    F4=History
│  Marked:    0│ │
│  Record:    1│ └
└──────────────┘
        DDC Number          Caption

>>      005                 Computer programming, programs, data
    M   005                 Computer programming, programs, data
    C   005.1-005.6         Computer programming and programs
    M   005.1 vs. 510       [Computer] Programming vs. Mathematics




  F7=Print                     ↑↓ Select    Ins/Del=Mark/Unmark    ↵View Record |
  Alt+D=DDC Functions
  Electronic Dewey  v1.00                     F1 Help  F8 Databases  F10 End
```

FIGURE 10

```
Database: EDEWEY ┌─────────────────────────────────────────────────
                 │    8>ip:"physics"
┌──────────────┐ │    9>
│RETRIEVED:   0│ │    F2=Indexes    F3=Index Labels    F4=History
│  Marked:     │ │
│  Record:     │ └
└──────────────┘



              No Records Found - Try a New Query.



                          NOTE

          You can use the Indexes to check how often
            a term occurs in the database. To do this,
          press <F2> and enter the term you want to look up.


  Electronic Dewey  v1.00                     F1 Help  F8 Databases  F10 End
```

to it in that index, in the middle of the screen, from which the user can move up and down the index as far as is required. Figures 12 and 13 show a search for "computer" as a Caption Phrase and its results. Pressing Enter from the browse index takes the user to the normal record list. Except for ip, which gives access to an approximation of the Relative Index in the printed edition, in that it includes not only the index phrase but also the appropriate class number, and pressing Enter in this case will lead the user to the record itself rather than to a record list. Figure 14 shows the browse index resulting from a search using F2, ip and computer*. It will be readily seen that there is a vastly increased flexibility of approach in comparison with the printed text, which is almost an embarras de richesse in knowing the best method to use.

The fact that the Relative Index can be searched in this way has an effect on the class numbers that can be found in the record lists that needs a little explanation, since it means that the lists include what EDDC calls built numbers. This is because the Index includes numbers that have been produced by synthesis, i.e., by using add instructions in the schedules and tables of the Classification. In the record list such numbers are shown with an I alongside them. Figure 15 shows a record list with six built numbers found as a result of a search for "concrete" in the basic index. The display for the individual record shows the nearest class number and caption, i.e., the record at which the add instruction to produce that synthesised number can be found. Figures 16 and 17 show the built number entry and the entry for the class number with the add instruction. Thus EDDC provides more numbers in its record lists than are actually found in the schedules and tables. Of course, EDDC remains a tool to help in number building–it does not itself build numbers by adding together elements from various parts of the classification as requested by the user and then present a synthesised number as a result. Such work remains the province of the human classifier.

Nor does this exhaust the ways in which EDDC can be used. There are also what are called the DDC functions. A list of these, as shown in Figure 18, can be called up by pressing Alt + D and highlighting the function required, or they can be accessed directly by the appropriate key combination. These functions can be accessed from both a record list and an individual record. The most exciting of these is undoubtedly Alt + H to display a number within its hierarchy in the schedules. An example of this is shown in Figure 19. From that point you can move up and down the hierarchy to a different level and by pressing Alt + H again view the hierarchy from that new location. And you can, of course, access any record at a different hierarchical level. This is really where a machine readable version of the Classification shows its power, as this is an excellent naviga-

FIGURE 11

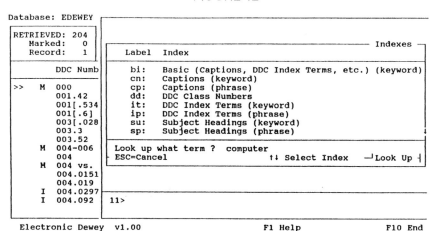

```
Database: EDEWEY  ┌─────────────────────────────────────────────────────
                  │  9>ip:"physics*"
 RETRIEVED:    5  │  10>
   Marked:     0  │  F2=Indexes    F3=Index Labels    F4=History
   Record:     1  └─
─────────────────────────────────────────────────────────────────
           DDC Number        Caption
─────────────────────────────────────────────────────────────────
 >>       215.3             Physics
          261.55            Science
          291.175           Religions and secular disciplines
          530               Physics
          621               Applied physics




  F7=Print                        ↑↓ Select   Ins/Del=Mark/Unmark   ↵View Record │
  Alt+D=DDC Functions
  Electronic Dewey  v1.00                      F1 Help  F8 Databases  F10 End
```

FIGURE 12

```
Database: EDEWEY  ┌──────────────────────────────────────────────────────────
                  │
 RETRIEVED: 204   │                                              ── Indexes ─┐
   Marked:    0   │
   Record:    1   │   Label  Index
─────────────────  │  ────────────────────────────────────────────────────────
          DDC Numb │    bi:   Basic (Captions, DDC Index Terms, etc.) (keyword)
                   │    cn:   Captions (keyword)
 >>    M  000      │    cp:   Captions (phrase)
       001.42      │    dd:   DDC Class Numbers
       001[.534    │    it:   DDC Index Terms (keyword)
       001[.6]     │    ip:   DDC Index Terms (phrase)
       003[.028    │    su:   Subject Headings (keyword)
       003.3       │    sp:   Subject Headings (phrase)
       003.52      │  ────────────────────────────────────────────────────────
    M  004-006     │  Look up what term ?  computer
       004         │  ESC=Cancel                      ↑↓ Select Index   ↵Look Up ┤
    M  004 vs.     │
       004.0151    │
       004.019     │  ──────────────────────────────────────────────────────────
    I  004.0297    │
    I  004.092     │  11>
                   └──────────────────────────────────────────────────────────

  Electronic Dewey  v1.00                  F1 Help                  F10 End
```

FIGURE 13

```
Database: EDEWEY  ┌──────────────────────── Index cp: Captions (phrase) ──
                  │ Compounds other than water (1)
┌─────────────┐   │ Comprehensive schools (1)
│RETRIEVED: 204│  │ Comprehensive treatment of nondominant aggregates * (1)
│  Marked:   0 │  │ Compressed-air transmission (1)
│  Record:   1 │  │ Compressible airflow (1)
└─────────────┘   │ Compression (1)
         DDC Numb │ Compton region (1)
  >>  M  000  .   │ Compulsive lying and defrauding (1)
        001.42    │ Compulsory education (1)
        001[.534  │ Compulsory labor (1)
        001[.6]   │ Computer (1)
        003[.028  │ Computer adventure games    computer fantasy games (1)
        003.3     │ Computer architecture (1)
        003.52    │ Computer communication (1)
     M  004-006   │ Computer communication vs interfacing and communic* (1)
        004       │ Computer communications (1)
     M  004 vs.   │ Computer communications networks (1)
        004.0151  │ Computer composition (2)
        004.019   │ Computer control (1)
     I  004.0297  ├───────────────────────────────────────────────────────
     I  004.092   │ 11>
                  │ ESC=Cancel   F2=Indexes
└─────────────────┘ ↑↓ Select   TAB=Copy
     Electronic Dewey  v1.00                                  ⅃ Issue Query ⅃
                                         F1 Help              F10 End
```

FIGURE 14

```
Database: EDEWEY  ┌──────────────── Index ip: DDC Index Terms (phrase) ──
                  │ Compulsive gambling  SA: mental illness
┌─────────────┐   │ Compulsive gambling--medicine          616.85227
│RETRIEVED:  1 │  │ Compulsive gambling--social welfare    362.25
│  Marked:   0 │  │ Compulsive lying  SA: mental illness
│  Record:   1 │  │ Compulsive lying--medicine             616.85845
└─────────────┘   │ Compulsory education                   379.23
    CLASS NUMBER  │ Compulsory education--law              344.079
                  │ Compulsory labor                       331.1173
         CAPTION  │ Compulsory military service            355.22363
                  │ Compulsory military service--law       343.0122
           NOTES  │ Computed tomography--medicine          616.07572
                  │ Computer access control                005.8
                  │ Computer access control--management    658.478
                  │ Computer applications                  t1--0285
                  │ Computer architecture                  004.22
                  │ Computer architecture--engineering     621.392
                  │ Computer art                           700
 DDC INDEX TERMS  │ Computer assisted instruction          t1--078
                  │ Computer awareness                     004
                  ├───────────────────────────────────────────────────────
                  │ 12>
                  │ ESC=Cancel   F2=Indexes
└─────────────────┘ ↑↓ Select   TAB=Copy
     Electronic Dewey  v1.00                                  ⅃ Issue Query ⅃
                                         F1 Help              F10 End
```

FIGURE 15

```
Database: EDEWEY
                     ┌──────────────────────────────────────────────────
                     │ 1>concrete
RETRIEVED:    47     │ 2>
   Marked:     0     │ F2=Indexes    F3=Index Labels    F4=History
   Record:     7     └
─────────────────────────────────────────────────────────────────────────
          DDC Number              Caption

     M   320                 Political science (Politics and government)
     M   341                 International law
         620.136             *Concrete
         620.137             *Reinforced and *prestressed concrete
         620.139             Artificial stones
     I   623.81834           Concrete--ship design
>>   I   623.818341          Reinforced concrete--ship design
         623.8207            Craft of specific materials
         623.845             Construction with masonry, ceramics, allied mater
     I   623.8454            Concrete--ship hulls
     I   623.84541           Reinforced concrete--ship hulls
     I   624.15336           Concrete--foundation materials
     I   624.15337           Ferroconcrete--foundation materials
         624.1832            Stone
   F7=Print                   ↑↓ Select    Ins/Del=Mark/Unmark    ⏎View Record
 ⌐Alt+D=DDC Functions
   Electronic Dewey  v1.00                    F1 Help  F8 Databases  F10 End
```

FIGURE 16

```
Database: EDEWEY
                     ┌──────────────────────────────────────────────────
                     │ 1>concrete
RETRIEVED:    47     │ 2>
   Marked:     0     │ F2=Indexes    F3=Index Labels    F4=History
   Record:     7     └ Ctrl+F3=Pull On/Off
─────────────────────────────────────────────────────────────────────────
     BUILT NUMBER:       623.818341

     NEAREST CLASS #:    623.818
     NEAREST CAPTION:    Design in specific materials

     DDC INDEX TERMS:    Reinforced concrete--ship design




   F5=Previous  F6=Next  F7=Print
 ⌐Alt+D=DDC Functions
   Electronic Dewey  v1.00      ESC Record List    F1 Help  F8 Databases  F10 End
```

FIGURE 17

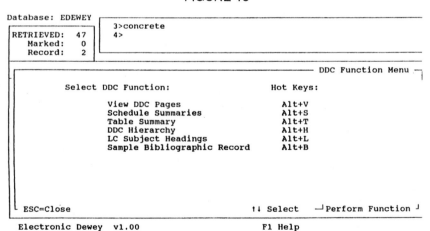

```
Database: EDEWEY ┌──────────────────────────────────────────────────────
               ┌─┐│  2>dd:623.818
RETRIEVED:   1 │ ││  3>
    Marked:   0 │ ││  F2=Indexes   F3=Index Labels    F4=History
    Record:   1 └─┘└  Ctrl+F3=Pull On/Off
              ─────────────────────────────────────────────────────────

       CLASS NUMBER:     623.818

            CAPTION:     Design in specific materials

              NOTES:     Add to base number 623.818 the numbers following 624.18
                         in 624.182-624.189, e.g., design in steel 623.81821

         LCSH TERMS:     Hulls (Naval architecture)




                      F7=Print
    └ Alt+D=DDC Functions
     Electronic Dewey  v1.00     ESC Record List    F1 Help  F8 Databases  F10 End
```

FIGURE 18

```
Database: EDEWEY ┌──────────────────────────────────────────────────────
               ┌─┐│  3>concrete
RETRIEVED:  47 │ ││  4>
    Marked:   0 │ ││
    Record:   2 └─┘└
              ┌─────────────────────────────────────── DDC Function Menu ─┐
              │                                                            │
              │      Select DDC Function:            Hot Keys:             │
              │                                                            │
              │          View DDC Pages                Alt+V               │
              │          Schedule Summaries            Alt+S               │
              │          Table Summary                 Alt+T               │
              │          DDC Hierarchy                 Alt+H               │
              │          LC Subject Headings           Alt+L               │
              │          Sample Bibliographic Record   Alt+B               │
              │                                                            │
              │                                                            │
              └ ESC=Close                      ↑↓ Select  ─┘Perform Function ┘

     Electronic Dewey  v1.00                      F1 Help
```

tional tool allowing movement from general to specific or vice versa in ways that cannot easily be done with a printed text. Some caution is needed where the notation is not properly hierarchical, as EDDC can only display a strict numerical hierarchy. So if Alt + H is used from the Dewey number 580 the hierarchy revealed shows 500 rather than 574 as the higher number. But this is a fault of the notation rather than the display mechanism, which shows a machine's need for regularity and predictability.

Another important DDC function is Alt + V, which allows the user to browse the full text of the DDC20 schedules and tables. The result of using Alt + V from Dewey number 624.1834 is shown in Figure 20. Once access has been made from a specific number the user can then browse backwards or forward from that point through the printed edition. The program will pause every so often to load a fresh segment from the disc. It is possible to use this facility to go right through all the schedules and tables.

A third DDC function enables use of the three summaries which appear at the beginning of Volume 2 of the printed edition of DC20, and this is initiated by using Alt + S. The user is then shown the first summary, the ten main classes. It is then possible to highlight one of these classes and by pressing Enter move to the second summary, the hundred divisions, with the highlight located at the start of that particular main class. Similarly by highlighting one division and again pressing Enter the user moves to the third summary, the thousand sections, in the same way. Pressing Enter a third time on one of those sections leads to a search on that particular Dewey number. At any point the user can return to a higher summary, or, by using Ctrl + Enter initiate an immediate class number search. Therefore, moving from the summaries to the appropriate schedule is much easier and faster and a very positive gain in the machine readable version.

The use of the summaries in this way leads to a consideration of another search technique that is only possible by automated means, which is the use of what EDDC calls restrictors. These are shown in Figure 21, and, as can be seen, they can be used with the Boolean operators to broaden or narrow searches by including or excluding specific parts of the classification. For instance, Figure 22 shows a search for any captions that include the word "physics" apart from the main physics class, 530. The only problem here is that such a search does not exclude manual entries in the 530 range, which is a pity and slightly reduces its value. That apart, the use of restrictors is a very powerful and useful search technique that is totally impossible by traditional means in the printed edition.

Returning to the consideration of DDC functions it will be noticed that as well as Alt + S to display the summaries the user can also use Alt + T

FIGURE 19

```
Database: EDEWEY   ┌─────────────────────────────────────────────────────
                   │ 4>dd:624.1834
RETRIEVED:    1    │ 5>
  Marked:     0    │
  Record:     1    └─────────────────────────────────────────────────────
```

```
┌──────────────────────────────────────────────── DDC Hierarchy ─┐
│    600      Technology (Applied sciences)                       │
│    620          Engineering and allied operations               │
│    624          Civil engineering                               │
│    624.1          Structural engineering and underground construction
│    624.18           Design and construction in specific materials
│    624.183            Masonry, ceramic, allied materials        │
│  > 624.1834             Concrete                                │
│    624.18341              Reinforced concrete (Ferroconcrete)   │
│    624.18342-624.18349  Specific concrete structural elements   │
│                                                                 │
│                                                                 │
│                                                                 │
│                                                                 │
│                                                                 │
│ ESC=Close                                      ↑↓ Select   ⌐View ┘
└─────────────────────────────────────────────────────────────────┘
```

```
Electronic Dewey  v1.00                        F1 Help
```

FIGURE 20

```
Database: EDEWEY   ┌─────────────────────────────────────────────────────
                   │ 4>dd:624.1834
RETRIEVED:    1    │ 5>
  Marked:     0    │
  Record:     1    └─────────────────────────────────────────────────────
```

```
┌──────────────────────────────────────────────── View DDC Pages ─┐
│  624.1834   Concrete                                            │
│       Class concrete and cinder blocks in 624.1832              │
│       See also 721.0445 for visual concrete                     │
│                                                                 │
│  624.18341  Reinforced concrete (Ferroconcrete)                 │
│       Class a specific concrete structural element of reinforced concrete in
│  624.18342-624.18349                                            │
│                                                                 │
│  624.183412  Prestressed concrete                               │
│                                                                 │
│  624.183414  Precast concrete                                   │
│                                                                 │
│  624.18342-624.18349  Specific concrete structural elements     │
│       Add to base number 624.1834 the numbers following 624.177 in
│  624.1772-624.1779, e.g., concrete shells 624.183462            │
│ ESC=Close      Ctrl+F3=Pull On/Off         Use ↑↓ PgUp PgDn to view text.┘
└─────────────────────────────────────────────────────────────────┘
```

```
Electronic Dewey  v1.00                        F1 Help
```

FIGURE 21

```
Database: EDEWEY  ┌──────────────────────────────────────────── Index Labels -
                  │
┌─────────────────┤  Restrictor      Record              Search
│ RETRIEVED:   4  │  Index Label     Sets                Example
│   Marked:    0  │
│   Record:    1  │  s1:             10 Main Classes     war and s1:200
├─────────────────┤  s2:             100 Divisions       tax and s2:330
│         DDC Numb│  s3:             1000 Sections       children and s3:155
│                 │  tn:             Table number        language not tn:T6
│ >>      500     │
│     M   500 vs. │
│     M   500 vs. │
│     M   500 vs. │
│                 │
│                 │
│                 │
│                 │
│                 │
│                 │
│                 ├──────────────────────────────────────────────────────────
│                 │  3>
│                 │  ESC=Cancel
└─────────────────┘

    Electronic Dewey   v1.00                    F1 Help              F10 End
```

FIGURE 22

```
Database: EDEWEY  ┌──────────────────────────────────────────────────────────
                  │  7>cn:physics not s2:530
┌─────────────────┤  8>
│ RETRIEVED:  12  │  F2=Indexes    F3=Index Labels    F4=History
│   Marked:    0  │
│   Record:    1  └─
├─────────────────┬──────────────────────────────────────────────────────────
│         DDC Number        Caption
│
│ >>      215.3             Physics
│         523.019           Molecular, atomic, nuclear physics
│     M   530 vs. 500.2     Physics vs. Physical sciences
│     M   530 vs. 540       Physics vs. Chemistry and allied sciences
│     M   530.41 vs. 548    Solid-state physics vs. Crystallography
│         621               Applied physics
│     M   621 vs. 530       Applied physics vs. Physics
│         621.4831          Reactor physics
│         631.43            Soil physics
│         T7--53            With physics
│         T7--539           Nuclear physics
│         T7--621           With applied physics
│
│  F7=Print                    ↑↓ Select    Ins/Del=Mark/Unmark   ─┘View Record │
└  Alt+D=DDC Functions
   Electronic Dewey  v1.00                      F1 Help  F8 Databases  F10 End
```

for the Table summary. However, unlike the Schedule summaries this is not interactive–the user cannot highlight a specific table in the summary to gain access to a record list. It simply lists the Tables found in the Classification. Searching for Table numbers using EDDC requires knowing the exact format to use–getting it wrong produces an error message. The format required is the Table number followed by a double dash and the required number, e.g., to search for the number for France in the area table requires the input of t2–44. The results of this search are shown in Figure 23. It is best to make this a Dewey number search using dd, i.e., dd:t2–44, so as not to retrieve entries with –44 in the notes field, e.g., 064. The search using dd retrieves only the last of the six entries on the record list in Figure 23. Using a single dash instead of a double dash does not produce an error message but the statement that no records were found, which is somewhat misleading. And searching the table for individual literatures requires a knowledge of whether the term sought is in Table 3A, 3B or 3C, since a search for a number as just t3 will fail. To add to the confusion in the Table summary the parts of Table 3 are given as Table 3-A, etc., with a hyphen. But a search using that hyphen will fail, and only one omitting it, e.g., t3a–3, will succeed. This is one area where a little bit more flexibility would ease matters for the user. In fact, the best way of searching the Tables is to make use of the tn (Table number) retrictor (see Figure 21). A successful search for the area number for France can be made by inputting "cn:France and tn:T2," and for the correct subdivision for fiction by using "cn:fiction and tn:T3." This is far easier than grappling with the intricacies of direct Dewey number searches of the Tables.

There are two further DDC functions that appear to have been added primarily for the American market, which are Alt + L to view LCSH and Alt + B to view a sample bibliographic record. As Figure 24 shows Alt + L displays the number of times that class number has been assigned in the OCLC Online Union Catalog and the five LCSH most frequently assigned to it with their percentages. The sample bibliographic record shows one record using that class number and the most frequently assigned LCSH. That works well when there is a high percentage use of one or two specific LCSH but produces, as Figure 24 shows, some rather bizarre results when a number of LCSH have each only been assigned once and there is no preponderance. While this is indeed something that cannot be done using a traditional approach with the printed schedules, there remains some question as to whether its value justifies the disc space taken up that could have been used for other purposes. How far should an aid to using one classification scheme provide material taken from a different system or code? As there are relatively few institutions in the United Kingdom that use both

FIGURE 23

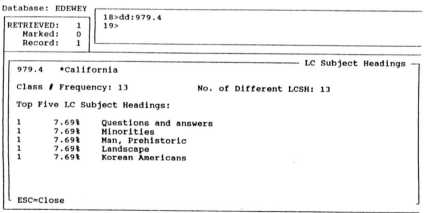

```
Database: EDEWEY
                 ┌─────────────────────────────────────────────────
RETRIEVED:    6  │ 12>t2--44
   Marked:    0  │ 13>
   Record:    1  │ F2=Indexes    F3=Index Labels    F4=History
                 └
─────────────────────────────────────────────────────────────────
          DDC Number        Caption

>>       064               General organizations in France and Monaco
         074               Journalism and newspapers in France and Monaco
         447.1-447.8       Geographical variations in France
     M   T2--3 vs. T2--4-T2 The ancient world vs. The modern world; extraterr
         T2--364           Celtic regions
         T2--44            France and Monaco




  F7=Print                    ↑↓ Select   Ins/Del=Mark/Unmark   ⏎View Record |
  Alt+D=DDC Functions
  Electronic Dewey  v1.00                   F1 Help  F8 Databases  F10 End
```

FIGURE 24

```
Database: EDEWEY
                 ┌─────────────────────────────────────────────────
RETRIEVED:    1  │ 18>dd:979.4
   Marked:    0  │ 19>
   Record:    1  │
                 └─────────────────────────────────────────────────
─────────────────────────────────────────────────────────────────
  ┌─────────────────────────────────── LC Subject Headings ─┐
  │ 979.4    *California                                      │
  │                                                           │
  │ Class # Frequency: 13         No. of Different LCSH: 13   │
  │                                                           │
  │ Top Five LC Subject Headings:                             │
  │                                                           │
  │ 1      7.69%    Questions and answers                     │
  │ 1      7.69%    Minorities                                │
  │ 1      7.69%    Man, Prehistoric                          │
  │ 1      7.69%    Landscape                                 │
  │ 1      7.69%    Korean Americans                          │
  │                                                           │
  │                                                           │
  └ ESC=Close                                                 ┘

  Electronic Dewey  v1.00                    F1 Help
```

Dewey and LCSH together, British librarians are unlikely to find these features of much help, but libraries where LCSH are assigned before a Dewey number might find greater benefit. It should be noted that LCSH as well as terms from the Relative Index are displayed on individual records as well. Examples can be seen on Figures 3 and 17.

Rather than occupy disc space with sample bibliographic records perhaps the opportunity could have been taken to make another feature, the Notepad, class number sensitive. You can open the Notepad by Alt + N, which gives you a blank area in the lower half of the view window. You can either enter text in the Notepad area yourself or you can copy the record you are viewing to it. It therefore acts as an aide memoire, but the contents remain the same until they are erased. If you open the Notepad while viewing a different record the same contents will be present. So it cannot be used for annotations on the use of a specific class number that will remain attached to that number, which is a pity. On the other hand, it can be used during number building to note the base number to which something should be added from another part of the schedules or tables—but a piece of scrap paper would serve that purpose just as well.

Some other features that are common to machine readable databases are present, such as online help. Others are not so common but rather useful, such as the facility to move the cursor on the screen to a different word or class number to start another search. This is a very interactive use of EDDC that is of course not possible with the printed text. Pressing F4 gives access to the last one hundred searches that have been entered in the query window. These can be saved so that they are available for the next session if required. The contents of previous searches can be tabbed down to the current query line and combined together using Boolean operators. It is very easy to construct quite complex search statements using this technique.

Records can also be marked, by using Insert, for subsequent printing or saving. Figure 25 shows a record list with four records marked, and shown as such in the results window. If the command to print is then chosen the default will be to print the marked records, though other print options can be chosen. Even so, multiple records are printed one per page. The format is very clear, as can be seen from Figure 26, but a bit wasteful of space if standard size stationery is being used. Marked, or indeed any, records can also be saved to a disc file for subsequent use.

This has been a quick tour of the major features of EDDC concentrating on the ways in which it differs from or leads to different search techniques from the traditional printed version of the classification. As has been shown, it gives far greater flexibility of approach, so much so that at first it may be

FIGURE 25

```
Database: EDEWEY
                      20>cn:engineering
RETRIEVED: 123        21>
   Marked:   4        F2=Indexes    F3=Index Labels   F4=History
   Record:  23

         DDC Number          Caption

           359.98            Artillery and guided missile forces; engineering
           359.982           *Engineering services
     .     620               Engineering and allied operations
           620[.00153]       Physical principles in engineering
           620[.00289]       Safety engineering
           620.0042          Engineering design
     .     620.1             Engineering mechanics and materials
       C   620.103-620.107   Engineering (Applied) mechanics
           620.11            Engineering materials
     .     620.19            Other engineering materials
       C   620.21-620.25     Applied acoustics (Acoustical engineering)
  >> .     620.4             Engineering for specific kinds of geographical en
           620.41            Engineering for specific kinds of geographical en
           620.44            Surface engineering
    F7=Print                      ↑↓ Select   Ins/Del=Mark/Unmark   ⏎View Record
    Alt+D=DDC Functions
    Electronic Dewey  v1.00                   F1 Help  F8 Databases  F10 End
```

FIGURE 26

```
--------------------------------------------------------------------------------
12/22/1993  15:12
Database:   EDEWEY (DDC 20 including changes through March 1993)
Query 20:   cn:engineering (123)
--------------------------------------------------------------------------------
--- Record #14 ---
   CLASS NUMBER:      620

        CAPTION:      Engineering and allied operations

          NOTES:      Class here manufacturing of products of various branches
                      of engineering

                      Class comprehensive works on manufacturing in 670

                      For chemical engineering, see 660

DDC INDEX TERMS:      Engineering

     LCSH TERMS:      Engineering
                      Automobiles
                      Production management
                      Materials handling
                      Sheet-metal work
```

difficult to decide which would be the most efficient and effective way of solving a particular problem. Those who already have some knowledge and experience of Dewey in print are likely to benefit far more than beginners who have not used Dewey before. It must always be remembered that this is the first time a general classification scheme has been presented in this way, and it says much for OCLC's previous expertise in online tools that it works so well.

There will no doubt follow further updates and releases that will still further improve or augment the CD-ROM product, now referred to consistently by OCLC as Electronic Dewey. An upgrade disc appeared in 1994 containing all changes including those in *DC&* published in March of that year, and also containing segmentation marks and a print version of the Editor's Introduction. A Windows version of the product is under development, and it is to be hoped that a LAN version is on its way. Whilst the printed version will most certainly be around for a long time yet, EDDC must certainly herald a revolution in the way classification is carried out. It cannot be that long before it will be possible to integrate the CD-ROM with a system for online assignment of classification numbers and other catalogue data or to move the data from one database to another seamlessly. Together with the [US]MARC format for classification and the recently published IFLA *Guidelines for subject authority and reference entries* Electronic Dewey takes us well on the way to the electronic age of classification.

Index

Indexing of the text was undertaken by the LIS 634 Abstracting and Indexing class (Spring, 1995) of Pratt Institute School of Information and Library Science (Visiting Associate Professor Alan R. Thomas, project coordinator; Robert Armitage, Terrie L. Ashley, Frank Collerius, Derek A. Coursen, Rodger Friedman, Frank J. Girello, Delritta R. Hornbuckle, Steven W. Knittweis, Edward D. Meisner, Ricki L. Moskowitz, John J. Patrisco, and Rick L. Perdew).

Haworth
DOCUMENT DELIVERY
SERVICE

This new service provides a single-article order form for any article from a Haworth journal.

- *Time Saving:* No running around from library to library to find a specific article.
- *Cost Effective:* All costs are kept down to a minimum.
- *Fast Delivery:* Choose from several options, including same-day FAX.
- *No Copyright Hassles:* You will be supplied by the original publisher.
- *Easy Payment:* Choose from several easy payment methods.

Open Accounts Welcome for . . .
- Library Interlibrary Loan Departments
- Library Network/Consortia Wishing to Provide Single-Article Services
- Indexing/Abstracting Services with Single Article Provision Services
- Document Provision Brokers and Freelance Information Service Providers

MAIL or *FAX* THIS ENTIRE ORDER FORM TO:

Haworth Document Delivery Service
The Haworth Press, Inc.
10 Alice Street
Binghamton, NY 13904-1580

or FAX: (607) 722-6362
or CALL: 1-800-3-HAWORTH
(1-800-342-9678; 9am-5pm EST)

PLEASE SEND ME PHOTOCOPIES OF THE FOLLOWING SINGLE ARTICLES:
1) Journal Title: _____
   Vol/Issue/Year:_____Starting & Ending Pages:_____
Article Title:_____
_____

2) Journal Title: _____
   Vol/Issue/Year:_____Starting & Ending Pages:_____
Article Title:_____
_____

3) Journal Title: _____
   Vol/Issue/Year:_____Starting & Ending Pages:_____
Article Title:_____
_____

4) Journal Title: _____
   Vol/Issue/Year:_____Starting & Ending Pages:_____
Article Title:_____
_____

(See other side for Costs and Payment Information)

COSTS: Please figure your cost to order quality copies of an article.

1. Set-up charge per article: $8.00
   ($8.00 × number of separate articles) _____

2. Photocopying charge for each article:

   1-10 pages: $1.00 _____

   11-19 pages: $3.00 _____

   20-29 pages: $5.00 _____

   30+ pages: $2.00/10 pages _____

3. Flexicover (optional): $2.00/article _____

4. Postage & Handling: US: $1.00 for the first article/
   $.50 each additional article _____

   Federal Express: $25.00 _____

   Outside US: $2.00 for first article/
   $.50 each additional article _____

5. Same-day FAX service: $.35 per page _____

   GRAND TOTAL: _____

METHOD OF PAYMENT: (please check one)

❏ Check enclosed ❏ Please ship and bill. PO # _____
(sorry we can ship and bill to bookstores only! All others must pre-pay)

❏ Charge to my credit card: ❏ Visa; ❏ MasterCard; ❏ American Express;

Account Number: _____ Expiration date: _____

Signature: ✗_____

Name: _____ Institution: _____

Address: _____

_____

City: _____ State: _____ Zip: _____

Phone Number: _____ FAX Number: _____

MAIL or *FAX* THIS ENTIRE ORDER FORM TO:

Haworth Document Delivery Service	**or FAX:** (607) 722-6362
The Haworth Press, Inc.	**or CALL:** 1-800-3-HAWORTH
10 Alice Street	(1-800-342-9678; 9am-5pm EST)
Binghamton, NY 13904-1580	